FACEBOOK® FOR SENIORS
QuickSteps®

About the Author

Carole Matthews has been a programmer, system analyst, manager, executive, and entrepreneur in the software business for many years. For the last 25 years, she has authored, co-authored, or managed the writing and production of more than 75 books. She lives with her husband, Marty, on an island in Puget Sound in Washington State.

FACEBOOK® FOR SENIORS
QuickSteps®

Carole Boggs Matthews

New York Chicago San Francisco
Lisbon London Madrid Mexico City
Milan New Delhi San Juan
Seoul Singapore Sydney Toronto

The McGraw·Hill Companies

Library of Congress Cataloging-in-Publication Data

Matthews, Carole Boggs.
    Facebook for seniors : quicksteps / Carole Boggs Matthews.
      p. cm.
    Includes index.
    ISBN 978-0-07-177265-5 (alk. paper)
  1. Facebook (Electronic resource)   2. Computers and older
people.   3. Internet and older people.   4. Online social
networks.   5. Social media.   I. Title.
    HM743.F33M27 2013
    004.67'80846—dc23

                                 2012040181

Facebook® for Seniors QuickSteps®

34567890   QVS QVS   10987654

ISBN   978-0-07-177265-5
MHID   0-07-177265-0

SPONSORING EDITOR / Roger Stewart
EDITORIAL SUPERVISOR / Patty Mon
PROJECT MANAGER / Harleen Chopra, Cenveo Publisher Services
ACQUISITIONS COORDINATOR / Ryan Willard
TECHNICAL EDITOR / Marty Matthews
COPY EDITOR / Lisa McCoy
PROOFREADER / Carol Shields
INDEXER / Valerie Perry
PRODUCTION SUPERVISOR / George Anderson
COMPOSITION / Cenveo Publisher Services
ILLUSTRATION / Cenveo Publisher Services and Erin Johnson
ART DIRECTOR, COVER / Jeff Weeks
COVER DESIGNER / Pattie Lee
SERIES CREATORS / Marty and Carole Matthews
SERIES DESIGN / Mary McKeon

To Marty, my partner in all things—you are my best friend.

To the Lorians, who warmly and enthusiastically encouraged me in writing this book.

To my Facebook friends who share their lives online, many of whom have contributed time and effort to place a part of themselves in this book. You all have been in my mind as I strove to make this book readable and authentic—and enjoyable. Thanks to all of you!

Contents at a Glance

1 2 3 4 5 6 7 8 9 10

Contents

Chapter 8   Using Facebook Apps and Games 145

Chapter 9   Creating Pages and Facebook Ads.. 177

10

Acknowledgments

This book is made more lively and interesting by the real-life Facebook experiences quoted in this book by friends and avid Facebook users. I am very grateful for the time and energy spent by these amazing people (alphabetically by first name): Ann Dotson, Deborah Koff-Chapin, Daniel Mulhaney, Del Hoffman, Ernestine Hoffman, Evelyn Yearwood, Freya Secrest, Gary Bouton, Helen Pohlabel Snyder, Jeremy Berg, John Cronan (also helped with Chapter 5), Marilyn Bochenek Hannahs, Mary Purtilo, Nancy Miller Johnson, Pat McClain Thomas, Ron Hays, Ruth Chaffee, Rue Hass, Susan Scann, and Suzanne Fageol.

I am, as always, indebted to the editing, layout, proofreading, indexing, and project management expertise of a number of people, only some of whom we know. I thank all of them and, in particular, acknowledge:

- **Roger Stewart**, editorial director and sponsoring editor of this book and the QuickSteps series

- **Patty Mon**, editorial supervisor

- **George Anderson**, production supervisor

- **Harleen Chopra**, project manager

- **Ryan Williard**, acquisitions coordinator

- **Valerie Perry**, indexer

- **Lisa McCoy**, copy editor

Finally, I want to acknowledge my husband, Marty, who helped with some parts of this book, but as an unrecognized contributor. You make my life so much easier and joyful!

Introduction

Writing about Facebook has been a kick! Not only has the doing of it been fun, but Facebook itself has become so visible and present in our lives, that it is almost like writing about an old friends—a well-known, old friend. Although I have been on Facebook for several years, only in the writing of it did I understand the variety and depth of relationships that one can experience in Facebook and how much influence it carries in our world.

Seniors, as you'll see in the book, are taking up Facebook with enthusiasm, waxing eloquently about nearly everything—and often. In these pages you'll learn how to use Facebook with ease and comfort, how to protect yourself, and how to expand your Facebook experience. Now's the time for learning how to do all this and more.

QuickSteps books are recipe books for computer users. They answer the question "How do I..." by providing a quick set of steps to accomplish the most common tasks for a particular situation.

The sets of steps are the central focus of the book. QuickFacts sidebars supply information that you need to know about a subject. QuickQuotes, contributed by senior friends and acquaintances, tell how topics are being used by real people. Notes, Tips, and Cautions augment the steps. The introductions are minimal rather than narrative, and numerous illustrations and figures, many with callouts, support the steps.

Facebook for Seniors QuickSteps describes in one book how you can use Facebook for work and pleasure. It not only covers core requirements, such as posting comments or updating profile information, but also more useful and fun activities, such as organizing friends, sharing photos and videos, creating Pages, sending private messages, chatting, keeping Facebook secure, tracking Facebook on your smartphone or other mobile device, and much more.

QuickSteps books are organized by function and the tasks needed to perform that function. Each function is a chapter, such as "Managing Your Friends." Each task contains the steps needed for accomplishing the function, along with the relevant Notes, Tips, Cautions, and screenshots. You can easily find the tasks you need through

- The table of contents, which lists the functional areas (chapters) and tasks in the order they are presented

- A QuickSteps To list of tasks on the opening page of each chapter

- The index, which provides an alphabetical list of the terms that are used to describe the functions and tasks

- Color-coded tabs for each chapter, or functional area, with an index to the tabs in the Contents at a Glance section (just before the table of contents)

Conventions Used in This Book

Facebook for Seniors QuickSteps uses several conventions designed to make the book easier for you to follow:

- A ✅ in the Contents references a QuickFacts sidebar.

- A 💬 in chapter sidebars shows a QuickQuotes by a contributing Facebook Senior.

- **Bold** type is used for words or objects on the screen that you are to do something with—for example, "Click **Start** and click **Computer**."

- ***Bold italic*** type is used for a word or phrase that is being defined.

- *Italic* type is used for a word or phrase that deserves special emphasis or that is a title, as for a book.

- <u>Underlined</u> type is used for text that you are to type from the keyboard.

- SMALL CAPITAL LETTERS are used for keys on the keyboard, such as **ENTER** and **SHIFT**.

- When you are expected to enter a command, you are told to press the key(s). If you are to enter text or numbers, you are told to type them.

- A pipe (|) indicates that you are to enter items in sequence. For instance, "Click ***yourname*** | **About** | **Basic Info Edit**" would tell you to first click your name for the Timeline page, then find and click About, then find and click Basic Info Edit.

Chapter 1

Stepping into Facebook

As seniors, we've seen a lot of changes. One of the most important is how the Internet has changed how we do many things—and one of the Internet tools most visible today is Facebook. From the largest and most disappointing stock offering in history, an Oscar-nominated movie, an enabler of revolution in the streets, and governments scrambling to shut Facebook down to stifle the flow of information, to less dramatic actions of grandmothers showing their friends photos of a new grandchild, Facebook is a versatile and dynamic Internet tool changing our vision of what our world may be. Seniors are right there, in increasing numbers, making use of Facebook to communicate, play games, and track what is going on with friends and family as well as interesting groups.

Facebook, now a publically owned website, was launched in 2004 (the movie *The Social Network,* shown in Figure 1-1, depicts its early days). Today it is perhaps the most visible social networking presence, although others are entering the competition for social networking. More than 900 million active users (http://en.wikipedia.org/wiki/Facebook) spend time on Facebook, some for hours a day. Facebook allows you to connect with other Facebook users—you choose which ones. You first set up your own webpage, which can be private for your designated family and friends or public where anyone can find you and initiate a connection. You can include a photo and personal

Figure 1-1: The movie **Social Network** *presents one interpretation of how Facebook was founded.*

information, or not, and then you can send invitations to others to be "your friend," or respond to others' invitations. You can correspond with all your "friends" at one time or individually, depending on your choice. You have to be over age 13 to use Facebook; most likely, that is not a problem if you're reading this book!

In this chapter we'll find out what Facebook is all about, prepare for and sign up for an account, set some basic

defaults and preferences, and build your initial profile. You also see how to get help, deactivate your account, and log in and out.

PREPARE FOR FACEBOOK

One of the ways you can prepare for Facebook is simply to wrap your mind around how Facebook is impacting our world. We'll start the chapter with ways to think about what Facebook is. Also, I am assuming in this book that you already have a computer and the correct equipment, and that you know the basics about wandering through Windows. However, you may not be signed up for an Internet connection or email account, both of which are required to use Facebook. You'll need to get both before you start; this chapter assumes you have both.

Connect to the Universal Facebook

Working with Facebook over the years, I have come to see it as something more than a sophisticated social networking tool. Indeed, as we witness the role Facebook has played in communicating about revolutions, earthquakes and tsunamis, royal weddings, and other global events, we can see and feel it becoming ever more visible in our lives. It is even changing our language—"facebooking" and "unfriend" are two new words now in our vocabulary. To me, Facebook displays a new form of *global human consciousness*. What do I mean by that?

After all, at one level Facebook is just a computer program using various forms of communications to connect people worldwide, including telephone wires, satellites, computers, and radio waves. It is a human tool—certainly not, one would assume, a thinking entity. But Facebook is also more *present* to the world than a single human mind—it is a connection of millions of minds entering information and communicating through one network. Its presence in the world is not a trivial thing. The implications are immense. One image I have of Facebook is that of a global breathing mechanism: on the inhale, information comes in and is digested and recognized; on the exhale, information in the form of millions of messages is sent racing around the globe. Another image might be that of a global nervous system: stimuli come in the form of billions of bits of information; responses go out in millions of messages along electronic neurons on the Internet. Each human becomes a node in this network—one receptor in a nervous system.

Experience Immediacy of Information

One impact of Facebook, of course, is the immediacy of information. Within a couple of seconds into the 2011 earthquake in Japan, Facebook was broadcasting news of it. During the subsequent tsunami, Facebook was sending photographs and videos, and family members were contacting each other. One friend of mine driving in Japan noticed how Facebook was tracking callers in Japan and displaying messages pertaining to the earthquake and tsunami. On her Facebook page she could view alerts from American officials targeted at Americans in Japan. This was a significant benefit to language and informational challenges in chaotic times. We can see what is happening in all parts of the world, from tribal Africa to the swamps of Louisiana, at the time it is happening.

This ability to connect and the immediacy of information seem stunning in their ramifications. An example is the 2011 Egyptian revolution—Facebook was credited to a large degree with outing a regime through enabling people-to-people communications. In days, a 30-year dictator was dethroned. What enables people to have the courage to change their lives in such a drastic way? One factor would surely be the confidence that they are not alone, that others (whom they don't even know) will support and join their actions—visible though online dialog. Today we can see the effects of Facebook in the struggle for political resolution in determining what kind of a country Egypt will become.

Envision the Viral Nature of Facebook

There is a viral nature to Facebook's passing on of information—no time to consider and analyze. It's just out there. How does this happen? Information passes from one person to a hundred friends, who each pass it on to another hundred friends in an explosion that can reach millions of people in a very short time. You share a comment on Facebook, and all your friends see it. Your friends comment on your post or click "like," and their friends see it, on and on. For people with thousands of Facebook friends, each one with friends or fans of their own, messages fly like bats out of a cave, darkening the sky. Global news, such as political intrigues, are everywhere, instantly.

Appreciate the Mirror of Your Life

Looking at what passes across your Home page or News Feed can be like a mirror—showing your life's voyage, old high school friends, previous wives and husbands, your family, and your changing friends over the years. I've found, and you'll find in the quotes throughout the book, that long-lost friends have resurfaced. Parts of our lives are again made current. Our lives become more of a whole, rather than segmented into current and past parts. It's quite amazing to see one's journey through a lifetime of friends and acquaintances.

Be Aware of Limitations

Facebook is a dynamic tool for finding information and learning about the world in real time, but it has its limitations, or at least some aspects that could be limitations if we're not aware of them.

Be Cautious About the Quality of Information

A hidden consideration is the quality of information you'll find on Facebook. Quality is mixed and reflects who we are as a species. Some of the information is authentic and reveals truth about events and the feelings of the sender. But some is intentionally deceitful, trying to hide truth and propagate lies. Some Facebook messages are inspirational, drawing us to a higher calling of ourselves; others, not so much. It's worth keeping in mind that Facebook is not a place to go for the "real skinny." It requires discernment and thought. Although we as a species now know what is happening on our planet immediately, we don't necessarily know what is happening, if you get my drift. And this uneven quality is who we are as humans. What you confront on Facebook depends on who your friends are.

Think About the Consequences of Selection

This fact, that what you are exposed to depends on your friends, has pros and cons to it. Your friends become a natural filter—you know about what your friends know about. You see opinions of your friends. You may not see opposing viewpoints if your friends share common viewpoints. Consequently, you will not see the whole picture—you only see one side of it. We can become more isolated and centered in our way of thinking unless we are forced to confront and deal with opposing viewpoints.

Note Facebook, as most online sites, changes its "face" frequently. It does this to improve its user interface, making it easier to use, correcting problems, adding new features, and so on. So this book, or any book, will never exactly reproduce your online experience. But it will be very similar so that you can follow along, allowing for the differences you'll no doubt encounter.

⟩⟩ Find a Public Facebook Page

Getting your Internet connection up and running and creating an email account are only beginning steps to getting started with Facebook. First, you will likely find that Facebook is most fun when you have an account, friends, and are connecting with others. But you *can* view pages on Facebook without an account as well. This will give you an idea of what Facebook is about. Then you can sign up, find friends, and set your initial defaults.

Facebook has private and public pages. The public Pages (capital P) are often used by celebrities, events, products, or groups for advertising purposes. You can create one yourself (see Chapter 9). Also, these Pages are available to non-Facebook viewers. They are very similar to your own Home page. To simply and quickly view a Page on Facebook, follow these steps.

1. Open your Internet browser, and type Facebook.com in the address bar. The Home page of Facebook will be displayed—you can see the form in Figure 1-2.

2. Scroll to the bottom of the page, and click **Pages** on the bottom link bar. You'll see a page of thumbnail images organized alphabetically.

3. Click the letter of the alphabet you want, and then click the thumbnail to see the Facebook public Pages for an individual or group, as shown in Figure 1-3.

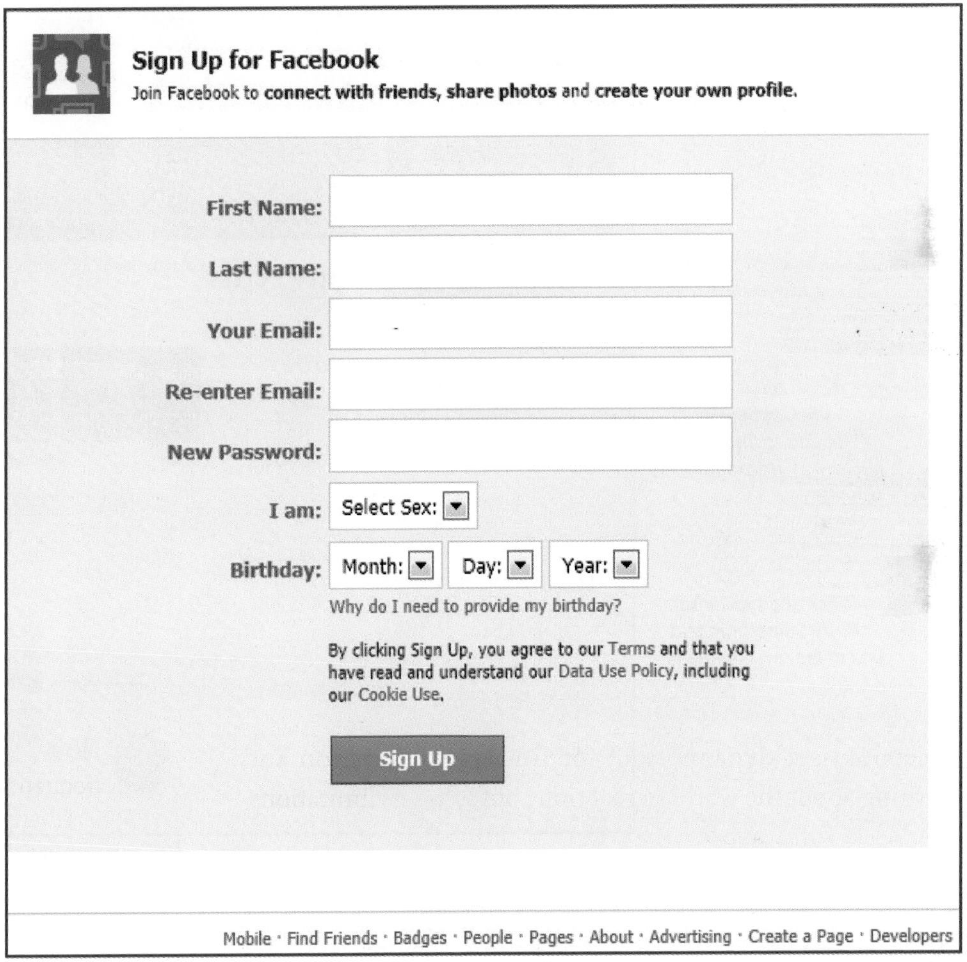

Sign Up for Facebook
Join Facebook to **connect with friends, share photos** and **create your own profile.**

First Name:

Last Name:

Your Email:

Re-enter Email:

New Password:

I am: Select Sex: ▼

Birthday: Month: ▼ Day: ▼ Year: ▼
Why do I need to provide my birthday?

By clicking Sign Up, you agree to our Terms and that you have read and understand our Data Use Policy, including our Cookie Use.

Sign Up

Mobile · Find Friends · Badges · People · Pages · About · Advertising · Create a Page · Developers

*Figure 1-2: **The Home page of Facebook is where you find a form or sign up for an account.***

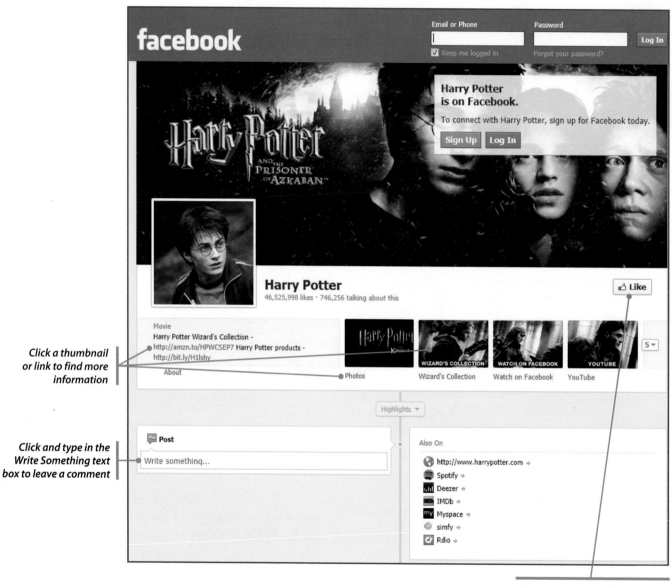

Click a thumbnail or link to find more information

Click and type in the Write Something text box to leave a comment

Click to indicate you like this page

Figure 1-3: *Similar to your own page, a Facebook Page contains navigational tabs and postings from the site.*

Pat Fights Being a Dinosaur with Facebook

I never thought about Facebook until my daughters flagged me as a technological dinosaur. They rummaged through my email contacts shouting, "Don't you want to be friends with your buddies?" I thought I was friends with them, but I quickly learned Facebook carries friendships to a dynamic new level.

Imagine yourself at a party chatting with varied acquaintances, friends, and family. Some you know well; others you have not seen in years, or know only tangentially. With some, you will have thought-provoking, personal exchanges. Some discussions will be in groups, about books or a football game. Others you will want to track day-to-day events. Facebook enables you to keep up with all, gaining an expanded sense of family and friendship.

I use Facebook for social networking and follow that old advice "Don't talk about sex, religion, or politics" when I write posts available to everyone. For private or select group conversations, I use Facebook messages. I encourage you to learn to use Facebook, set your privacy comfort level, and start reconnecting. Post pictures—they speak thousands of words. Oh, and don't spy on your kids. It's counterproductive.

Pat T., 68, Colorado

GET A FACEBOOK ACCOUNT

In this chapter you will get a Facebook account, perhaps saving a lot of the entering of data until later, if you choose. Chapter 2 explains how to input your personal profile in detail after your account is set up, so if you want to wait until later to enter personal data,

do so. I actually recommend this in order to simplify the sign-up process and to have time to consider the implications of entering that data. Facebook creates a special "Welcome" environment that enables you to enter data easily when you are first establishing your site. This chapter covers the Welcome environment. However, you may find that entering your information at that time is inconvenient or you're not yet comfortable doing it right then. So, Chapter 2 covers how you enter the same data once your Welcome environment is unavailable.

Note You may not want to use your normal email account for your Facebook account, having greater privacy if you use a separate account from your regular email. You can quickly set up a new account using **web mail**. Web mail is the sending and receiving of email over the Internet using a browser, such as Internet Explorer, instead of an email program, such as Windows Live Mail. There are many web mail programs, such as Windows Live Hotmail (hotmail.com), Yahoo! Mail (mail.yahoo.com), and Google's Gmail (gmail .com). As long as you have access to the Internet, you can sign up for one or more of these services, usually getting the basic features (simple sending and receiving of email) for free.

Sign Up for an Account

Setting up your beginning account is easy. You simply fill in an initial form with basic information, and then fill in the holes later with your personal data in your own Facebook page. If you find that you are not ready to fill in the details, you can skip some steps and do it later—"Skip" will be an option. To get started you'll need an email address.

1. Open your browser, such as Internet Explorer, type facebook .com in its address bar, and press **ENTER**. The Facebook Sign In page is displayed, shown earlier in Figure 1-2.

2. Fill in the form with your name, email address, and a password. Enter your gender and birth date (needed to verify that you are old enough to register). Click **Sign Up**.

3. You may (or may not) have to type in the security check words designed to keep **bots**, or robot/drone computers, from pretending to be a person to access Facebook illegally. If the words are hard to distinguish, you may have to reenter them more than once. It's a pain, but worthwhile. (The illustration contains one error in the typed code—can you find it? The answer is below.) Click **Sign Up**. The three-step page for completing your webpage will be displayed.

4. The first step in finalizing your webpage is to find your friends. If you want Facebook to look in your email files and find your friends, enter your email address and email password, and click **Find Friends**. Otherwise, scroll to the bottom and click **Skip This Step**—there will be other opportunities to find your friends. You'll have to verify that you want to skip this step.

5. Step two allows you to enter your profile information. If you choose to do so now, type your high school, college,

or university; the years you graduated from each; and then your employer. You may prefer to not enter dates that would reveal your age—in that case, you might want to wait and enter this later. Click **Save & Continue**. If you want to skip this step, click **Skip**—you'll have another opportunity later.

- If you choose to enter the data now as you type school and employment data, you'll see a list of possibilities (schools with the same names, for instance) presented to you; click the correct one if it is listed.

- Also, if you enter profile information at this point, you may see pictures of people you may or may not know and be asked if you want to add any as friends. Click any images of people who you know and want as friends in Facebook, or just click **Skip** or **Save & Continue** again.

6. The third step allows you to insert a picture of yourself onto your webpage. You can insert a photo or graphic using one of two techniques. Click **Upload A Photo** to find and retrieve a picture from your hard disk. Click **Browse** to locate the picture, and double-click it when found. Alternatively, click **Take A Photo** to take the photo with your webcam (the instructions for doing this are in this chapter in the section "Get Your Photo"). If you upload or take a photo, click **Save & Continue**; otherwise, click **Skip** to do this later. At this point you'll see the Welcome To Facebook page of your new Facebook webpage.

7. However, there is one more step. You'll need to go to your email inbox, where you should see two email messages from Facebook. Double-click the **Just One More Step** email and click the link. You will automatically be confirmed and your Facebook page displayed, as shown in Figure 1-4.

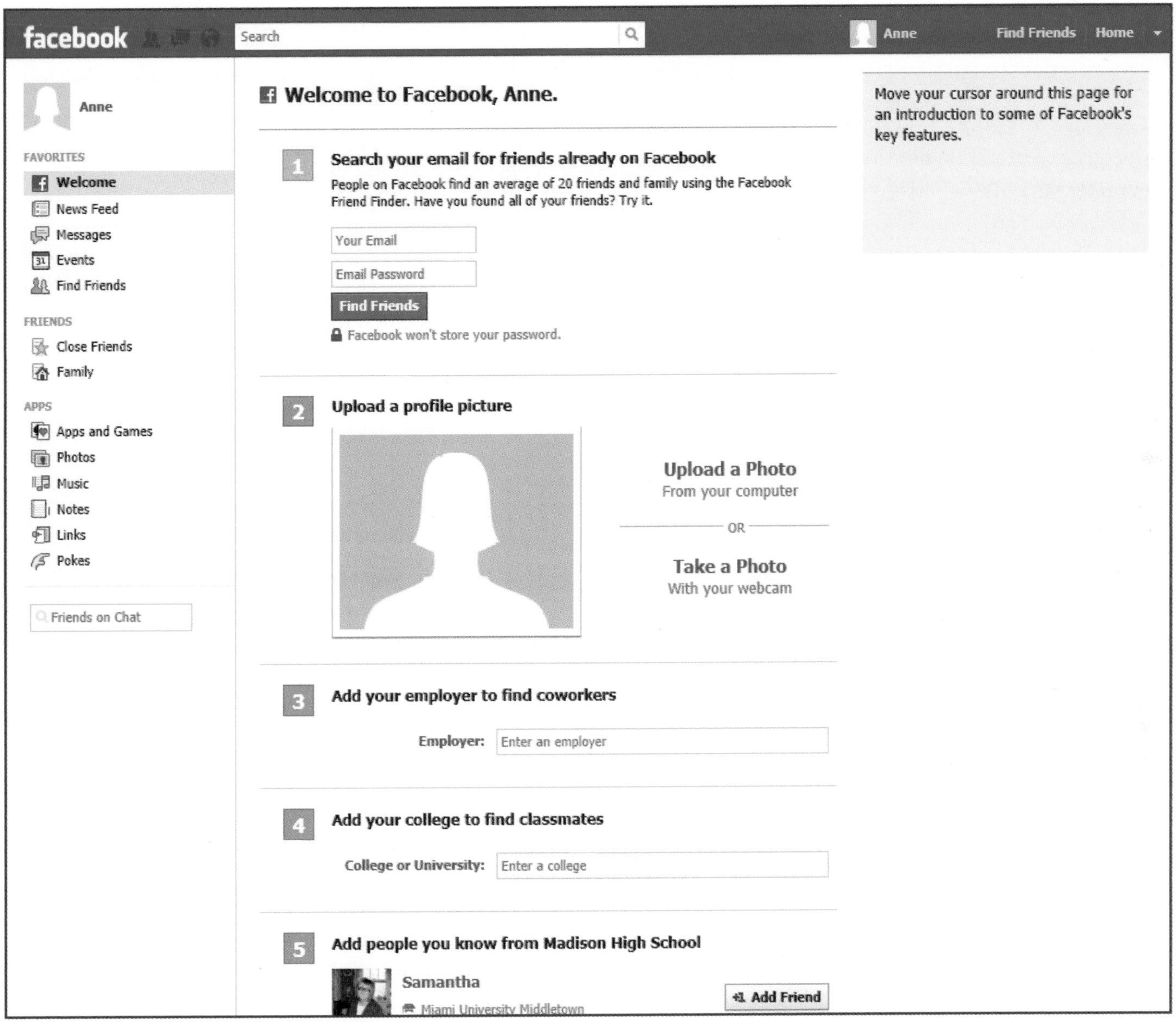

facebook   Search   Anne   Find Friends   Home

Anne

FAVORITES
- **Welcome**
- News Feed
- Messages
- Events
- Find Friends

FRIENDS
- Close Friends
- Family

APPS
- Apps and Games
- Photos
- Music
- Notes
- Links
- Pokes

Friends on Chat

Welcome to Facebook, Anne.

1   **Search your email for friends already on Facebook**

People on Facebook find an average of 20 friends and family using the Facebook Friend Finder. Have you found all of your friends? Try it.

Your Email

Email Password

Find Friends

🔒 Facebook won't store your password.

2   **Upload a profile picture**

Upload a Photo
From your computer

OR

Take a Photo
With your webcam

3   **Add your employer to find coworkers**

Employer: Enter an employer

4   **Add your college to find classmates**

College or University: Enter a college

5   **Add people you know from Madison High School**

Samantha
Miami University Middletown   **+1 Add Friend**

Move your cursor around this page for an introduction to some of Facebook's key features.

*Figure 1-4: **When your email has been confirmed, your Facebook account is ready for you to enter the rest of your profile information.***

Note The Welcome to Facebook email allows you to click either the **Get Started** link or one of the three links in the body to begin your setup. You can come back to this email at any time. (In Facebook, to return to this beginning page, you can also just click **Home** in the upper right of the screen, and then **Welcome** in the left column.)

If you have chosen to skip entering your friends or profile, you can see how to do it in "Enter Personal Information in the Welcome Page" in this chapter, or refer to Chapter 2 to see how to do it at some future time.

Tip Incidentally, the missing colon is the error in the illustration.

Open Facebook the Easy Way

To place a Facebook tab on your Internet Explorer browser so that you can quickly find your webpage whenever you open the browser:

1. With your Facebook account opened in your Internet Explorer browser, find and click the down arrow on the Home icon (in IE 8), or right-click the **Home** icon (in IE 9) and, in either case, click **Add Or Change Home Page**.

2. Click one of the following options, and then click **Yes**. (Click **No** if you don't want Facebook to open automatically when you open the browser.)

- **Use This Webpage As Your Only Home Page** When you open your browser, this tab will be the only one that opens.

- **Add This Webpage To Your Home Page Tabs** This adds a tab for Facebook to the other tabs currently available when you open the browser. This is the set of tabs displayed when you open your browser.

- **Use The Current Tab Set As Your Home Page** This makes the current set of tabs available by default whenever you open the browser.

3. If you selected one of the options and clicked Yes, the next time you open your browser, a tab with the Facebook webpage will appear. If Facebook is not displayed, click the tab name (click **Login** and click **Facebook**) to open it.

Enter Personal Information in the Welcome Page

When you signed up for your Facebook account, you had the opportunity to fill in personal information. After activating an account, Facebook welcomes you with a page, shown earlier in Figure 1-4, that leads you through finding friends, filling in your profile, and specifying which information may be displayed to the public. (If you don't see it immediately, click **Welcome** on the left side.) On each step described next, just click the appropriate button, such as **Find Friends** or **Upload A Photo**. It is very straightforward, as you'll see in the following sections.

However, unlike a lot of things in life, you will always be able to enter or modify your profile information. Chapter 2 describes how to change your profile information, even after you've gone "live."

> **Tip** If you should lose your place after completing a section of adding personal information, click **Home** in the upper-right menu bar and click the **Welcome** link on the left column. You should be returned to the Welcome To Facebook page. Eventually, the Welcome link will disappear or become unreliable—there are other ways to access and change all the information, such as to click **yourname | About**.

Find Friends in Your Email List

If you type an email address that has a contact list associated with it, Facebook will import the email addresses and find those contacts who also have Facebook pages. You will be able to choose which contacts you want to import into Facebook. To do this, you'll need your email address and password. After you have chosen them to be your friend, an invitation is sent to each. They then confirm you as a friend before they appear on your list of friends.

1. In the Welcome page, type your email address and password into the text boxes, and click **Find Friends**. A window showing a list of people containing Facebook pages will be displayed.

2. Click the check boxes beside the names you want as friends, and click **Add As Friends**. You can also click **Select All Friends** to import all individuals in the list.

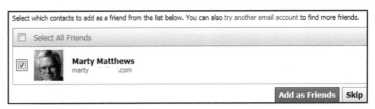

3. Repeat these steps with other email addresses if you choose.

To return to the initial page, you may need to click your browser's back arrow button a couple of times or click **Home** on the menu bar and **Welcome** on the left sidebar. In this case, you'll see that Find Friends is no longer displayed on the page, but you can still add friends easily.

Find Friends by Name

You may want to add friends not on your email list. You can ask Facebook to search for friends using either name or email address.

1. Under Find People You Know (see Figure 1-5), type the person's name or email address, and click the **Search** icon. If you have typed the name, a list of candidates will be displayed. You'll need to search through the list and find the one you want. If you typed the email address, the exact person is displayed.

2. Click the image, and on the person's page, click **Add Friend**. A request will be sent to them to be your friend. When they get your message and accept you, you'll see a message on your Facebook page confirming the friend status.

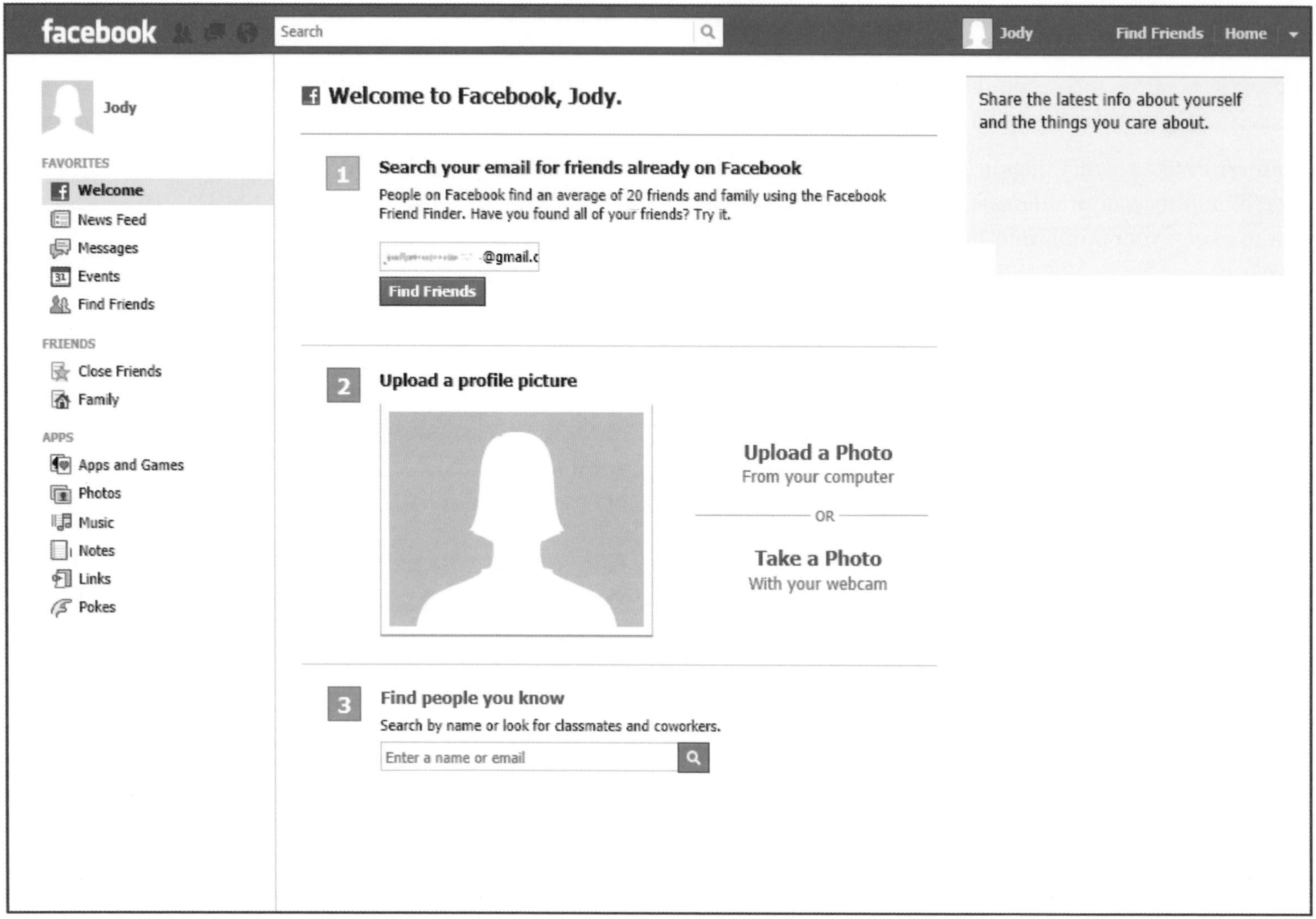

facebook 👥 💬 🌐 | Search 🔍 | 👤 Jody   **Find Friends** | Home ▾

👤 Jody

FAVORITES
- 📘 **Welcome**
- 📋 News Feed
- 💬 Messages
- 📅 Events
- 👥 Find Friends

FRIENDS
- ⭐ Close Friends
- 🏠 Family

APPS
- 🎮 Apps and Games
- 📷 Photos
- 🎵 Music
- 📄 Notes
- 🔗 Links
- 👈 Pokes

📘 **Welcome to Facebook, Jody.**

1 **Search your email for friends already on Facebook**
People on Facebook find an average of 20 friends and family using the Facebook Friend Finder. Have you found all of your friends? Try it.

[................@gmail.c]

Find Friends

2 **Upload a profile picture**

Upload a Photo
From your computer

———— OR ————

Take a Photo
With your webcam

3 **Find people you know**
Search by name or look for classmates and coworkers.

[Enter a name or email] 🔍

Share the latest info about yourself and the things you care about.

Figure 1-5: The Welcome page allows you to enter information and find friends using the same initial entry format.

QuickQuotes

Deborah Expands Her Networks

I'm a visual artist. The image orientation and relational aspects of Facebook present a dynamic landscape of family and friends from around the world and different phases of my life. Facebook keeps me aware and connected in new and expanded ways.

An example of this is an experience I had meeting Joan, who was attending a workshop of mine in New York. We agreed to connect through Facebook—just a casual intention.

Subsequently, in Japan while presenting another workshop, the big earthquake forced me to leave prematurely. I found myself in Hong Kong for three days because those flights were unavailable. As I sat wondering what to do, I posted on Facebook, "Guess what! I'm in Hong Kong for three days!" Soon after, Joan responded, "You're in Hong Kong? Come stay with me!" Over the three days I held a surprise workshop; met a rich and rewarding group of colleagues in Hong Kong; and formed a strong, personal friendship with Joan.

Joan also needed a mentor for a project she was embarking upon. I knew just the person, Joe. Joe, retiring from an academic career, found that this invitation to mentor Joan in her project gave him a sense of new possibilities. Rich outcomes from one casual connection on Facebook!

Deborah C., 61, Washington

Get Your Photo

Placing a photo on your Facebook page makes it more interesting and lets others, especially people who have not seen you in person for a while, know that you are the person they are trying to reach. You must have either a digital photo or a webcam to take your photo.

1. On your Welcome page under Upload A Profile Picture, click **Upload Photo** to use an existing digital photo.

2. Click the **Browse** button on the right of the text box to open Windows Explorer and browse for your photo file. When you find it, double-click the photo or click the photo and click **Open**. The photo will appear on your page.

–Or–

1. To use a webcam photo, click **Take A Photo**. The Take A Profile Photo window will open and display the Adobe Flash Player Settings dialog box.

2. Click **Allow** to let Facebook access your camera, and use the icons on the bottom to adjust how Facebook is using your camera.

- The leftmost icon allows hardware acceleration (which you probably want).
- The second icon contains privacy permission allowing Facebook to access your webcam photo.
- The third icon allows you to set the amount of storage that can be used for the picture.
- The fourth icon, which really doesn't apply here, allows you to set the sound source and the volume level.
- The rightmost icon allows you to select the camera that you want to use.

To save the camera settings in the dialog box, click **Remember**.

1. Look into the camera, and when you like the image, click the **Camera** icon, and then wait for the countdown (3-2-1) while your photo is taken (smiling is optional, but lighting is critical!).

2. To save the picture, click **Save Picture**. To do it again, click the **X** in the upper-right corner to delete the picture and start over.

Note If you find you want to change your profile photo in some way, either by adding a new one or changing the position of the image (for instance, perhaps the top of your head is shaved off or your face is too near the left side of the frame), see Chapter 2 for how to do it.

Tip When taking a profile picture with a webcam, after clicking **Remember** in the Adobe Flash Player Settings dialog box, that dialog box is not shown again. If you want to return to the settings dialog box, right-click the **Camera** icon and click **Settings**.

Add Profile Info and Fill in Your Friend List

While you still have access to the Welcome page, you can fill in more of your friends. Getting connected with others is how you will truly experience the benefits of Facebook. The following instructions, depending on how much information you have already entered, may display slightly different numbering and titles of the Welcome page items than what you have on your page. However, the differences will be obvious. When you add someone as a friend, an invitation is first sent to them. They must agree to be your friend. To find more friends:

1. Under Add Your Employer To Find Coworkers, type the name of your employer in the Employer text box. A list of names with thumbnail images will be displayed, with others who work for that employer. You may want to click **See All Suggestions** to see more names. Click **Add Friend** for any that you know and want as your friend. An invitation will be sent to each person informing them that you want to be a friend.

2. Under Add Your College To Find Classmates, type the name in the College Or University text box. A list of potential classmates will be displayed. Again, you may want to click **See All Suggestions** to see more names. Click **Add Friend** for anyone whom you want as a friend.

3. Under Add Your High School To Find Classmates, type the name in the High School text box. Again, a list of people will be displayed. Click **See All Suggestions** to see additional names. Then click **Add Friend** for those classmates you'd like as a friend.

4. Under Add More People You Know, you'll see a list of people who are friends with anyone you have already selected as being a friend. This is a good way to find people you might not think about otherwise. Again click **Add Friend** to send a request to be your friend.

Fill in Basic Information

Before you go too much further, it is good to enter other important information. Security is an important element in entering this information, and Chapter 10 discusses security in detail. I'll cover some of the basics here, but Chapter 10 is the place to go for more answers. Before you start, think about how much information you feel comfortable revealing. For example, it's really not a good idea to reveal all information about yourself because of the problems around identity theft. Your exact location and birth date are examples of information I would never reveal.

To get to this information, which is discussed in more detail in Chapter 2, follow these steps:

1. Click your name in the upper-right menu bar.

2. Scroll down until you see Basic Information. Click **Edit**. The form shown in Figure 1-6 is displayed.

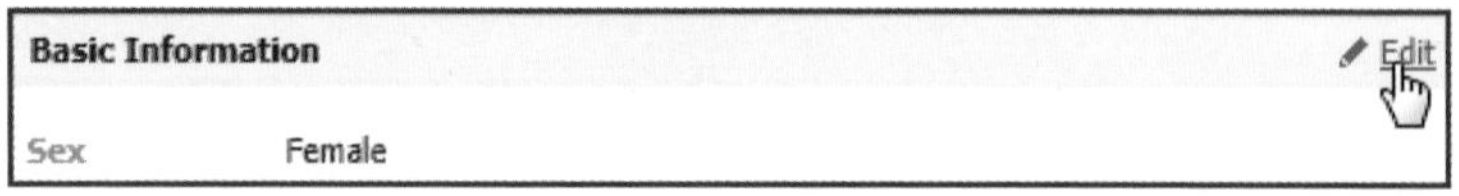

Basic Information	✎ Edit
Sex	Female

3. Here is where you need to ask yourself some basic security questions. Here are our recommendations:

- When showing location, we recommend that you don't enter your exact location. It's better to specify a city close to you in the same state.

- It's better not to display your whole birthday. You can choose to display the whole thing, only the month and day, or not at all.

- Be careful what you reveal about yourself, such as the names of children or grandchildren. You want a balance between revealing enough of yourself to be interesting and authentic, and not revealing too much so that someone can take advantage. You can choose where the balance feels right to you.

4. Click **Save Changes** when you are finished.

Figure 1-6: **Basic Information contains the bare minimum of profile data.**

Final Thoughts on Entering Personal Information

You can also edit settings for your mobile phone and find more friends. Chapters 2 and 5 give you information on how to configure these settings. This section has given you a quick overview of how to set your initial profile. Remember that you can change these settings and more at any time.

FIND USEFUL TIPS

Here are a few useful tips that you may find are needed sometime during your Facebook life. For instance, Facebook has a Help Center that can be enlightening. It gives you tips on how to do more common tasks, such as adding friends or troubleshooting problems. Although you cannot directly contact Facebook to discuss specific problems, you can search through a myriad of questions that have already been answered and enter a new question of your own, which the gods of Facebook may opt to answer—or not.

Access the Help Center

The Help Center is a system of questions and answers plus user discussions. Frankly, it is not a great help system. It is hard to find the answers to specific questions—and you need to have the right question or it is no help at all. The discussions often reflect a high level of frustration of people trying to figure out unique problems. However, for the most common needs, it will probably work for you. To access and use Facebook Help:

1. Click the down arrow to the right of Home on the menu bar, and click **Help**. You'll see another menu.

2. You'll see a small dialog box asking what help you want. You can either click a specific Help topic, such as Manage Your News Feed, or click in the Search For Help text box and type your own topic. To get a greater understanding of the Help feature, click **Visit The Help Center** link at the bottom. The window shown in Figure 1-7 is displayed.

3. On the left is a navigation bar containing links to the overall concerns. For instance, Facebook Basics will give you information on the overall use of Facebook. If you want to view help for games, click **Apps, Games And Credits**.

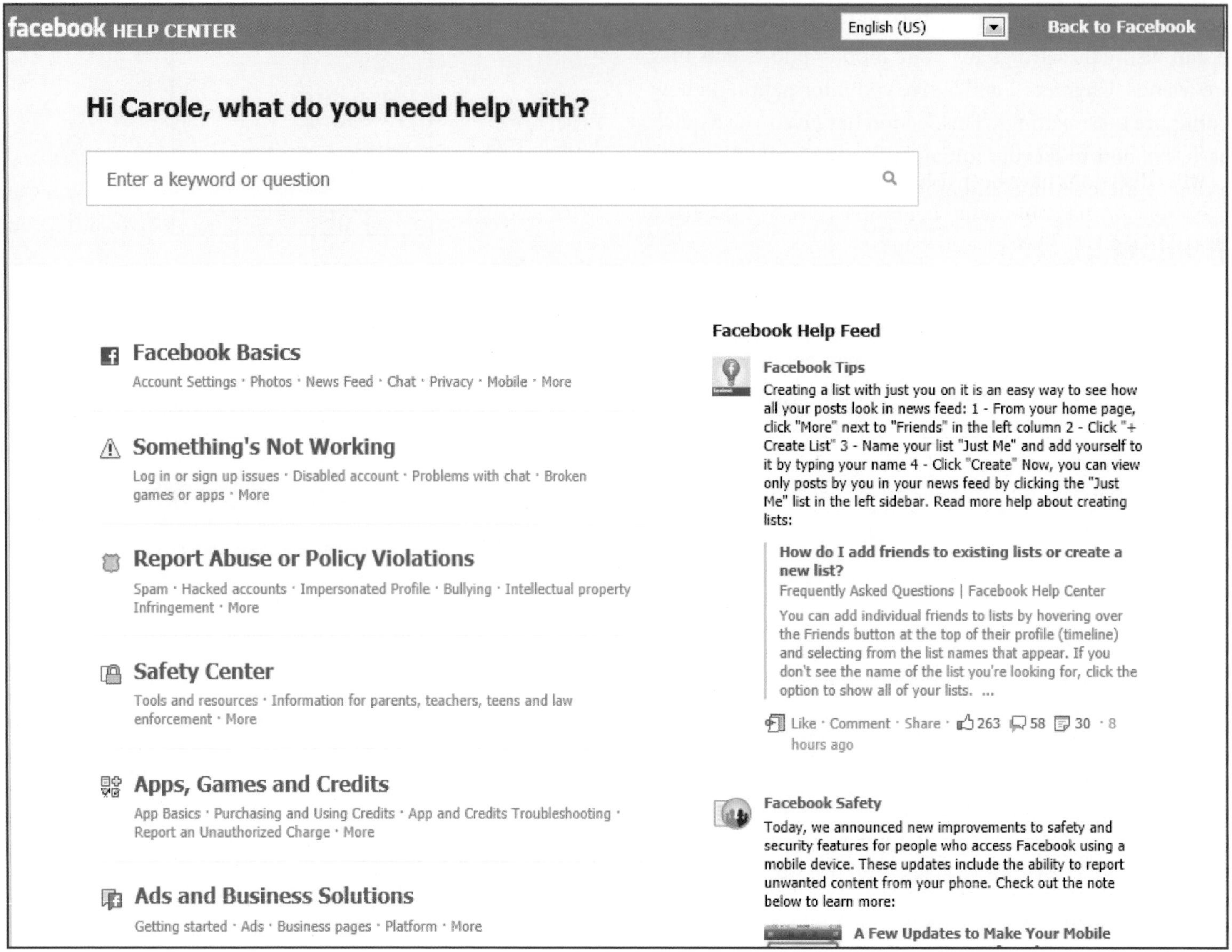

facebook HELP CENTER

English (US) ▾   **Back to Facebook**

Hi Carole, what do you need help with?

Enter a keyword or question   🔍

Facebook Help Feed

 Facebook Basics

Account Settings · Photos · News Feed · Chat · Privacy · Mobile · More

⚠ **Something's Not Working**

Log in or sign up issues · Disabled account · Problems with chat · Broken games or apps · More

🛡 **Report Abuse or Policy Violations**

Spam · Hacked accounts · Impersonated Profile · Bullying · Intellectual property Infringement · More

🔒 **Safety Center**

Tools and resources · Information for parents, teachers, teens and law enforcement · More

▦ **Apps, Games and Credits**

App Basics · Purchasing and Using Credits · App and Credits Troubleshooting · Report an Unauthorized Charge · More

 Ads and Business Solutions

Getting started · Ads · Business pages · Platform · More

Facebook Tips

Creating a list with just you on it is an easy way to see how all your posts look in news feed: 1 - From your home page, click "More" next to "Friends" in the left column 2 - Click "+ Create List" 3 - Name your list "Just Me" and add yourself to it by typing your name 4 - Click "Create" Now, you can view only posts by you in your news feed by clicking the "Just Me" list in the left sidebar. Read more help about creating lists:

How do I add friends to existing lists or create a new list?
Frequently Asked Questions | Facebook Help Center

You can add individual friends to lists by hovering over the Friends button at the top of their profile (timeline) and selecting from the list names that appear. If you don't see the name of the list you're looking for, click the option to show all of your lists. ...

👍 Like · Comment · Share · 👍263 💬58 📋30 · 8 hours ago

Facebook Safety

Today, we announced new improvements to safety and security features for people who access Facebook using a mobile device. These updates include the ability to report unwanted content from your phone. Check out the note below to learn more:

A Few Updates to Make Your Mobile

Figure 1-7: The Help Center, always available, contains links to information you may find useful.

4. Beneath the list of overall topics is a link to the Community Forum. Click it and you will see the Community Help topics for specific areas of Facebook. Which topics are displayed depends on the selected link on the left—Community Forum at the bottom is the default. Click a link to find out what questions have been asked by the community. At the bottom of the community help topics, you'll see links to My Questions, My Answers, and Questions I'm Following. These allow you to track your questions and answers, and those of other community members.

5. To return to your Facebook page, click **Back To Facebook** in the upper right of the menu bar. (You may have to click **Facebook Help Center** on the upper left first.)

Deactivate Your Account

When you deactivate your account, it is unavailable to others. You can reactivate it at a future time. If you find that you want to make your Facebook account inactive, here is how you do it.

1. Click the down arrow to the right of Home, and click **Account Settings**.

2. Click **Security** on the left column. Then beneath the list of Security Settings, click **Deactivate Your Account**. The Are You Sure You Want To Deactivate Your Account? page is displayed.

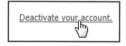

3. Click a **Reason For Leaving** option—this is required. You can optionally click **Other** and then click in the text box and type a message. Click the **Email Opt Out** check box if you do not want to receive further emails from Facebook.

4. Click **Confirm**. Or you can click **Cancel** to change your mind. You'll need to enter your password to confirm it is really you and then a security code.

Reactivate Your Account

Once you have deactivated your account, you can easily restore it: Simply log in to your account with your email address and password.

Terminate an Account

You can also, with a bit of difficulty, terminate a Facebook account if you are sure you will never want it again. When you do this, all information on your Facebook account is no longer available. You cannot be found in a search. You cannot reactivate the account or retrieve any content. (Some comments that you have posted to others will still be visible on their sites, however.)

1. From the down arrow to the right of Home on the menu bar, click **Help** and then click **Visit The Help Center**.

2. In the Search text box at the top of the Help Center page, type <u>terminate an account</u>. You'll see a list of Frequently Asked Questions (FAQ) results.

3. Click **How Do I Permanently Delete My Account?**

Help Center Search

"terminate an account"

FAQ Results

▸ How do I permanently delete my account?
If you deactivate your account from your Security Settings page, your profile (timeline) disappears from the Facebook service immediately. People on Faceb...

4. In about the third paragraph down you'll see a link to permanently delete your account.

> If you do not think you will use Facebook again and would like your account deleted, keep in mind that you will not be able to reactivate your account or retrieve any of the content or information you have added. If you would like your account **permanently deleted with no option for recovery**, log in to your account and then submit your request here.

▷▷ Log In and Out

It's a good thing to officially log out of your Facebook account, especially if you are not the only one using your computer, or if there are others who can peek at your computer monitor. If your Facebook page is open, anyone can see what is on it. This may not be a problem, but if it is, log out.

- To log in, just type facebook.com in the browser address bar, enter your email address and password, and click **Log In**.

Email or Phone	Password	
youremail.com	••••••••	**Log In**
☑ Keep me logged in	Forgot your password?	

- To log out, click the down arrow to the right of Home on the menu bar, and click **Log Out**.

✓ QuickFacts

Reviewing a Facebook Glossary

Facebook has its own vocabulary. Here are some common words you'll encounter:

- **Chat** You can "chat" with someone else who is online at the same time. You indicate that you want to chat, and a dialog box opens, allowing the two of you to hold a person-to-person, written conversation.

- **Friend** A friend is someone you usually know, but may not, whom you have judged to be able to view your personal information, your Timeline Wall, and your postings. Usually this is someone imported from your email contact list, but you can also find their Facebook page (usually because you have friends in common) and ask to be their friend.

- **Like** When you see a comment, photo, or posting of someone else's that you like or agree with, you can click a Like link that allows you to indicate your pleasure without writing anything. It shows to others that you have read their comments or viewed a photo or video and acknowledge it.

- **Newsfeed** When your friends (or others, not necessarily your friends, where you have commented on a Facebook page) post something to be shared, it is shown on your Home page. You see a stream of comments from everyone you have as friends on Facebook. You can see comments and happenings from old and new friends, from organizations you follow, and from individuals playing games you play. It is the primary focus of Facebook.

- **Poke someone** This is an irritating way to say "Here I am" to your friends. If you have to do this at all, do it sparingly. When you poke someone, a "poke" icon appears on their page with the ability to remove it or "poke back."

(continued)

- **Postings**   This is a comment you type and share with others. It can be in response to another's posting or a new one of your own. This is how you communicate with all your friends at once and others on Facebook.

- **Profile**   Your personal information is your profile. Your education, home, family, job, contact information, and so on are how you communicate with others about yourself. It is displayed on your Timeline protected by your audience selectors—a way of setting privacy by selecting who will see your personal information. Some of your personal information, such as your name and profile picture is by default set to Public and cannot be hidden without hiding the site.

- **Tagging**   You can tag a photo, post, pages, events, groups, or applications. When you do, you place a link in your News Feed that lets others link through your post to the tagged source. This enables you to draw attention to elements in Facebook that you like and want others to see.

- **Timeline**   Facebook's "album" approach to displaying the content of your Wall, including previously posted comments, photos, and replies from others. The information about you is posted according to the date it was entered into Facebook. You can add information about your life into the Timeline so others can see what has happened to you in the various years. A Timeline replaces the Profile page in earlier releases of Facebook.

- **Wall**   The Wall is the area on your Timeline or older Profile page where you share information about yourself, and others post on your page. It is the content you see when you display your own Timeline or Profile pages or click a friend's Facebook page. It is what others see when they click your name. It contains personal photos, videos, posts and postings from others, and your list of friends You get to it by clicking your own name in the upper-right menu bar.

Chapter 2

Customizing Your Facebook Site

One of the fun things about Facebook is having your own webpages. When you open an account on Facebook, you are given your own webpage, which you can customize to a limited degree according to your own desires. This chapter takes a look at the standard Facebook pages, and then leads you through setting some preferences. If you find that you are confused about what pages are used for what, you can't find what you're looking for, or you are hesitant about which information to reveal or keep hidden, this chapter will make your Facebook life easier.

EXPLORE YOUR FACEBOOK PAGES

Once you have entered some data, invited friends, and set yourself up in Facebook, the Welcome page shown in Chapter 1 will go away. The remaining set of pages allow you to "do the business" of Facebook, such as the Home page shown in Figure 2-1. You'll see that there are five primary pages for you to understand:

- **Home** Displays your News Feed and gives you access to Facebook's many links. No one else can see this but you.

Left column · Center column · Right column · Ticker/Chat sidebar

Menu bar

Links to other views and pages

Indicates who is online · Hide/Show sidebar

Figure 2-1: When your screen is maximized, you'll see a Ticker/Chat column in the Home and Timeline pages.

- **Timeline**   Displays your personal profile information, your Wall (where personal comments are shared), your friends, and photos. Your friends will see this.

- **Find Friends**   Offers several ways for you to invite new friends.

- **Account Settings**   Includes a menu of options that allow you to, for instance, change your general account information and set account preferences.

- **Security Settings**   Allows you to set security for your Facebook information.

These pages contain many common links and bits of information, but they are specialized for particular uses.

> **Note**   Timeline has replaced the older Profile page (see "Work with an Alternate Profile Page"). This book assumes you are using Timeline. However, you may be one of the people who have not converted to Timeline. If this is the case, you'll find Tips throughout the book directing you to the features using the Profile page. It is recommended, however, that you convert to Timeline. Once you're used to it, you'll find it more intuitive and visually interesting to use.

Understand Your Home Page

When you want to know what's going on in your friends' worlds, go Home! Your Home page is known primarily as the place where your *News Feed* is displayed. A News Feed is the flow of information your friends are choosing to share. It is also a place where you can create and post your own comments (as is your Timeline page). You can reach other pages in Facebook from the Home page—it is your starting place. The page itself is divided into three or four columns with a menu bar at the top.

Understand Screen Sizing

The first thing to be aware of is that the contents of the window change depending on the size of your window. For instance, if your Home page is "maximized" (when your window fills the screen and the Maximize status is active in the upper right of your window), you'll see four columns, as shown in Figure 2-1. The fourth column is a sidebar containing the ticker or activity of your friends and a list of friends currently online and available to chat. However, if your window is "not maximized" (where your window is smaller than the screen and the Restore status is active), you'll see three columns, shown in Figure 2-2.

To confuse things further, if the window is not maximized, the columns rearrange themselves. For instance, the Ticker is now crammed into the third column and the Chat list is in the left column. This book assumes the "not maximized" version for most of the discussion, without the sidebar.

Display the News Feed on Your Home Page

You can get to your Home page from anywhere in Facebook by clicking **Home** in the upper-right menu bar or by clicking the **Facebook** logo on the left of the menu bar. If your News Feed is not showing, click **News Feed** beneath your profile photo.

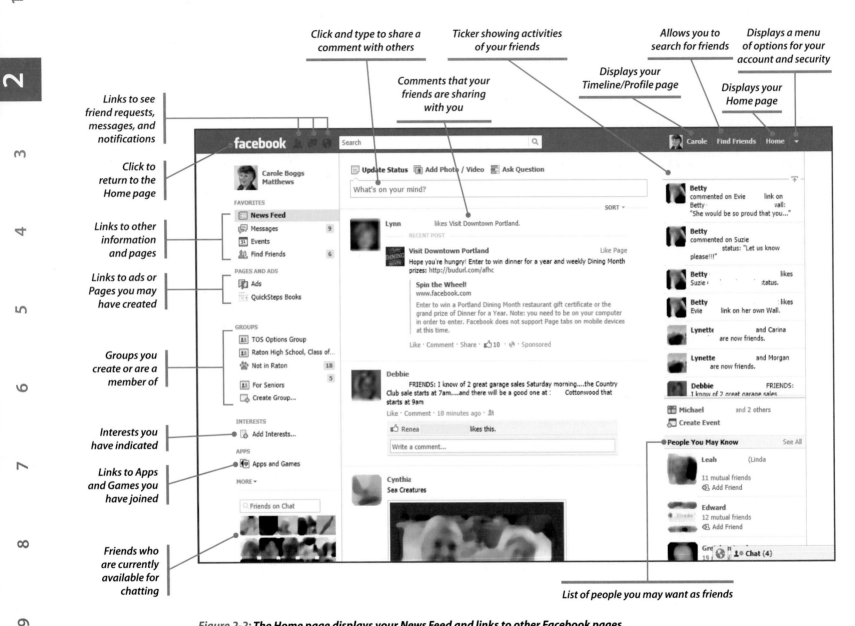

Click and type to share a comment with others

Ticker showing activities of your friends

Allows you to search for friends

Displays a menu of options for your account and security

Comments that your friends are sharing with you

Displays your Timeline/Profile page

Displays your Home page

Links to see friend requests, messages, and notifications

Click to return to the Home page

Links to other information and pages

Links to ads or Pages you may have created

Groups you create or are a member of

Interests you have indicated

Links to Apps and Games you have joined

Friends who are currently available for chatting

List of people you may want as friends

Figure 2-2: *The Home page displays your News Feed and links to other Facebook pages.*

2

View the Home Page Menu Bar

Here are some of your options along the menu bar:

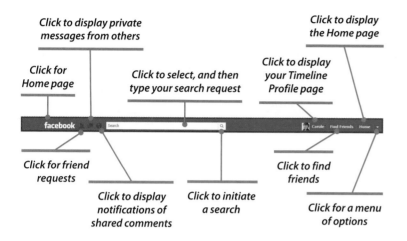

Click to display private messages from others

Click for Home page

Click to select, and then type your search request

Click to display your Timeline Profile page

Click to display the Home page

Click for friend requests

Click to display notifications of shared comments

Click to initiate a search

Click to find friends

Click for a menu of options

- **Facebook** The logo in the upper-left corner is displayed on all pages. Click it to return to the Home page.

- **Friend Requests** This is where you can see outstanding requests from others to be your friend. Just click the name and a request dialog box will appear. You can also click **Find Friends** on the left column of the Home page for the Find Friends page. Chapter 3 discusses managing your friends in more detail.

- **Messages** Lists private messages you have had with others. You can click a message to see it in its entirety. You can also click **Send A New Message** in the dialog box to send your own message to someone else. You'll find more on sending messages in Chapter 4.

- **Notifications** Lists friends who have commented on or in some way interacted with one of your postings or status changes. You can see how to set notifications later in this chapter.

- **Search** Allows you to search Facebook for friends or groups. Just click in the text box, type a name or email address, and a list of matching friends is displayed as you type. The search results are displayed below the text box.

- **Your Name** Displays your Timeline/Profile page, which is the page others see when they click your name. You can share your own thoughts here as well as on the Home page.

- **Find Friends** This command leads you through finding and inviting others to be your friend. After you are established, this command displays likely candidates to be your friends that are friends of your friends, went to your school, or work in the same company. You are told the number of your friends who are friends with the suggested person.

- **Home** Displays the Home page. This is where you see what your friends have shared. You can communicate with them here, sharing your own thoughts or commenting on a friend's posting, clicking "like," or linking to others in a variety of ways.

- **Down arrow icon** Displays a menu of options relating to your Facebook account. For example, you can establish advertisements, establish settings for your account and privacy, access the Help Center, and log out.

Filter Views, Navigate, and Chat with the Left Column

You can change your Home page's center column, navigate to other pages, and chat online by clicking an option in the left column. In addition, you can see a number of items contained within the option; for example, on my Messages option there are nine messages.

- **Favorites**   The Favorites options immediately below the profile picture are Favorites filters that change the contents of the center column. For instance:
  - **News Feed**   Displays the stream of posts from friends.
  - **Messages**   Shows the contents of your private messages.
  - **Events**   Shows events you've created or been invited to.
  - **Find Friends**   Shows the Friend Finder page
- Beneath the Favorites are several other groupings and links to other pages. You may not find them in the order listed here, and you can change the order in which they appear.
  - **Apps and Games**   Apps, including the addictive games, are initially listed below the Favorites. Apps are covered in Chapter 8.
  - **Groups**   Figure 2-2 shows links to a number of groups. When you initially sign up, you'll not have any groups, but you will be able to click **Create Group**. Groups are addressed in Chapter 7.
  - **Friends on Chat**   Shown on the bottom of the left column (in the non-maximized window), this displays friends who are currently online. If they have a green square in the lower-right corner of an image, they are

available for you to chat with them. Hover your pointer over an individual image to see who it is.

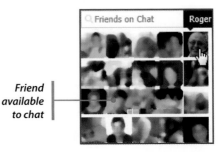

Friend available to chat

Tip   To extend the list of groupings, such as the Groups or Apps link, hover your pointer over the title and then click **More**; the list of links will expand in the center column. Reduce the list again by clicking your browser's back arrow. Some groupings will not have more to view.

QuickQuotes

Nancy Counsels Parents About Facebook

As a grandparent and family counselor, I have found Facebook quickly becoming an issue of serious concern for families in my community. It was clear to me that I needed to learn about Facebook if I was going to be able to help my clients. I didn't want my private life to be visible to my clients, so I was hesitant, and frankly untrusting. I could easily see why parents struggle with their own lack of knowledge while teens fearlessly charge ahead.

(continued)

Update Status, Add Content, and Ask Questions

In the top of the center column on the Home page is a menu bar where you can add your own content to the stream of News Feed. You can add a comment, add a photo or video, create a photo album, or ask a question. Here's how:

> 📝 Update Status   🖼 Add Photo / Video   📊 Ask Question

- **Update Status**   Click **Update Status** to add a comment to the News Feed. The text box will open. You can type your comment, set your privacy option, and click **Post** to publish it.

- **Add Photos or Videos**   Click **Add Photo/Video** to get the options to upload a photo or video, create a webcam, or create a photo album. Chapter 6 discusses how to do these.

- **Ask Question**   Click **Ask Question** and a text box is displayed where you can ask a question or poll your friends for a survey. Chapter 4 looks at this in detail.

Change News Feed View and Share and Add Items with the Center Column

The center column on the Home page is where the News Feed is displayed. This is the content of all the sharing that is being done by your friends that you are allowed to view (a person can restrict who views content, so you may not see everything a friend is posting). Here are your options:

- **Change News Feed View**   To the right of the News Feed, click the **Sort** down arrow. It will display a menu showing Top News and Most Recent; if you click one, the other will become the link. Top News displays postings that Facebook thinks are the most interesting. It uses an algorithm involving the number of people viewing a post or responding in some way to determine this. Of course, Facebook's assessment of "interest" may have nothing to do with your own judgment of your most interesting posts! When you click **Most Recent**, you'll see the most recent postings of all your friends.

> SORT
> ✓ **Top Stories**
> Most Recent

> 📌 **Note**   The difference between the News Feed on your Home page and the Wall on your Timeline (or Profile if you don't have Timeline) page may be hazy to start with. Your News Feed is just a continuous stream of postings, videos, or photos shared by your friends, or notifications when friends click Like or type comments on another person's post. Your own shared comments are in the News Feed as well. The News Feed is the universe of sharings from your friends. The Wall, on the other hand, is personal. It is about you. It shows your postings or threads of conversations on which you have commented or "liked." If you personally are tagged, responded to, or acknowledged among your friends, you'll likely see it on the Wall.

View Events, Facebook Ads, and Other Miscellaneous Links

The right column contains several types of links. On the non-maximized page, you'll see the ticker at the top of the right column. On the maximized window, you'll only see ads and events, since the Ticker/Chat sidebar contains the Ticker. If you have events, you'll see them listed as well as Facebook ads. Additional requests from friends and other appeals and informational links may be found here.

⫸ View Your Timeline Page with Its Profile and Wall

Your Timeline, shown in Figure 2-3, is where your personal Wall contains comments and activities, and personal profile information is shown, along with a list of your friends and your own activities. Your Timeline can be seen by those you specify in your privacy or audience selection settings. You can restrict access to this or not. This is also true with postings on your Wall—you can determine who may see them. You can find out how to change your profile information later in this chapter in "Manage Your Profile."

One consideration about hiding or revealing information is your purpose for using Facebook and how well you know your "friends." Facebook may be a casual social networking tool that you use for a broad community of friends or, conversely, a way to connect personally with family and close friends. If you decide to only allow people to be your friends that you personally know, you can feel freer about revealing personal information about yourself. If you befriend all who request to be your friend, you may be more cautious about what you reveal.

1. To view your Timeline with your Wall and personal information, click **Your Name** on the menu bar.

> 💡 **Tip** You can also display your Timeline from the Home page by clicking your profile picture.

2. To access major items on the Timeline click one of the following (see Figure 2-3):

Friends 181   Photos 5   Map 1   Likes 19

- **Friends** Located beneath the Timeline cover photo or beneath your profile photo in the left column, it shows a page of all your friends.
- **Photos** This is located immediately below your cover photo and name and lets you view and add photos.
- **Maps** Displays locations you have pinned to the map.
- **Likes** Displays all the Facebook pages you have "liked."
- **Now** Or you can click a specific year to see your Wall for that time period.
- **Status** This is located below your profile photo and allows you to add a comment of your own to your Wall. You can also just click in the What's On Your Mind text box.

📄 Status	📷 Photo	📍 Place	📖 Life Event
What's on your mind?			

Your Timeline cover image

Lets you change your profile information

Displays a log of all your activity—your postings, photos, likes, and other such activities

Click a year to see activity posted then

Your Profile photo

Profile information you choose to display

Click to add a comment, photo, place, or special event you want to share

Click to see all your friends

Click a friend's image to see their Timeline

Figure 2-3: **Your Timeline is where you see your own Wall activity and change your personal profile.**

- **Photo** Located below your profile in the left column, this lets you add a photo or video, use the webcam, or create a photo album.
- **Place** Add a location to your Timeline.
- **Life Event** Add notice of an event in your life worth recording in the Timeline.

3. Immediately below your profile image is your profile. Click **About** to change or modify personal information. You can also click **Update Info** below the Timeline cover photo to do the same. See "Manage Your Profile" later in this chapter to find how to change and save your profile information. Chapter 3 considers this in more detail.

The Timeline is divided into two columns. As you scroll down the Timeline, you will see your activity for each year. If your Timeline page is maximized, you'll also see the Ticker/Chat sidebar to the right.

Work with an Alternate Profile Page

Facebook revised how it displays profile and Wall information in 2011 when it implemented the Timeline design which replaced the Profile page. Facebook maintains that all users eventually will be converted to the Timeline, but they are slow to actually do it. "Timeline" in this book is used interchangeably with "Profile." When Profile refers to the older version, it will be clear from the context.

Figure 2-4 shows the older version of the Profile page and where you find common features on it. There are still many people who have this page instead of the updated Timeline.

Convert to Timeline

If you have an original Profile page and would like to convert to a Timeline, you can do so in a couple of ways:

If you have this message on your Profile page, click **Get Timeline**.

1. From any page click the down arrow to the right of Home and click **Help | Visit The Help Center**.
2. Type How do I get timeline in the Search text box. As you type a list of possible links will be shown. Click **How Do I Get Timeline**. A message is displayed.
3. In the message, click **Introducing Timeline | Get Timeline**.

Scan Your Account Menu

The Account menu contains access to several vital functions within Facebook. You get there by clicking the down arrow to the right of Home in the menu bar. Your options may vary.

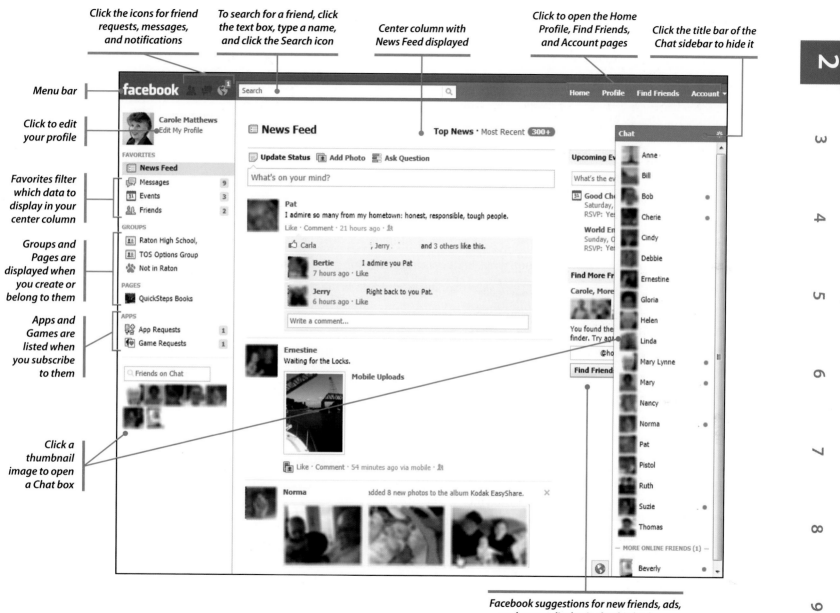

Click the icons for friend requests, messages, and notifications

To search for a friend, click the text box, type a name, and click the Search icon

Center column with News Feed displayed

Click to open the Home Profile, Find Friends, and Account pages

Click the title bar of the Chat sidebar to hide it

Menu bar

Click to edit your profile

Favorites filter which data to display in your center column

Groups and Pages are displayed when you create or belong to them

Apps and Games are listed when you subscribe to them

Click a thumbnail image to open a Chat box

Facebook suggestions for new friends, ads, and events display in the third column

Figure 2-4: *Some people still use the original Profile page rather than the newer Timeline.*

- **Use Facebook As**   This allows you to switch identities between your personal page and a Page you set up—for maintenance or promotion, for example. For instance, I can switch my personal Carole Matthews identity with my Page, QuickSteps Books. This allows me to enter comments and other activities as QuickSteps Books rather than as Carole Matthews.

- **Promote Your Page**   Discussed further in Chapter 9, this allows you to set up a Page and advertise or use it to promote yourself or a business.

- **Account Settings**   This lets you set your primary account options. These are your official names and contact information with Facebook, and not what is necessarily displayed. Refer to "Change General Account Settings" later in this chapter for more information.

- **Privacy Settings**   This allows you to determine what personal information you will display or hide. Chapter 10 explores this in more detail.

- **Log Out**   Discussed in Chapter 1, this is how you exit Facebook.

- **Help**   Discussed in Chapter 1, this is Facebook's help system.

MANAGE YOUR PROFILE

After you have created your Facebook account and entered your basic profile, you can return and fine-tune it, plus add new information. When considering what to place on your Facebook profile, there is always a line between displaying too much about yourself and not enough. You want your account to be interesting and to be personal enough that people know who you are, but at the same time, you don't want to enable identity thieves and other unscrupulous people who would do you harm. Unfortunately, they are present and active on Facebook. But you don't need to be too skittish either. Check Chapter 10 for more information.

⏩ Update Your Basic Profile Information

On your Timeline page, basic profile information is displayed beneath your profile photo on the left. It includes whatever you want, but often your location, birth day and month, high school and university, and work experience. To protect your information, you can control who sees each item of information you enter. Also read "Check Privacy Controls" after you're done here.

1. To change or modify personal information, click **Update Info** beneath the Timeline cover photo. You'll see a page similar to the one shown in Figure 2-5.

2. For each item you will see an icon that controls privacy, also known as the audience selector. Click it and select the level of privacy, or the audience, you want:

- **Public**   Everyone can see the information.

- **Friends**   Only your friends can see the information.

- **Only Me**   You are the only one who can see the information.

- **Custom**   Allows you to set a custom setting for this information. You can select specific groups of people or individuals to whom you can either show or hide the information.

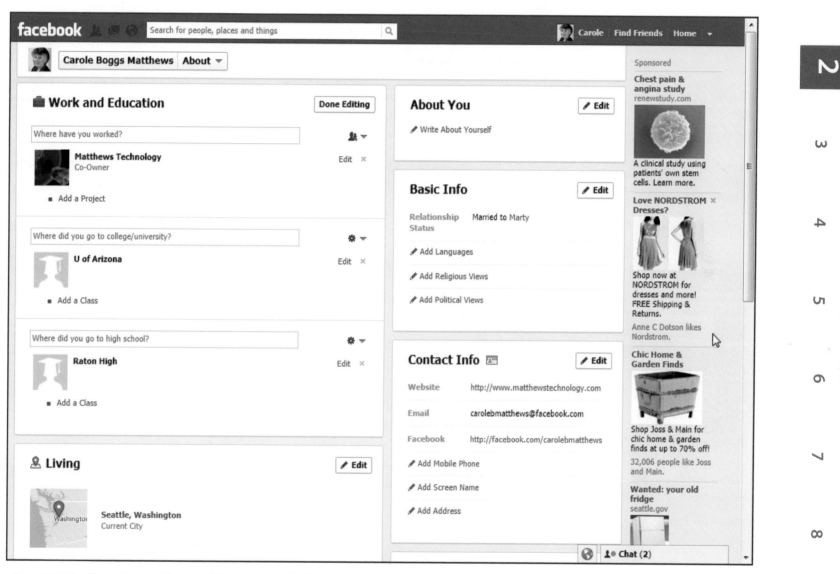

Figure 2-5: You'll want to consider what information to display in your Timeline/Profile page.

- **Named groups**   Lists you have created and assigned to specific friends that can be treated with a single privacy setting (for instance, all my "Close Friends" can see all my postings).

3. To the right of the item click **Edit**.

4. Fill in the information as you want others to see it, and click **Save Changes**.

5. Consider the following:

- **Work And Education**   Identifies where you work and went to high school and college. This is one way you will find friends (and they can find you). One of the first uses of Facebook for me was to connect with high school friends in the weeks leading up to a class reunion. I found friends I had not talked to in years. (I'm not going to say how many years!) To enter this information, just click in a text box and type your employer, college or university, or high school.

- **Living**   This is important for people to figure out in searches whether you are the one they want to find. It asks for your "home" and your current city. However, it is also an important bit of information that can be misused. Protect your location by putting a city near where you live, but perhaps not the exact city. I do not live in Seattle, but I do live in the state of Washington, for example. That and my profile picture should assure that people looking for me can find me.

- **Relationship And Family**   Lists your relationships, such as spouse or partner, and any children or other family members. It also asks for anniversary and birthdates of family members. I would flatly not give these out, protecting the privacy of my family.

- **Pages**   Identifies any Pages (capital P) that you have created. Pages are created to promote people or products. They are used primarily for business purposes. I have one for the QuickSteps Books series, for example.

- **About You**   Allows you to write an essay or a short paragraph about yourself. Examples of what you might post are a brief bio, a list of your most endearing traits or interests, a statement of your activities, or a poem you particularly like. What do you want others to know about you? This gives others insight into what makes you tick—what you are most eager for others to know about yourself. You can click the Audience Selector to control who sees it.

- **Basic Info**   This includes the following information:
  - **Gender**   This may be obvious from your name, but if not, this might be important for people to find you when searching among all those who have similar names.
  - **Birthday**   This is a key bit of information needed for people to steal your identity. Consequently, I do not like my birthday revealed to anyone who doesn't have a need to know. However, you can choose to share only the month and day or nothing at all.
  - **Interested In**   This lets you identify what your sexual orientation is. If you are looking for a partner, this might be helpful.
  - **Relationships**   You can supply this information if it is not already identified.
  - **Languages**   This lets you list languages you can use other than the one being displayed.
- **Religion And Political Views**   This allows you to share your religious and political philosophies. This reveals a more intimate description of you by describing personal interests or passions.
- **Contact Info**   This allows you to set up your mobile phone numbers, instant messaging addresses, home or business address, and a website address. For each address you can click the **Audience Selector** to select to whom you want to show the information. Again, you

want your friends to be able to connect with you, but you don't want to threaten your security. So be selective, both for which addresses you reveal and to whom you reveal them. I only show my email address and website Uniform Resource Locator (URL). If someone wants to know my address or phone numbers, they can ask me.

- **Favorite Quotations**   This allows you to write a quotation or poem to which you really relate.

6. When your basic profile information is complete, click **Done Editing** at the top of the left column.

7. You can click *your name* on the menu bar or your profile photo to see how your profile now looks.

Tip   If you have not updated to the Timeline, you can update your profile information from your Profile page by clicking **Edit Profile** in the right column of your Wall.

Note   When you enter information such as your workplace or school, Facebook tries to find friends for you that have the same identifying information. This can be a quick way to find friends that you may not otherwise think about.

Check Privacy Controls

To quickly review your privacy controls so that you are aware that your information won't be shown to the public right off the bat, follow these steps (privacy is discussed further in Chapter 10).

1. To the right of Home on the menu bar, click the down arrow, and then click **Privacy Settings**. You'll see the Privacy Settings page.

2. Scroll down to see the settings, such as How You Connect, and click **Edit Settings**. You'll see the current settings, which, by default, are initially set to a combination of Everyone, Friends Of Friends (people who see you from a friend's site), and Friends (only your own friends), as seen in Figure 2-6 for How You Connect.

3. I recommend initially allowing access to just Friends until you have had a chance to work with Facebook and understand who will be viewing your information. Reset the combination by clicking **Friends**.

4. Click **Done** to make it official.

⯈⯈ Add a Profile Picture

If you did not enter a profile photo as described in Chapter 1 in the Welcome page, you can do it using the Timeline page,

Figure 2-6: Facebook provides a recommended way of controlling who will see your page, but you can customize it according to your own comfort zone, as you see here in the How You Connect dialog box.

the primary place where you can access the ability to insert a profile photo from files on your disk or to take a webcam photo. (See Chapter 5 to learn how to work with photos in general.)

1. On the menu bar, click your name to see your Timeline page.

2. On the Timeline page, mouse over your profile photo, and click **Edit Profile Picture**. A menu of choices for editing your profile picture is displayed.

3. You have these choices, described in the following pages:

- **Choose From Photos**   This allows you to choose from other photos you have already uploaded. Click **View Albums** to see all your photos.

- **Take Photo**   This enables you to use a webcam to take a photo.

- **Upload Photo**   This leads you through uploading a photo from your computer.

- **Edit Thumbnail**   This is used to reposition the image in the frame—perhaps your head is too high or too much to one side, for instance.

- **Remove**   This allows you to delete this photo.

Choose from Current Uploaded Photos

To choose from your current uploaded photos:

1. On the Timeline page, place your pointer over your profile photo, and click **Edit Profile Picture**.

2. On the menu, click **Choose From Photos**. You see your current profile pictures. Click the one you want.

3. If you don't see the picture you want, click **View Albums**. You'll see the list of albums. Click an album to find the photo you want, and then click the photo you want to make your profile photo. You may have a couple of options depending on your photo:

   • Beneath the photo, click **Make Profile Picture**. (You may have to click **Options** first.)

   • Drag the transparent box where you'd like the photo to be. You can change the size of the box by dragging the corners. To crop the photo for your profile photo, click **Done Cropping** beneath the photo when you're ready.

Take a Picture with Your Webcam

Chapter 1 describes this process as you would do it from the Welcome page. Here is how you take a photo of yourself using the webcam with the Edit Profile Picture menu.

1. Click **Take Photo**. The Take A Profile Photo window will open and display the Adobe Flash Player Settings dialog box.

2. Click **Allow** to let Facebook access your camera, and use the icons on the bottom to adjust how Facebook is using your camera:

   • The leftmost icon allows hardware acceleration (which you probably want).

   • The second icon contains the privacy permission allowing Facebook to access your webcam photo.

   • The third icon allows you to set the amount of storage that can be used for the picture.

- The fourth icon, which really doesn't apply here, allows you to set the sound source and the volume level.

- The rightmost icon allows you to select the camera that you want to use.

To save the camera settings in the dialog box, click **Remember**.

3. Look into the camera, and when you like the image, click the **Camera** icon, and then wait for the countdown (3-2-1) while your photo is taken (smiling is optional, but lighting is critical!).

4. To save the picture, click **Save Picture**. To do it again, click the **X** in the upper-right corner to delete the picture and start over.

Add a Photo from Your Disk

To upload a photo from your computer using the Edit Profile Picture dialog box:

1. Click **Upload Photo** to use an existing digital photo.

2. Using Windows Explorer, browse for your photo file. When you find it, double-click the photo or click the photo and click **Open**. The photo will appear on your page.

Reposition Your Profile Photo

If you want to change the way your image is positioned in the profile picture (for instance, perhaps the top of your head is shaved off or your face is too near the left side of the frame), follow these steps:

1. On your Timeline page, move your pointer over your profile picture, and click **Edit Profile Picture | Edit Thumbnail**.

2. In the Edit Thumbnail dialog box, place your cursor over the image and drag it where you want it to be.

3. Click **Scale To Fit** to automatically resize the photo so that it fits the space better.

4. When it is positioned the way you want, click **Save**.

Thumbnail Version

Drag the image to adjust.

☐ Scale to fit.

We use this version of your picture around the site.

QuickQuotes

Ron Catches Up with Family and Old Friends

I first started using Facebook a couple of years ago when the media started reporting its phenomenal growth. The first thing that I discovered was that my grown children were on Facebook. More importantly, they were willing to friend me. Since no one in my family calls home regularly, Facebook now has allowed me to read and see photos of the events in their lives. Soon I discovered cousins that I hadn't seen for years were regular Facebook commenters. I got to see pictures of them, their grown children, and their families. One cousin posted some old photos of her mom and dad, my aunt and uncle, and my grandmother. They were fascinating to see.

I turned my attention to old friends. In the 1970s and 1980s, I was a member of a small intentional community. Most of us moved to different parts of the country and lost touch with each other. Using Facebook's search function, I found many old friends. We don't write on each other's Walls often, but it's great to leave a comment now and then. Some of their children, who I remember as teenagers, friended me. Now seeing them grey haired and balding, I realize that maybe I'm a little older myself.

Ron H., 62, Oregon

MANAGE YOUR ACCOUNT

Your account contains information to manage your Facebook pages. When you click the down arrow next to Home on the menu bar and then **Account Settings**, you will see the page of account options seen in Figure 2-7. The items along the left of the page display the detailed options for each category:

 Note When seeking information about some of the account options, check Chapter 3 for more about editing friends, Chapter 9 for using Facebook as a Page, Chapter 10 for privacy settings, and Chapter 1 to log out and the Help Center.

- **General** The default tab, this contains your personal information and is explained in this chapter.

- **Security** Contains preferences about browsing and other security issues. Chapter 10 discusses this setting.

- **Notifications** This is where you identify which actions will result in notifying you by email or by a text message on your cell phone. See "Set Notifications" in this chapter.

- **Subscribers** Places a "Subscribe" button on your Timeline, which allows others to receive your public posts, even if they are not friends. See Chapters 3 and 4.

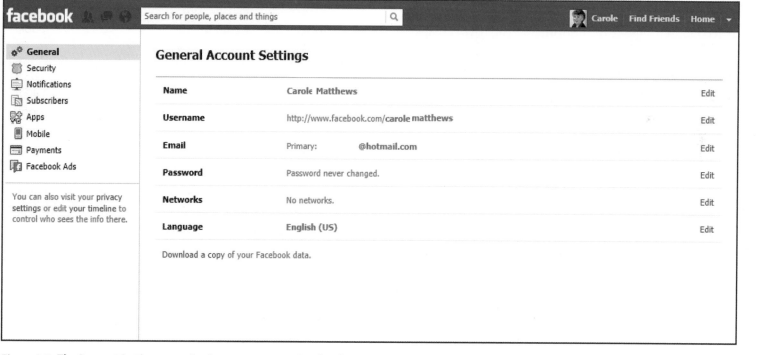

*Figure 2-7: **The Account Settings page is where you set your Facebook account preferences.***

- **Apps**   Allows you to edit certain preferences about the apps you use. Chapter 8 discusses this further.

- **Mobile**   This is where you identify and connect Facebook to your mobile (cell phone) device. See Chapter 5 for more information.

- **Payments**   Establishes and tracks your financial and credit card information in case you want to play games or purchase something, such as an ad, on Facebook.

- **Facebook Ads**   This is where you can set two permissions for how Facebook handles third-party ads and your personal information, and to whom your actions in social ads will be displayed. See Chapter 9 for more information.

Change General Account Settings

Your account settings are the information you have revealed to Facebook. These are used to facilitate your relationship with Facebook.

1. Click the down arrow to the right of Home on your menu bar, and then click **Account Settings**.

2. Click the **General** tab if it is not selected by default. You have these options (with each one, click **Edit** to open the change options):

   - **Name**   Allows you to change your first, middle, or last name. If you are married or divorced, you might want to do this so people who know you under another name can find you. You can also change how your name is displayed or use an alternate name if you have one. You must enter your Facebook password. Then click **Save Changes**. Incidentally, you must wait 24 hours so Facebook can run a security check on your name change.

 Tip   When changing your name, you can also enter an alternative name. You might want to do this to let others recognize you by a name you may no longer use, such as a maiden name or nickname. When you enter an alternative name, you can also choose whether it is to be shown on your profile along with search lists and friend requests. The default is to only use that name in searches.

- **Username**   Allows you to create and change a username. Your account must have been verified before you can set up a username. You can only change a username once, so you want to be very careful about what you select. Your username is used to create a unique Facebook URL, such as www.facebook.com/*username*. People who navigate to your Facebook pages will be able to see your username.

Username	Your account must be verified before you can set a username.
	If you have a mobile phone that can receive SMS messages, you can verify via mobile phone. If not, please try to register your username at a later time.
	Close

- **Email**   Records a change in your email. This is the address by which you are contacted by Facebook, and it must be a valid email address. Email sent to this address is also duplicated in the Messages area. You can also add another email address. When your friends download their own information (see "Archive Your Facebook Data"), you can choose whether your email address may be included in the downloaded information.

- **Password**   Changes your password. You must remember your old one before you can enter a new one. (If you forget, you can ask Facebook to allow you to reset it at the time you log in.) You should change your passwords periodically, perhaps annually at the very least. Also, a combination of letters, numbers, and punctuation in the six characters required will ensure that you have a strong password.

- **Networks** Allows you to join an organization or other network.

- **Language** Allows you to identify which language you want as your primary one and to select a translation App if you need Facebook translated. See "Set Your Language" in this chapter.

Tip The translator can be found by clicking the World icon to the left of the Chat bar on the bottom of the third column (or the Ticker/Chat sidebar in a maximized window).

Set Your Language

You can establish which language is your primary one while you're using Facebook. You can also request a translator if needed.

To set your language to one other than what is on the page:

Scroll down to the very bottom of any Facebook page (you may want to select a short one), and click the current language link next to the Facebook copyright date. A menu will appear. Click the language you want.

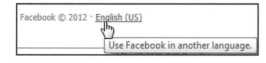

–Or–

1. Click the down arrow to the right of Home, and then click **Account Settings | General**. The Language page is displayed.

2. Click **Edit** to the right of the Language item.

3. Click the **Choose Primary** down arrow, and click the language you want.

4. Click **Save Changes**.

Archive Your Facebook Data

Facebook allows you to copy or archive the data you have on Facebook. Your data will grow to be an immense storehouse of valuable photos and videos, including those placed on your Wall by friends; your profile information, including your contact info and groups; collections of your thoughts that you have shared on your Timeline Wall, private messages, and chats; names and comments of friends (and their email addresses if they give permission); notes you have written or events you have responded to—all the memories you have built up.

This is valuable information, and you are urged to protect it by taking care with how it is stored and revealed. You will not be able to download other people's photos or videos from their pages or any of their private postings or personal information.

1. Click the down arrow to the right of Home on your menu bar, and then click **Account Settings**.

2. Click the **General** option on the left if it is not selected by default.

3. Beneath the Language option, click **Download A Copy Of Your Facebook Data**. The Download Your Information page is displayed.

4. Click **Start My Archive**.

Download Your Information
Get a copy of what you've shared on Facebook.

Easily download and browse through a personal archive of your Facebook photos, posts and messages. Learn more about downloading a copy of your information.

Start My Archive

5. You will be sent an email. Reenter your password, and enter any security codes requested.

Note You can download an "expanded" version of your data, which includes information such as IP addresses you have used, pending friend requests, dates you changed your status, event history, and more profile information, including all your phone numbers and account settings you have changed.

⏩ Set Notifications

When there is activity on Facebook, you can elect to receive notifications by email or text messaging. Luckily, there is one place you can go to set all your notifications. A key to setting all notifications or a summarized group of them is the Email Frequency check box. By default, it is designed to send you a defined set of notifications, not all—which would be considerable. When this is checked, you periodically are sent one email or text message grouping with any notifications you have into one message. This is very nice to have. However, if you want to receive notifications for all your Facebook activity, clear

the check mark and *all* notifications will be marked to be sent to you. Replacing the check mark in the Email Frequency check box restores the original settings. To selectively edit a category, you can open just its specific edit box, as explained here.

1. On a Facebook page, click the down arrow to the right of Home on the menu bar, and then click **Account Settings**.

2. Click the **Notifications** option on the left. The Notifications Settings page will open, as shown in Figure 2-8. You'll see your email address where notifications will be sent and the Email Frequency option.

3. A check mark placed by default in the **Email Frequency** check box reminds you that a summary notice will be sent to you instead of individual notifications. If you don't want this, clear the check mark. I recommend you do not clear the check mark.

Email Frequency:
☑ Send me important updates and summary emails instead of individual notification emails [?]

4. Then, to set the conditions for notifications you want, or to review those that are set by default, scroll down through the categories of notifications. The envelope icon to the right of a category with a number indicates the number of options set in that category.

🔲 Facebook   ✉ 3

5. Click either **Edit** or the **Envelope** icon to open a category's edit box so that you can review or change the individual settings. Doing this displays the settings and resets all the notifications to be "turned on" or selected.

6. To remove notifications you do not want, clear the individual check boxes. Click the individual check boxes to turn them on or off separately.

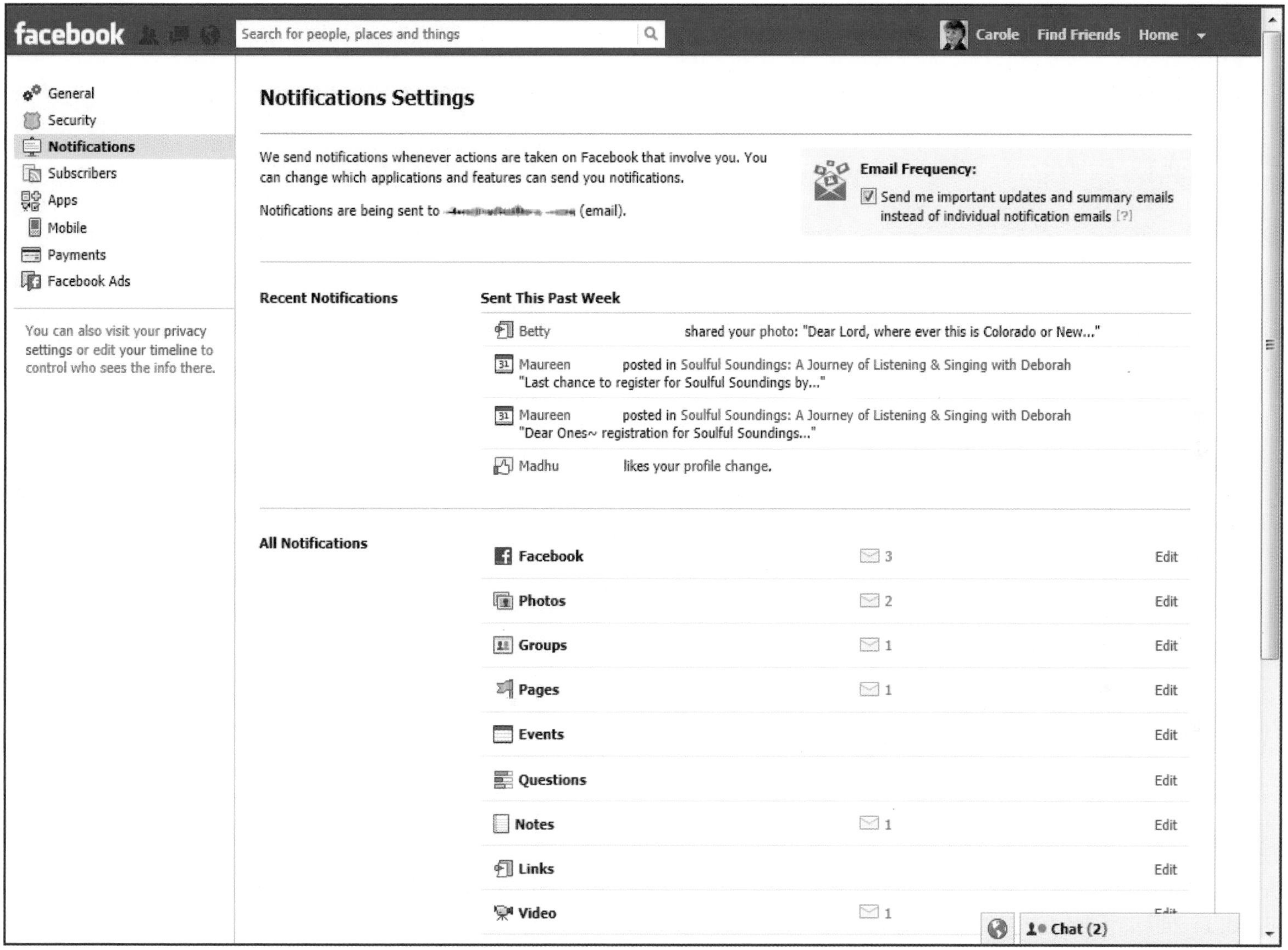

facebook ⚋ ⚏ ⊕   Search for people, places and things   🔍   👤 Carole   **Find Friends**   **Home**   ▾

Notifications Settings

- ⚙ General
- 🛡 Security
- 🖥 **Notifications**
- 📇 Subscribers
- 🎛 Apps
- 📱 Mobile
- 🗔 Payments
- 🎞 Facebook Ads

You can also visit your privacy settings or edit your timeline to control who sees the info there.

We send notifications whenever actions are taken on Facebook that involve you. You can change which applications and features can send you notifications.

Notifications are being sent to ⟶⟵⟶⟵ (email).

📨 **Email Frequency:**

☑ Send me important updates and summary emails instead of individual notification emails [?]

Recent Notifications

Sent This Past Week

📧 Betty   shared your photo: "Dear Lord, where ever this is Colorado or New..."

🗓 Maureen   posted in Soulful Soundings: A Journey of Listening & Singing with Deborah "Last chance to register for Soulful Soundings by..."

🗓 Maureen   posted in Soulful Soundings: A Journey of Listening & Singing with Deborah "Dear Ones~ registration for Soulful Soundings..."

👍 Madhu   likes your profile change.

All Notifications

📘 **Facebook**	✉ 3	Edit
📷 **Photos**	✉ 2	Edit
👥 **Groups**	✉ 1	Edit
🚩 **Pages**	✉ 1	Edit
🗔 **Events**		Edit
📊 **Questions**		Edit
📄 **Notes**	✉ 1	Edit
📧 **Links**		Edit
🎥 **Video**	✉ 1	Edit

🌐   👤● Chat (2)

Figure 2-8: You can set your defaults for how you are notified about activities in Facebook.

7. Here are your options:

- **Facebook** Sets notification status for activities that typically occur on your Facebook site, such as being added as a friend or friend requests.

- **Photos** Establishes when notifications are sent if you have activity involving photos, such as to upload a photo via email, receive a comment on a photo or photo album, someone else comments or responds to your comment, or someone tags your photo or you in another photo.

- **Groups** Defines when you are notified for activities within groups to which you belong, such as a name change, if you are made an administrator, if you are added to a group, and more.

- **Pages** Defines when you are notified for certain Page activities, such as when you are made a Page Admin, someone suggests a Page to you, a reply is made to a discussion you're in, a weekly Admin report is emailed to you, or a Page's email settings are changed.

- **Events** Defines the conditions under which you are informed when activities happen in an event that you either are attending or creating, such as the event is cancelled or the date is changed.

- **Questions** Specifies the activities under which you are notified on a question you have asked or answered.

- **Notes** Defines whether you are notified when you are tagged in a note or comments are made.

- **Links** Defines whether you are notified when someone comments on a link you have initiated or commented on or shares a link you posted.

- **Video** Specifies the activities under which you are notified on a video you have posted or commented on.

- **Help Center** Specifies when you are notified when a question you posted is replied to or when your question is identified as the "Best Answer" to a question.

- **Wall Comments** Specifies when you are notified when someone comments on your Wall or makes a comment after you.

- **Other Updates From Facebook** Specifies whether you want to be notified when friends or products have updates or when you have a special research invitation from Facebook.

- **Credits** Specifies whether you want to be notified when you've purchased credits or an order is completed.

- **Translations** Determines whether you want to be notified when there is progress in a translation or approval for the translation.

- **Other Applications** Determines whether you want notifications from Apps you are using.

8. For each type of notification, click either the **Email** or **SMS** check box (the latter is only visible if your mobile phone is added to Facebook) to clear or place a check mark in the box, depending on your preferences. A check mark in the box indicates that a notification will be sent; no check mark indicates that no notification will be sent.

9. When you've finished setting the check marks as you wish, click **Save Changes**.

Chapter 3 _____

Managing Your Friends

The main thing about Facebook is its ability to connect you with friends. That is the whole reason that Facebook exists: to provide a place for the gathering of friends, a way for conversations to take place, and a platform for presenting visual aspects of one's life—photos and videos. In this chapter you will learn how to find friends and to manage them. Chapter 4 deals with the conversation part of Facebook.

FIND AND VIEW FRIENDS

Finding and viewing friends can be one of your most important jobs in Facebook. You need to be friends with someone before you can drop in on them and find out what they are up to. Your friends, and sometimes their friends, are those with whom you will communicate when you share posts or send messages. You will see their postings as well. Consequently, defining what a "friend" is to be in your Facebook site is important to making sure your information is protected and your friends are who you want them to be. See "Understanding the Concept of Friends" QuickFacts.

✓ QuickFacts

Understanding the Concept of Friends

When you create a Facebook site, you accumulate friends. Friends are people you know with whom you want to communicate. You can communicate in a number of ways (see Chapter 4):

- You can share a comment with all your friends at once.
- You can share comments with selected friends.
- You can send a private message to one or more friends.
- You can chat online.

When you invite someone to be your friend, a request is sent to them by Facebook. When they confirm that they know you and want to be your friend, they are added to your list of Facebook friends.

When a friend is added to your list of friends, depending on your privacy settings, he or she has access to your profile and to all the comments, photos, and videos that are posted to your site. Likewise, depending on your friend's privacy settings, you have access to all of her or his comments, photos, videos, and friends. Your News Feed on your Home page is updated constantly with postings from your friends, such as that shown in Figure 3-1. Your private messages or online chats are not public.

When you first start using Facebook, you can start with a few friends that you know are already on Facebook. You can find names for friends from an existing email contact list, or by searching for friends, or simply typing in their email address and asking to be shown their page.

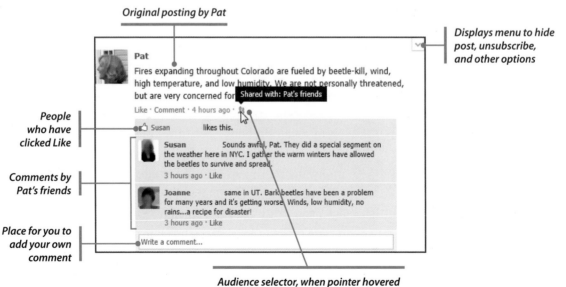

Figure 3-1: *This posting shows how a friend posts a comment and is responded to by others.*

Find Friends Using Email Contacts

When you download contacts from your email provider, Facebook stores them all, even those you do not select to be friends. Facebook uses them to suggest names to you or others later. Facebook does not share these names with others, and it does not actually invite anyone on the imported list unless you say to do so, but it keeps them stored. Although Facebook likes to have these downloaded names handy to make things easier to find friends, you don't have to accommodate this if it makes you uncomfortable. You can delete them, as you'll see later.

To find friends using the Friend page:

1. From your Home page, click **Find Friends** in the left column under Favorites (notice that neither clicking Friends on the Timeline nor clicking Find Friends on the menu bar gives you the same result).

2. Under Add Personal Contacts As Friends, choose the email provider—for example, Windows Live Hotmail (see Figure 3-2)—that contains the contact list you want. After getting the names from one servicer, you can select additional ones if you use several email providers (such as Yahoo!), or you can include an email provider not listed (for example, Google's Gmail) by clicking **Other Email Service**. Click **Other Tools** to use means other than email lists to find friends.

3. Enter your email address and, if needed, a password and click **Find Friends**. A list of potential names with thumbnail images will be listed. It is highly likely that you don't want all names on your email list to be friends.

Figure 3-2: The Friend page enables you to import your contacts from web-based email providers.

4. Click just the check boxes next to the thumbnails that you want.

5. When you have selected all that you want, click **Add As Friends**. You will see a message that all selected names have been sent an invitation from you to be a friend.

6. You may also see a list of people who are in your contact list, but are not on Facebook. Since all are selected by default, click **Select All/None** to deselect everyone.

7. If you know a listed person who might like to be on Facebook, click the thumbnail next to the name and click **Send Invites**. Invitations to join Facebook will be sent to the selected people. Otherwise, click **Skip** to void this way of inviting your friends.

▶▶ Manage Your Imported Contacts

Facebook stores all your imported contacts, but you can delete selected contacts or all of them.

1. From your Home page, click **Find Friends** in the left column.

2. At the top of the Add Personal Contacts As Friends list, click **Manage Imported Contacts**. A list of your outstanding invitations and imported contacts will be displayed.

> See how it works or manage imported contacts.

3. You have these options:

   • To delete all imported contacts that have not been invited, under Contacts Imported (Not Yet Invited), click the **Select** down arrow, and click **All**. Then click **Delete Selected**.

   Contacts Imported (not yet invited)

   Select: All ▼ Delete Selected

   Displaying 551 contacts

   ☑ Bob

   ☑ Thomas

   • To delete selected imported contacts, click in the check box beside those you want deleted, and click **Delete Selected**.

> **CAUTION!** Facebook warns you about deleting all your imported names. They use the names to make your suggested friends more relevant, and this list is synced to your iPhone contact list. Your iPhone will no longer include these contacts (although if your friends include the email addresses in their profile, you'll still see the contact information). If you go ahead and delete your imported names, you'll need to open Facebook on your iPhone, click the **Friends** icon, and click **Sync**.

▶▶ Invite People Facebook Suggests

Facebook automatically provides *suggestions* for people you might want to consider as a friend based on your current friends, work, schools, or other networks. You'll see suggestions in several places. Also, you may want to suggest a friend to someone else. Often, the more established Facebook users suggest newbies to other Facebook users to help a novice get going. It is a friendly thing to do. (However, you may find that you do not want to confirm someone suggested to be your friend and don't want to see them in the future. In that case, you can block them, as you'll see later.) When the invitation is sent to be your friend, the invitee must confirm they also want to be your friend or the "friendship" will not happen.

1. From your Facebook Home page, click **Find Friends** in the left column.

2. On the Friends page, scroll down to the People You May Know list. Click **See All** on the upper-right area of the list of thumbnails to see all candidates.

People You May Know — See All — Marty — +1 Add Friend

3. If you find someone you want as a friend, click **Add Friend**. A request will be immediately sent. As soon as your new friend confirms your request, you are officially friends.

Respond to a Friend's Request

You will receive requests from friends to be a friend. You must give your permission before a person can claim you as a friend. When you become friends, you can view each other's Facebook pages.

Normally, you will see both a notice in your Friend Requests list and an email notifying you that you have a request to be a friend. Whether you get an email depends on your notification settings. By default, the request is sent via email, provided you haven't reset this.

1. From any page click **Friend Requests** in the menu bar.

2. To immediately confirm that you want to be a friend, simply click **Confirm**. The notice will be sent to the sender and you will have a new friend.

3. If you're not sure, click **Not Now** to hide the request. You will be asked if you know the person. Click **No** to stop requests from this person; click **Yes** to hide it only. You may also have an Ignore option. Click **Ignore** to have the person still visible, but inactive. To add this person later, click the name and then click **Add Friend** from his or her Timeline.

Suggest One Friend to Another

You can suggest someone as a friend to one of your friends. Invitations will be sent to both people and either one can confirm the other as a friend. To suggest someone as a friend to another person:

1. In your list of friends, click the photo of the friend to receive the suggestion.

2. Beneath the menu bar, to the right of the Friends and Message buttons, click the gear icon down arrow and then click **Suggest Friends**. A list of your friends will be displayed.

3. In the resulting list, click the friends you want to suggest. You can select more than one.

- You can type their name in the **Find Friends** text box.

- You can scroll through your list of friends.

- You can click **Filter Friends** and click a network that shows just friends connected with that criterion.

4. Click **Send Suggestions**. Both friends will receive an invitation to be a friend.

Suggest Friends for Marilyn

Both Marilyn and the friends you choose will receive a friend suggestion from you.

Find Friends: Start Typing a Name

Filter Friends ▼   **All**   Selected (0)

6 Recommended Suggestions

Lynn   Marty   Paul

Paul   Susan   Virginia

All Suggestions

Amy   Angelo   Ann

Ann   Anne C   Anne

Send Suggestions   **Cancel**

▷▷ Respond to Suggestions from Other Friends

When you are new to Facebook, you likely will be sent suggestions from other friends. They may be helping you to get established on Facebook and suggest friends to help your experience be more robust.

1. You may first receive an email alerting you to the request that you have received. Click the link in the email to go directly to the request.

2. If you want to be friends with the suggested person, click **Add As Friend**. If not, click **Ignore**. If you decide that you want to proceed, you will need to confirm the invitation that will be sent to the requested friend. If you are not sure at the moment or you decide not to be a friend with the suggested person, nothing will happen.

facebook

Hi Marty,

Carole Matthews suggests you add Daniel as a friend on Facebook.

Send request:

Add Friend

Daniel

Thanks,
The Facebook Team

To view this friend suggestion and send a friend request, go to:
http://www.facebook.com/n/?reqs.php&mid=44a2ab0G

Note If you delete or ignore a request to be a friend, the requestor will not find out. The request will simply be removed from your list of friendships waiting to be confirmed.

Marilyn Connects from Afar

My first Facebook friend request came by email three years ago when we were vacationing in Croatia, so I signed up. Since we were there, my account said my language was Hrvatski (Croatian), which amused us. Eventually, I changed it to English. Since then I have loved keeping tabs through Facebook with many friends living or visiting abroad.

At first I was unaware of privacy settings, but wasn't concerned since I haven't put much info on my Page. Now, I allow Friends Only to access my information (I think).

Photos are an interesting part of my Facebook interactions, especially of kids. I only have posted two photos, and I am uncomfortable uploading photos of my grandkids—just to be safe. I rarely search for friends; I only respond to requests from others. Among my friends are family members from other parts of the country, and I appreciate knowing what is going on with them. Many of my friends are politically active, and they share information that I particularly enjoy. Usually I check my Wall once a day; otherwise, it gets overloaded if I wait too long. Facebook isn't something critical to my life, but is an interesting distraction.

Marilyn, 62, New Mexico

Use Search to Find a Friend's Facebook Page

You can use the Search feature in Facebook to find friends.

1. On any page, click in the **Search** text box on the menu bar; type a name, location, school, or other criteria; and click

the **Search** icon (the magnifying glass). As you type, a list of matching possibilities will be displayed.

- If you want to see more results, click **See More Results For** at the bottom of the list.
- To display the desired result, click the thumbnail image or name.

Tip If you are finding it tough to find a person by name, try using an email address.

Set Search Privacy

If you want to restrict who may see you in a search, you can specify the category of people that are allowed to find you in a search.

1. On any page, click the down arrow to the right of Home on the menu bar. Click **Privacy Settings**.

2. To the right of How You Connect, click **Edit Settings**. A menu is displayed.

How You Connect
Control how you connect with people you know.   Edit Settings

3. Select the category of friends that you want to be able to find you in a search: everyone, friends of your friends, or just your own friends.

4. Click **Done** when you've chosen. If you restrict the search to those who are already your friends or friends of friends, you will be invisible to others searching for you.

How You Connect

	Friends of Friends
Who can look you up using the email address or phone number you provided?	👥 Friends of Friends ▼
Who can send you friend requests?	🌐 Everyone ▼
Who can send you Facebook messages?	🌐 Everyone ▼
Learn more	Done

Search Friends by Location, School, Work, or Interest

You can search for friends filtered by location, one of your schools, a mutual friend, or an employer.

1. From any Facebook page, click **Find Friends** in the menu bar.

2. Click the check box containing the value you want, or enter another value, such as another city for the Hometown field or another high school for the High School field. A menu will display the possible candidates—click the one you want. A list of your friends and friends of friends matching those criteria is displayed.

Hometown
Denver

🏙️ **Denver, Colorado**
Denver, Colorado

Denver City, Texas
Denver City, Texas

🗺️ **Denver, North Carolina**

3. Scroll through the list and click **Add Friend** for those people you want as friends.

Tip To use the Search text box, first click in the text box and then type the name you want. As you type, a list matching your search criteria will be displayed. Click the name you want. Using the email address works best if the friend is not in your friend list.

⏩ Find Friends of Friends

One of your best sources of friends is the friends of friends.

1. On your Timeline page, click **Friends** beneath your name. A list of friends will be displayed.

Friends 186

2. Click the thumbnail of a friend who has friends you know and would like to invite to be your own friend. Depending on whether your friend has Timeline installed, you'll see their Timeline (friends link below their name) or Wall (friends listed down the left column with the link on top).

3. Click whichever **Friends (*no.*)** link is available in order to display the entire list of friends. Hover your pointer over a person's name to see more information about them.

Friends (57)

Nancy
Owner at Raising Responsible

Nancy
Owner at Raising Responsible Rascals
43 mutual friends

✓ Friends | 💬 Message

4. Scroll through the list, click the photo of the person, and click **Add As Friend** for those persons you'd like to invite to be your friend. You'll be shown a menu of categories to add the friend to. Click the one you want.

5. You'll see the button change to "Friend Request Sent."

Invite Someone Not on Facebook by Email

You may have friends who are not on Facebook but you know would love it. In that case, you can directly invite a friend to join Facebook and then become your friend.

1. From your Home page, click **Find Friends** on the leftmost column.

2. Scroll down within Add Personal Contacts As Friends, and click **Other Tools | Invite A Friend By Email**. The Invite Your Friends dialog box will open as shown in Figure 3-3.

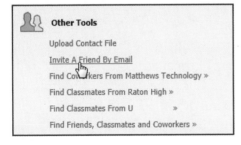

3. Click the **To** text box to select it, and type the email address of the friend you want to invite. Then click the **Message** text box and type your message.

4. Click **Invite Your Friends**. The invitation will be sent.

Manage Your Invites

To keep track of who you have invited and delete those who are not responding:

1. From your Home page, click **Find Friends** on the left column.

2. At the top of the Add Personal Contacts As Friends list, click **Manage Imported Contacts**. A list of your outstanding invitations will be displayed.

3. You have these options:

   - To delete someone you have already invited who has not yet responded, click the check box and click **Delete Selected**.

   - To send someone you have invited a reminder about your invitation, click the check box and click **Send Reminder**.

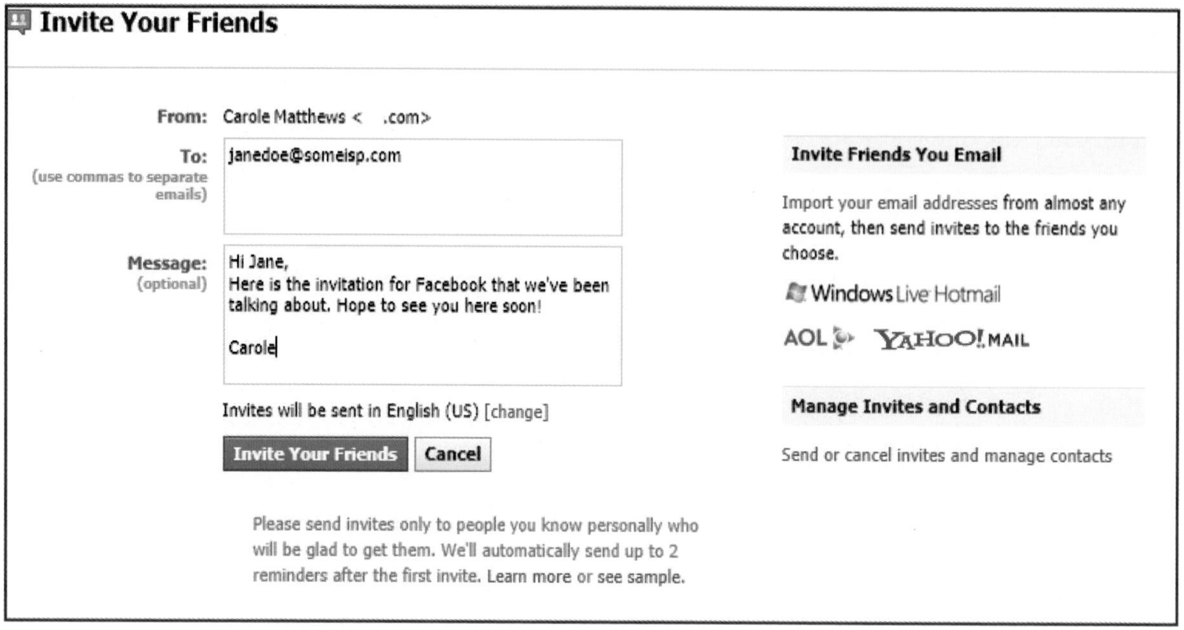
Invite Your Friends
From: Carole Matthews < .com>
To: (use commas to separate emails)
janedoe@someisp.com
Message: (optional)
Hi Jane,
Here is the invitation for Facebook that we've been talking about. Hope to see you here soon!
Carole
Invites will be sent in English (US) [change]
Invite Your Friends
Cancel
Please send invites only to people you know personally who will be glad to get them. We'll automatically send up to 2 reminders after the first invite. Learn more or see sample.
Invite Friends You Email
Import your email addresses from almost any account, then send invites to the friends you choose.
Windows Live Hotmail
AOL
YAHOO! MAIL
Manage Invites and Contacts
Send or cancel invites and manage contacts

***Figure 3-3:* You can send an invitation to someone not yet on Facebook.**

View All Your Friends to Find One

To see a list of all your friends or friends of friends and find a specific one:

1. Beneath your name on the Timeline page, click **Friends**.

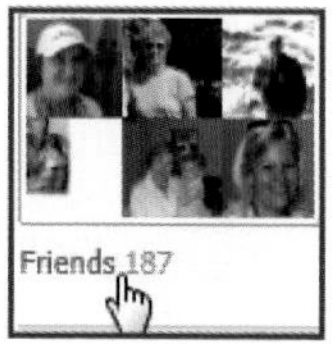
Friends 187

2. You have these options:
   - To quickly find a particular friend, click in the **Search** text box and type the name. As you type, your Friend list will be searched and the appropriate candidates listed. Click the one you want.
   - To search by city, hometown, school, workplace, interest, or friend of friend, click the down arrow on the Search text box. Click the criteria you want. A search page will open with a text box for your criteria. Type the criteria you want, such as the city name. Another menu of possible candidates will be displayed, such as names of cities and states. Click the menu for the exact criteria. The matching friends or friends of friends will be displayed. Click the one you want.

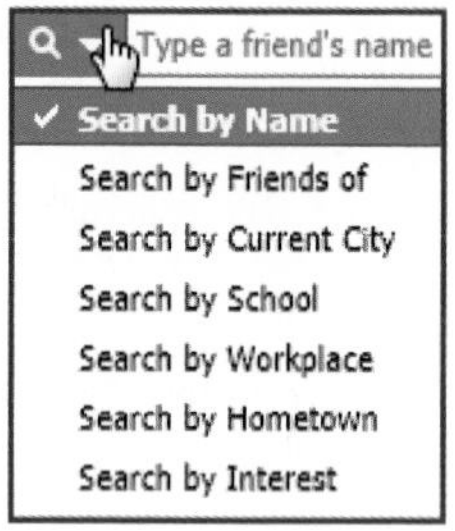
Type a friend's name
Search by Name
Search by Friends of
Search by Current City
Search by School
Search by Workplace
Search by Hometown
Search by Interest

MANAGE YOUR FRIENDS

Once you have accumulated your friends, you'll want to know how to organize and manage them. You can put them in lists, track what they are up to, hide their posts or delete them, delete friends, and control what you see from them.

Controlling Your News Feed Content

You have several ways that you can control what pops up on your News Feed and Ticker sidebar from your friends. Here is summary of the potential actions you can take:

- **Sort What Appears** Click the **Sort** menu at the top of the News Feed and select between **Most Recent** and **Top Stories**. This prioritizes your News Feed between what is happening right now and what might be the most interesting to you based on your past preferences (see Chapter 2 for more information).

- **Organize by List** Lets you see posts from people only on a list. So you can see just the stories from your family, or your investing club, or so on. This allows you to follow the thread of a conversation, or see what one particular set of friends are now up to. (See "Organize Your Friends with Lists.")

- **Hide a Person's Posts or Type** Often you'll have a friend whose posts are not to your taste. One example is that some friends will be addicted to games and share about them, and other friends don't appreciate them at all. You can hide all posts from that friend, or the app or game he or she subscribes to. (See "Hide, Unhide, or Unsubscribe Posts.") Hiding something can always be undone.

- **Turn Off Posts for Your News Feed** You can control whether a friend's posts show up in your News Feed by toggling **Show In News Feeds** on and off from the person's Friends button on their Profile page. (See "View a Regular Profile Page" or "View a Friend's Timeline Page.")

- **Select Which Kind of Posts You'll See** You can control what types of posts you'll see in your News Feed from a friend; for instance, live event happenings, games, photos, comments or likes, music and videos, and other activity. So if you want to stay connected with a friend but don't want the games, you can choose that (see "Set What You See from a Friend").

Understanding Types of Lists

There are several kinds of lists created either by you or by Facebook:

- **Default lists** Facebook creates these lists. These are *Close Friends,* those friends you want to closely track; *Acquaintances,* more distant friends you don't want to see on your News Feed all that often or to track closely; and *Restricted,* friends who will only see your public posts (public posts are shown to anyone, even people who are not your Facebook friends).

- **Smart lists** Facebook creates these automatically from common traits you share with many friends, such as for the city you live in, or your hometown, where you have many friends, or a hobby. Family is an example of a smart list. These lists are automatically updated when you add a friend that matches the trait.

- **Custom lists** You can create these lists to track friends or to send posts selectively. Examples are a club to which you belong, family members, and so on.

- **Friends list** This is simply the list of all your friends—they are automatically added to it because they are confirmed friends. You can use it to find names to add to other lists.

⟫ Organize Your Friends with Lists

You can organize your friends into lists and track people separately by list. When you add a friend, you have the option of adding them to a group. This is particularly useful if you have a large number of friends from different parts of your life—for example, friends from high school, college, work, investment club, political party, and so on. Grouping your friends into lists has these advantages:

- You can prioritize posts that you see on your Wall, for instance, seeing those of close friends and family or not seeing those of more distant acquaintances.

- You can share messages with a list of friends rather than individually or all. This way, you keep your communications relevant to a group.

- You can vary your privacy by list so that friends in one list may have more restricted access than another list.

> **Note** Your lists of friends are not visible to others. Only you can see them or know about them. The only exception is the Family list. In that case, when you add a family member to your Family list, a notice is sent to him or her to invite them to add you to their Family profile.

Create a List of Your Friends

To create a custom list:

1. On your Home page, scroll down to the Friends group on the left column. You may need to click **More** to see it.

2. Click **More** again to see all the lists that currently exist on your Facebook site. They will be displayed in your center column.

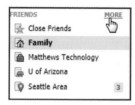

3. Click **Create List** on the top of the center column. The Create New List dialog box is displayed.

4. In the text box, type the list name.

5. In the Members text box, begin typing the names of the friends you'd like to add. As you type, a list of candidates will be displayed, as shown in Figure 3-4. Click the one you want, and repeat until you've added all the friends you want to the list.

6. Click **Create**. The new list is added to the Friends lists.

*Figure 3-4: **You can group your friends into lists of common characteristics, such as those from your hometown, your church, or reading club.***

Add Friends to a List

You can add friends to a list as you invite them to be your friend, or afterward. Sometimes you'll create a new list and want to add friends to it after the fact. To add or delete friends on a list, you must first display the list and then make your changes.

1. Find the thumbnail image of the person you want to add to a list. You can either click **Find Friends | Manage Friends List** from the Home page, or click **Friends** from the Timeline.

2. Hover your pointer over the name of the person until a profile box appears.

3. Hover your pointer over the **Friends** button. A list of lists is displayed, shown in Figure 3-5.

Figure 3-5: *You can easily add a friend to a list, change their posting status, or "unfriend" them.*

4. Click the list you want, or click **Show All Lists** for a longer list of lists.

–Or–

1. From your Home page, scroll down to the Friends list and click the name of the list. This displays the posts of people on the list in the middle column.

2. On the right column, beneath On This List, click in the text box and type the name of the person you want to add to the group. As you type, candidates will be displayed. Click the name you want.

Delete Friends from a List

To delete a friend from a list:

1. On the Home page scroll down to the Friends lists, and click the name of the list containing the friend you want to delete.

2. On the right column, to the right of On This List, click **See All**.

3. Find the friend on the list you want to delete, hover your pointer over the thumbnail image, and click **Delete**. The name is not deleted as one of your friends, only as someone belonging to the list being displayed. If you make an error, they can quickly be added back using the previous section.

4. Then click **Finish** to restore the list view.

Manage Your Friends List

Your Friends list is simply the list of all your friends. This is another way to find and add people to a list.

1. From your Home page, click **Find Friends** in the left column. The Friends page is displayed.

2. Click **Manage Friend List** in the upper-right corner of the center column.

3. Hover your pointer over the name of the person until a profile box appears.

4. Hover your pointer over the **Friends** button. A list of lists is displayed, shown earlier in Figure 3-5.

5. Click the list you want, or click **Show All Lists** for a longer list of lists.

Control Who Sees Your Friends List

1. From your Home page, click **Find Friends** in the left column. The Friends page is displayed.

2. Click **Manage Friend List** in the upper-right corner of the center column.

3. Click **Edit** in the upper-right corner of the center column.

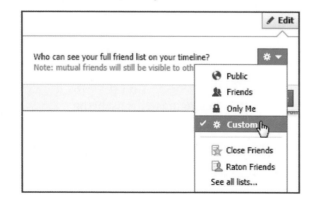

4. Click who will be able to see your Friends list: everyone, only friends, only yourself, or a custom setting—for example, friends of friends, or only people on a list.

View Posts from Friends on a List

To view postings from friends on a specific list, display the Home page. On the left column, find and click the list name under Friends (you may have to click **More** to see the list you want). When you click the list name, the postings from people on that list are displayed in the center column.

Delete a List

Deleting a list does not delete the people on the list. It simply removes that way of viewing your friends' postings or communicating with them.

1. From the Home page, scroll down to the Friends lists, and click the name of the list you want (you may have to click **More** to see it).

2. Click **Manage List** on the upper right to display a menu.

3. Click **Delete List**.

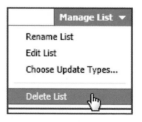

Post to a List

When you post a comment, video, or photo, you can direct it to be shown only on selected friends' Walls by selecting a list.

1. On your Home page or Timeline, click in the **Status** text box and type your comment.

2. Click the **Friends** button and click a list name. (Click **See All Lists** if the one you want is not displayed on the menu.)

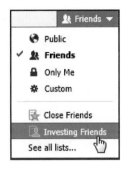

Evelyn Tracks Family

I started on Facebook when I realized that *everybody* is on Facebook and I could see what my grandchildren are up to! Now my two sisters and I, as well as many of our children and grandchildren, use Facebook fairly frequently, sometimes several times a day, to, in effect, just say "Hi!"

I really enjoy the pictures that people post and to see pictures of kids that don't live nearby. Of course, I *love* seeing my own grandchildren's pictures as they perform or play sports. Mostly we comment on what is happening in the world, what we think of the weather or current news, or what one or the other of us or our friends has posted. None of it is terribly important—we still do have phones for that—but it is a great way to stay in touch and let each other know what we're thinking about and doing. It is a great way to just acknowledge that we are thinking about each other.

Evelyn Y., 65, New Jersey

View a Friend's Page

The Timeline page is what you see when you go to a friend's page. Depending on the friend, you'll see a variety of creative and interesting sites, each helping you to touch into the personality and interests of the person you are viewing. Some people spend a lot of time on their Facebook pages, and others are just barely present. It's all good!

View a Friend's Timeline Page

Figure 3-6 shows an example of an updated Timeline page. To find out what is happening on a friend's Timeline:

1. Click the friend's thumbnail photo to see their Facebook page. You will see your friend's Timeline with their basic profile beneath their photo and a divided center column of photos, friends, and activities beneath, with a Timeline on the right column. You have these options:

   • Click **About** beneath the profile photo and info to see detailed profile information.

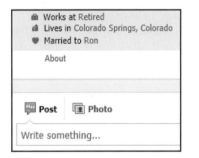

   • Click and type in the **Write Something** text box on the left, and click **Post** to leave a message for the friend that is seen by all who visit her or his site.

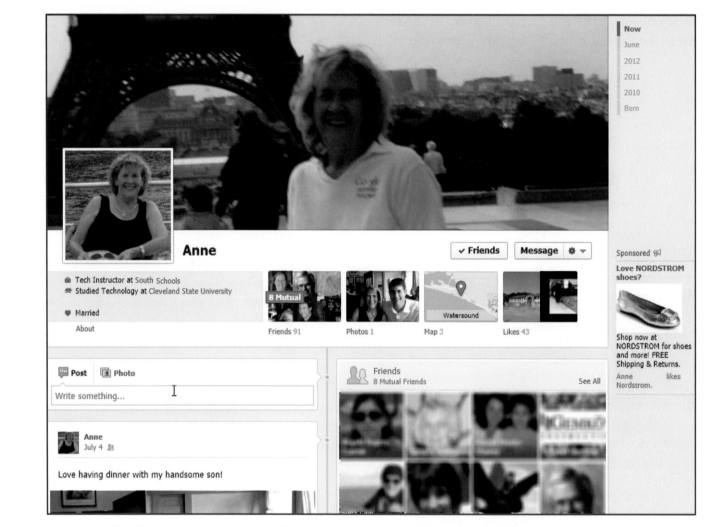

Figure 3-6: A Timeline page shows a more visual presentation of your personal interactions with Friends.

- Click **Photo** to upload a photo or video on your friend's Timeline, or use the webcam.

- Beneath the friend's name, you can click **Friends** to see the list of friends, **Photos** to see all the photos they have added to their site, **Map** to see where they have been, and **Likes** to see what pages or ads they support (this friend likes 70 sites).

- Click the **Friends** button above the Likes link to display a menu where you can add the friend to a list, control whether you see their posts in your News Feed, suggest friends to them, or unfriend them.

- Click **Message** to the right of Friends to send a private message to the friend.

- Click the gear icon down arrow for a menu. You can add this friend to an Interest list, see all the communications you have in common with this one, "poke" your friend, suggest friends to them, report them for illegal activities, or block them from your site. (See Chapter 4 for more information on these features.)

2. To return to your own site, simply click *your name* for your Timeline, or **Home** in the menu bar.

Set What You See from a Friend

You can distinguish between the many kinds of posts that a friend may send you. For instance, perhaps you have a close friend that you really want to track on Facebook, except for the games they play. You can choose to see everything except games.

1. Click the friend's thumbnail photo to see their Facebook page. You will see your friend's Timeline with their basic profile beneath their photo.

2. To the right of their name, click **Friends | Settings**.

3. Beneath What Type of Updates, click to clear any check marks beside the type of post you want to repress, such as Games. A check mark means you will see it on your News Feed; no check mark means you will not see it.

Hide, Unhide, or Unsubscribe Posts

Sometimes you'll find a friend or an application that shares or posts too much. Perhaps the information is just something you don't want on your Facebook page. Some people, for instance, do not play games and get a lot of postings about games, or during the political season, a lot of unsolicited opinions clog the Facebook space. You can hide or unsubscribe from one or a group of postings by a friend or application.

Hide or Unsubscribe Posts

On your Home page, in the News Feed stream, mouse over the posting that you want to hide or unsubscribe from. Click the down arrow that appears. You have these options (some may not be displayed if they do not apply to the post):

- **Hide Story**   Hides the individual post from your News Feed.

- **Report Story Or Spam**   Removes the post and reports it as illegal, offensive, or spam. (Reporting a post doesn't mean that it will be removed from Facebook, since while the post may be offensive to you, it may be okay within the guidelines of Facebook.)

- **Subscribed To** *name of person*   Allows you to control what level of posts you want to see: all posts, most of them, or only the "important" posts.

- **Unsubscribe From** *name of person*   Hides this post and all future posts from this person or app.

- **Unsubscribe From Status Updates Activity By** *name of person*   Prevents this post and all future posts from this person or app from being shown (only appears in the post if it is from an application, including games).

 Tip   If you receive text messages that someone has updated their Facebook status and you would like these to stop, just reply with the word "unsubscribe" the next time you receive a post about that person. You'll get a confirmation telling you that the unsubscribed status is successful.

Unhide Posts from Friends

1. On the Home page, mouse over **News Feed** in the left column. A **Pencil** icon will appear (click the pencil and a menu option will appear).

2. Click **Edit Settings**. An Edit News Feed Settings dialog box will open listing all the friends and apps from whom you are hiding or unsubscribing.

3. Next to the friend's name, app, or page you'd like to reinstate, click the **X** to remove it from the block list.

4. Click **Save** to complete the process.

Block or Unblock Someone from Your Site

If you have a friend that you must block from your site—perhaps they are posting insulting or politically incorrect statements—you can do so. Once a person is blocked, they will no longer be your friend or be able to post on your site. One exception: You can still interact with them in common games and applications. This is a confidential action—the blocked person will not know that he or she has been blocked.

Block a Person from Your Site

1. Click the down arrow to the right of Home on the menu bar, and then click **Privacy Settings**.

2. Scroll down and to the right of Blocked People And Apps, click **Manage Settings**.

3. In the Block Users area, either type the name of the person in the Name text box, or type the email address in the Email text box, and then click **Block**.

4. You'll be shown a list of people with common names. Click **Block** by the name you want to block.

Unblock a Blocked Person

1. Click the down arrow to the right of Home on the menu bar, and then click **Privacy Settings**.

2. Scroll down, and to the right of Blocked People And Apps, click **Manage Settings**.

3. Beneath the Block Users area, the names of blocked persons will be listed. Click **Unblock** next to the name you want.

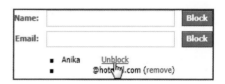

Delete a Friend Request Not Yet Confirmed

You may find that you want to retract an invitation to someone to be your friend that has not been responded to. You'll want to wait long enough for the friend to respond to your invitation. But if time goes by and the person still does not respond, you may decide to withdraw it.

1. In the Search text box, type the name of the invited person. You'll be shown a list of persons matching your criteria.

2. Click the thumbnail of the person you want. On the upper right will be a Friend Request Sent button.

3. Beneath their profile photo, click **Cancel Request | Confirm**.

4. To return to your own page, click the **Facebook** logo or **Home**.

Your invitation will no longer be displayed on their site.

Note If you are wondering what has happened to an invitation to be friends that you remember sending to someone, you can tell your friend status by going to the person's page and looking at the button on the upper right of the page. If it is *Friends,* you know you are already a confirmed friend; if it is *Friend Request Sent,* an invitation has been sent but not confirmed; and if it is *Add Friend,* you are not friends and have no invitation outstanding.

▷▷ Control Which Friends See You

When you create a posting, you can determine who will see it. You can either hide a posting from specific people, including a list you've created, or you can make it visible to them.

1. Click in the **What's On Your Mind** text box on the top of the center column of your Home page, and type your comments. When you click the text box, the default audience setting (Public usually) will appear along with the Share command.

2. Click the **Audience Selector** down arrow, and a menu will open.

📝 **Update Status** 🖼 Add Photo / Video

It is July and I am really tired of the Seattle rain! Does anyone else feel that way?

👤+ 📍   🌐 Public ▼   Post

         ✓ 🌐 **Public**
         👥 Friends
         🔒 Only Me
         ⚙ Custom

         ⭐ Close Friends
         🏠 Family
         See all lists...

3. Click the degree of privacy you want:

- **Public**   Anyone can see it
- **Friends**   Only your confirmed friends can see it
- **Friends Except Acquaintances**   Only friends who are not merely acquaintances
- **Only Me**   For your eyes only
- **Custom**   More choices are displayed
- *Named List*   Only friends assigned to a list can see this post

▷▷ Make a Post Visible or Hidden to Specific People

When you specify that a post is visible to specific people, it will be invisible to everyone else, as defined by your privacy settings. If you specify a post to be hidden, it will be visible to everyone else.

1. Click in the **What's On Your Mind** text box on the top of the center column of your Home page, and type your comments. When you click the text box, the default audience setting (Public usually) will appear along with the Share command.

2. Click the **Audience Selector** down arrow, and a menu will open.

3. Click **Custom**. The Custom Privacy dialog box will open, as shown in Figure 3-7.

4. To make the post visible only to specific friends, under Make This Visible To, click the **These People Or Lists** down arrow, and click **Specific People Or Lists**. Click in

Figure 3-7: Using the Custom Privacy feature, you can make a post visible or hidden only to specific individuals.

the blank text box and begin to type the name of a friend or list. As you type a list of names will be displayed. Click the ones you want included. Repeat this sequence.

5. To make the post hidden only to specific friends, under Hide This From, click the **These People Or Lists** down arrow, and click **Specific People Or Lists**. Click in the blank text box and begin to type the name of a friend or list. As you type a list of names will be displayed. Click the ones you want excluded. Repeat as needed.

6. Click **Save Changes**.

SET UP AN EVENT

You can create an event and invite your friends. The event can be a private affair or a public one. It can be a casual social party or a more formal business gathering. Once you have created the event and invited people, you can then track RSVPs.

▷▷ Create an Event

To create an event:

1. On your Home page, click **Events** beneath your profile photo. The center column will display existing events you've created or been invited to.

2. On the top of the center column, click **Create Event**. A Create Event page is displayed. You can see an example of a completed one in Figure 3-8.

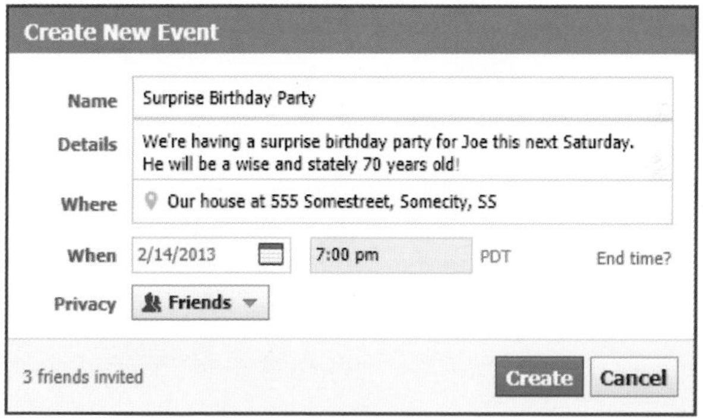

3. Set the parameters of the event:

- In the **Name** text box, type a name for the event.
- Click the **Details** text box and type a description of the event in more detail.
- Click the **Where** text box to set the location or other identifying information.
- Click the **When** calendar and find the date you want.
- Click the **Time** down arrow and set the time.
- Click **End Time** to be able to set a date and time that the event will end.

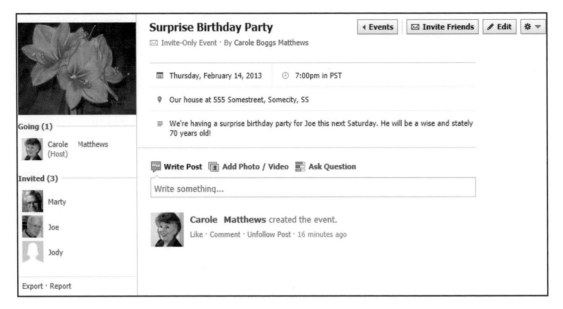

Figure 3-8: Setting up an event is easy and allows you to manage inviting and tracking RSVPs.

- Click **Privacy Setting** and select the recipients of the invitation. You can choose Public, where everyone sees the invitation; Friends, where the invitation goes out to your friends; or Invite Only, where you invite specific friends.

- Click **Invite Friends** to choose your guests. The Invite Friends dialog box will appear. Put a check mark next to each name you want to invite. Click **Save**. (See "Invite Your Friends" for additional information on this dialog box.)

- If you have chosen Invite Only, you will see two additional options. Clear the check marks to deselect whether the guests can invite additional friends and whether the guest list is displayed on the Events page.

4. Click **Create** to make it final.

5. On the invitation page, you can add a photo or video to make it more attractive. You can ask a question to poll those invited, and you can update the invitation with ongoing posts on the Events page itself.

Invite Your Friends

After you've created an event, you can invite additional friends.

1. Click **Events** on the Home page to view the events. If you have more than one event, scroll to the event you want and click it. The Events page will open. On the left you'll see those you've previously invited and those who have accepted so far.

Going (1)

Carole Matthews (Host)

Invited (3)

Marty

Joe

Jody

2. On the upper right of the page, click **Invite Friends**. The Invite Friends dialog box is displayed, as seen in Figure 3-9.

3. In the Search box, type the invitee names, and a list of matching friends is displayed. Then click the names of the friends you want to invite, and then click **Save**.

–Or–

Scroll down the list of names and place a check mark by those you wish to invite. Click **Save** to save the selections.

–Or–

Click the **Search By Name** down arrow and choose a list name or group name. You may have to click **Show More** to find the list or group you want. Place a check mark by the names of those you want to invite. Click **Save**.

4. Click the down arrow and choose **Selected** to review all the friends on your invitation list.

5. When you click **Save**, the invitations are sent.

Figure 3-9: *Inviting friends to an event is as easy as can be.*

Respond to an Event Invitation

To respond to an event invitation:

1. On your Home page, click **Events** on the left to view the list of events to which you are invited or have created. If you have more than one event listed, click the event you want to see.

2. In the upper right of the page, click **Join**, **Maybe**, Or **Decline**. The RSVP To This Event dialog box will be displayed. Your name will be placed in the appropriate slot: Going, Maybe, or Declined.

Cancel Your Event

To cancel an event that no longer seems like a good idea:

1. From your Home page, click **Events** in the left column to see your event. Click the event name that you want to cancel.

2. On the Events page, click the gear icon down arrow and click **Cancel Event**. You will be asked to confirm you really want to cancel this event. When you respond **Yes**, all information is lost.

Chapter 4

Socializing with Friends

Once you have friends, you can explore the reason Facebook exists: its capacity for socializing and engaging with friends. You can communicate with all your friends at once, with one or more privately, or with a list of friends. This chapter explores the relational and conversational aspects of Facebook—how you connect and communicate with your friends.

SEND AND RECEIVE MESSAGES AND POSTS

The most direct way of communicating with friends is by posting comments and sending private messages.

▶▶ Post a Comment

You can share a comment with all of your friends or some of them. Consequently, it's important to realize that what you post may be visible to your friends, and their friends, depending on your audience selected and whether a friend has responded to you.

Share a Comment with All Friends

1. To post a comment on your Wall from either your Home or Timeline page to all of your friends, click in the **What's On Your Mind** text box, and type your comment. As you type the Post command will appear.

📄 Status	📷 Photo	👤 Place	📖 Life Event
What's on your mind?			

2. Click **Post** to post the comment to all your friends.

> **Tip** If you press **ENTER** to move down to the next line, Facebook will instead post your comment. To move to the next line without posting the comment, press **SHIFT+ENTER**.

Select Your Audience for a Post

Your post will automatically be assigned a default audience category to which a typical post is sent. The default is the previous audience you selected for a post. Selecting an audience is how you set your privacy. To reset the audience for a particular post, on either your Home or Timeline page, click in the **What's On Your Mind** text box, and type your comment. As you click in the text box, an Audience Selector icon and the Post command will appear. When you mouse over the Audience Selector icon, you'll see which category is the default for your post. To change it:

1. Click the Audience Selector icon, and click select one of these options:
   - **Public**   Everyone on Facebook can see the post.

- **Friends**   All of your confirmed friends can see the post.
- **Friends Except Acquaintances**   All of your friends except for those you've assigned to the Acquaintances category can see the post.
- **Only Me**   Restrict the post to your eyes only (a note to yourself).
- **Custom**   Hide or show the post to specific people, lists, or groups.
- *Name of list*   Select a specific group or list to see the post.

Send a Post to Specific People

To send a post to certain people, lists, or groups:

1. Click the Audience Selector icon | **Custom**.

2. Under Make This Visible To, click the **These People** down arrow, and click the group of people you want to have read your post:

   - If you want to select only some people or lists of people, click **Specific People Or Lists**, and in the text box that appears, type the name of the person or list you want. If you want to select multiple people, after selecting the first person, just continue typing the name of the next person. The additional people will be added to the list in the text box.

- If you want to send it to a list or group (see Chapter 3), type the name of the list or group, and click it when displayed.

3. Click **Save Changes** to save the audience setting.

Hide the Post from Specific People

To hide your posting from certain people, lists, or groups:

1. Click the Audience Selector icon | **Custom**.

2. In the Hide This From text box, begin typing the names of people, lists, or groups you do not want to see this post. As you type a list appears with the matching candidates on it. Click the name you want. Repeat this for multiple names. You can hide the post from some and make it visible to others at the same time.

3. Click **Save Changes** to save the audience setting.

⏩ Send and Receive Private Messages

Sometimes you'll want to send a message to just one or a few persons, but not to everyone on a list or group. Facebook's message function allows you to send a private message to up to 20 designated people at one time. When you send a message, it appears in the addressee's Messages page. Depending on how the addressee has adjusted their notification settings, he or she may also receive an email.

There are several ways to do this—from the menu bar, the Home page, or the Friend page.

Send Messages from the Menu Bar or Home Page

1. From any Facebook page click the **Messages** icon on the menu bar, and click **Send A New Message**.

–Or–

From your Home page, click **Messages** in the leftmost column, and then click **+New Message** above the messages in the center column. The New Message dialog box is displayed, as shown in Figure 4-1.

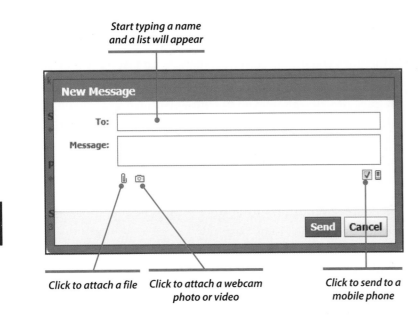

Start typing a name and a list will appear

Click to attach a file *Click to attach a webcam photo or video* *Click to send to a mobile phone*

Figure 4-1: You can send a private message to selected persons.

2. If he or she is a Facebook friend, type the name of the person to whom you want to send a message. As you type, a list of matching candidates will appear. Click the one you want:

- If you're going to send the message to more than one person, after you've selected a name, type another name, select the one you want, and so on. You can send to up to 20 names.
- If you're sending this to a non-Facebook friend, type the email address.

3. When you've completed the addressees, click in the **Message** text box, and type your message.

4. Click **Send** to send it.

Send Messages from a Friend's Page

1. To display the friend's page, click *your name* on the menu bar, click **Friends** below your name, and then find and click the friend's picture.

2. Beneath the Timeline image, click **Message**. You'll see the Message dialog box.

Tip If you have not installed Timeline, you'll find the Message button on your Profile page in the upper right corner.

3. In the text box at the bottom of the messages, or in the Message text box, type your message. You have these options:

- Click the **Paperclip** icon to attach a file.
- Click the **Camera** icon to take a photo or webcam video.

4. Click **Send** to send the message.

CAUTION! Once a message is sent, it cannot be unsent or deleted. It's just out there.

Look at and Reply to Messages

You can tell if you have a message because you'll see a red square with the number of messages waiting for you on your Messages icon in the menu bar. You may also be notified that you have a message at your primary email address or on your Facebook Wall. Your messages and chats are available in one place, organized by friend. You can access messages in two ways:

1. Click the **Messages** icon on the left of the menu bar.

–Or–

Click **Messages** under Favorites on your Home page.

2. Click the name of the friend whose messages you want to see.

3. Click in the text box at the bottom of the messages, and type your message.

4. Click **Reply**.

–Or—

If you place a check mark in the check box next to Reply, just press **ENTER** to send the message.

QuickQuotes

Ernestine Chats Using Her iPhone

I love Facebook because it's such a great communication tool without expending a lot of effort. It helps me keep in touch with friends and relatives without having to type out individual email messages or send letters. I share news and photos from my home computer or, when on the road, from my iPhone. And I enjoy seeing what my friends and relatives are posting about what is going on in their lives. My 88-year-old mother is on Facebook too, and she looks forward to my "posts"!

Facebook is also great for finding old friends and relatives. I've found several people that I had lost track of and now feel connected to again.

Another feature I like is the Chat box. I can see which of my friends are online at the same time I am, and can send or receive messages that are private.

Ernestine, 68, Washington

⊳⊳ Chat with Online Friends

Chatting is a way to communicate in real time with friends who are on the computer now. Only your own friends who are willing to be seen online will be available to you for chats. However, if a friend is not online at the moment, your chat will still be available to them as a message, which they can access later when they are online. The chats are private—just another form of messages. Figure 4-2 shows an example of a chat. When you send a chat to a friend, a Chat dialog box pops up on your friend's Facebook window. Your chats are stored in your Messages page, so the conversations don't go away. You can see which of your friends are online in two ways:

- There is a Chat bar on the bottom of your Facebook pages, which tells you how many friends are currently signed on. Click the **Chat** bar to see a Chat sidebar displaying a list of your friends.

  👤● Chat (2)

- When your Facebook window is maximized, you'll see a Ticker/Chat sidebar on the right—with the Ticker on the top of the sidebar and the Chat sidebar on the bottom. If the window is not maximized, you can activate the Chat sidebar by clicking the Chat bar at the bottom of the screen. A green circle indicates that a friend is online and available to chat; a white rectangle indicates that a friend has downloaded an app such as iPhone or Messenger and can probably receive messages on a mobile phone; no symbol indicates that the friend is currently offline.

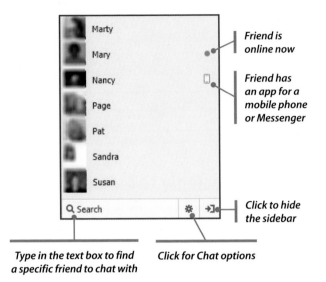

Friend is online now

Friend has an app for a mobile phone or Messenger

Click to hide the sidebar

Type in the text box to find a specific friend to chat with

Click for Chat options

Start a Chat

To initiate a chat, check to see whether the friend with whom you want to chat is online. Or, if you're in the mood to chat and don't care with whom, just see who is available at the moment. You can also send a chat to someone not online and they will see it later when they are online.

1. On any page, click the **Chat** bar (a number in it tells you how many people are online at the moment) to see which friends are online—there will be a green circle to the right. Click the thumbnail image of the friend with whom you want to chat.

   –Or–

   Click in the **Chat** search box and type the name of the friend you want to chat with. Click the thumbnail that appears.

   A Chat dialog box will appear, as shown in Figure 4-2.

2. Click in the lower text box, and type your greeting. Then press **ENTER** to send it.

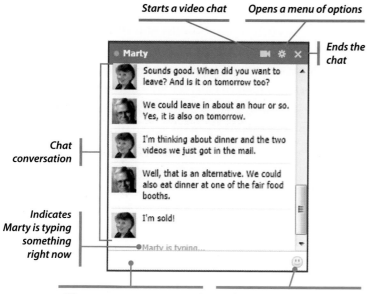

Starts a video chat *Opens a menu of options*

Ends the chat

Chat conversation

Indicates Marty is typing something right now

Where my responses are typed *Opens a selection of emoticons*

Figure 4-2: Chatting with online friends occurs in real time and is fun.

3. Continue the chat in the same way. When you're finished and have said your good-byes, click **X** to close the Chat dialog box.

Control Your Chat Availability

You can control whether others can see that you are online and available for chats.

On the Chat bar, click **Options** (the gear icon). You can turn your chat online status on and off:

- Click **Go Offline** to turn off your chat image.
- Click **Go Online** to turn on your chat image.

If you are in the middle of a chat, you can click **Options | Go Offline To** *name* to be unavailable to your chat partner right now. (You are seriously ticked off!)

Add Friends to a Chat

You can have "group" chats by adding names to the Chat box. You simply open one Chat box and add names to it.

1. Click the **Chat** bar in the bottom-right corner of your Facebook page. A pop-up dialog box will appear showing thumbnails of who is available. (If your Ticker/Chat sidebar is open, you can use that.)

2. Type the name in the bottom text box or click the thumbnail of the first person with whom you want to chat.

3. Add people to the chat by clicking **Options** (the gear icon) | **Add Friends To Chat**. A small text box opens beneath your first friend's name.

4. Type each additional friend's name.

5. When you have added all you want, click **Done**. A new Chat box will open containing the names of everyone you've added.

6. Click in the lower text box and begin your chat.

Use the Like Function

The Like function on Facebook allows you to signal that you like or approve of a post, page, or ad. When you click **Like**, you are counted as a person who has connected in some way with what is being posted. Exactly what happens depends on what you like.

- If you like a friend's comment, video, or photo, you are simply saying, "I like what you've posted." You are added to a counter beneath the comment, photo, or video that you like. If someone clicks the counter, they will see your name. You will also see a posting on your Timeline that you like it. Your friend may be notified that you like it, depending on his or her notification settings. When someone else comments on something you like, you are notified.

> Like · Comment · 25 minutes ago ·
> 👍 5 people like this.

- If you like a Page, you are forming more of a relationship with it, which is displayed on your Timeline. You may see postings in your own News Feed, and your friends may see it too on theirs. Your name may be displayed on the Page, and if there are advertisements about the Page, you may be featured in it. You can edit this by "unliking" it if you want your support to remain private. Liking a Page is one way to track what is happening on the Page.

Carole liked Rotary District 5050 Conference.

- If you like an ad or content in the third column of a Facebook page, you are forming a connection with a business brand, product, or organization. (Ads are a way you can advertise a business, product, organization, or person. Ads usually support a Page—see Chapter 9.) Although Facebook does not share your personal information, your name may be used in an ad and be seen on your Timeline page, on your friends' News Feed pages, and on the advertised Page's page or ads. The Page can post to your News Feed or send you messages. So be sure you're up for having your name associated with the advertisement. Again, you can control this by "unliking" the ad.

Love NORDSTROM shoes?
Shop now at NORDSTROM for shoes and more! FREE Shipping & Returns.

Anne likes Nordstrom.

CAUTION! If you find you don't want to continue a "Like" status, you can unlike it. To do this, click **Unlike** displayed with the link where you indicated a Like in the first place. If you want to unlike a Page or ad, go to the Page or ad and you'll see "Like" indicating you have liked that Page or ad previously. Click **Like | Unlike**. You can also remove it from your Timeline or restrict access by adjusting your privacy settings (see Chapter 10).

Share a Photo, Link, or Video

Sharing enables you to show others photos, links, or videos that you like or dislike by putting a shared item where they can see it. You determine where while sharing. If you see something that you'd like to share with others:

1. Click **Share** beneath the link, photo, or video. A dialog box will open, as shown in Figure 4-3.

2. Click the **Share** down arrow to select where your message will be seen. You can choose your own Timeline, a friend's Timeline, a group, on your Page, or within a private message. There are these considerations:

   - If you choose one of the Timelines, you can set your audience.

   - If you choose groups or a private message, audience settings are unavailable since you've already determined the selection by the choice.

   - You cannot choose Group unless you belong to a group.

3. If you want change your audience from the displayed default, click the **Friends** down arrow and choose Public (displays shared item to everybody), Friends, Friends except for those you've assigned to the Acquaintances list, only yourself, Custom, or a list. Here are some considerations:

   - The audience selector defaults to the last audience you selected when posting. If you change it, the default is updated to what you now choose.

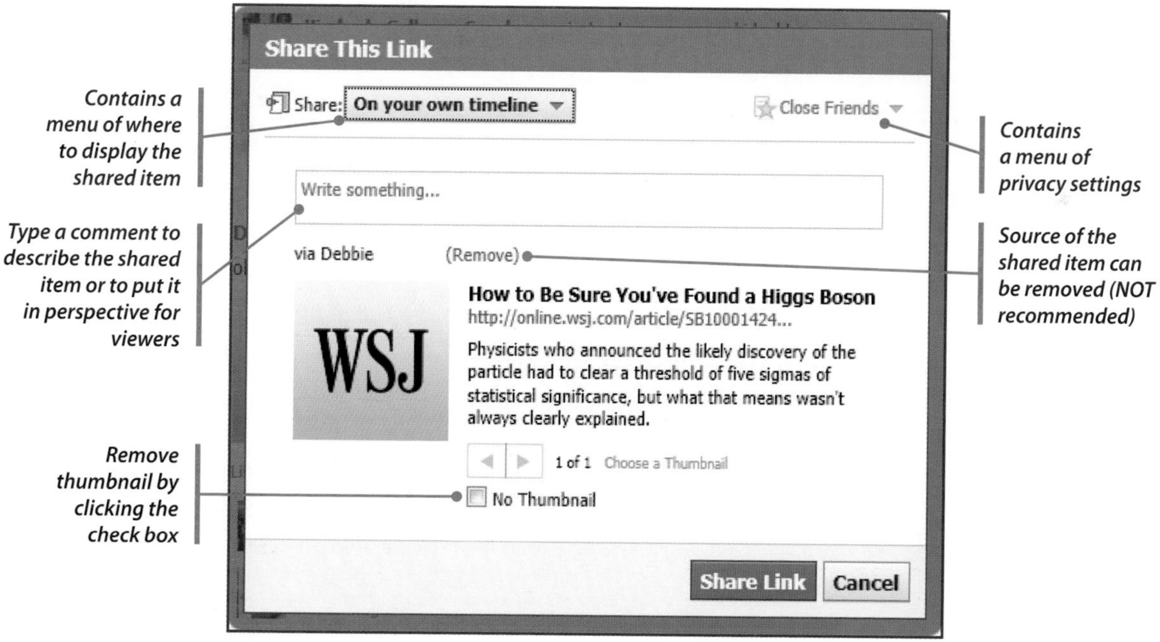

Contains a menu of where to display the shared item

Type a comment to describe the shared item or to put it in perspective for viewers

Remove thumbnail by clicking the check box

Share This Link

Share: **On your own timeline** ▼   ⭐ Close Friends ▼

Write something...

via Debbie   (Remove)

How to Be Sure You've Found a Higgs Boson
http://online.wsj.com/article/SB10001424...

WSJ

Physicists who announced the likely discovery of the particle had to clear a threshold of five sigmas of statistical significance, but what that means wasn't always clearly explained.

◄ ► 1 of 1 Choose a Thumbnail
☐ No Thumbnail

Share Link **Cancel**

Contains a menu of privacy settings

Source of the shared item can be removed (NOT recommended)

Figure 4-3: You can share a video, photo, or link on your News Feed or from a friend's page.

- People who see your shared item, can also see who you have selected to be your audience.

- In the Custom dialog box you can choose to hide the message from certain people or to make it visible. (See Chapter 3 to see how to work with the Custom feature.)

- You can include up to 20 people in one message. (If you want to send this to more than that, send multiple messages.)

4. If you want, click in the **Write Something** text box, and type a message that explains or describes what you are sharing.

5. If you see and then click **Remove**, you can delete the name of where you found the shared item. But we recommend that you give credit and openly reveal your source. (Remove is unavailable for some shared items.)

6. Likewise, if you see and click **No Thumbnail**, you can remove the visual thumbnail, but that may also remove an interesting element. (No Thumbnail is also unavailable for some shared items.)

7. Click **Share** *item*.

Poke a Friend

Poking a friend is just a way of saying "Hello" or "Notice me!" When you poke someone, a poke alert appears on their profile. Pokes are popular with the younger set, but most seniors find them a bit lame.

1. Click a friend's thumbnail.
2. Click the **gear** icon beneath the Timeline image, and then click **Poke**.

You can poke or be poked by a friend, friend of a friend, or someone on a shared network. The "poke" will be displayed in the right column. Click it to **Poke Back** or the **X** (to remove the poke). If you remove a poke, it cannot be recovered.

Keep Up with Birthdays

One of the most fun activities in Facebook is tracking birthdays of friends. It's a small but caring way to say "I'm thinking of you" to distant friends or even acquaintances. And it is a good way to remember important birthdays! Chapter 8 discusses one app to help you manage birthday lists.

View Birthdays

You can scan through the list of names with upcoming birthdays. On the special day, you can wish them a happy birthday, if your friends reveal their birthdays in their profiles.

Scan for Birthdays

1. On your Home page, you'll see today's birthdays listed on the right column (until you click the link to wish them a happy birthday).

2. To see all upcoming birthdays, click the **Events** link in the leftmost column. The Events page is displayed. You'll see birthdays listed for today (if there are any), this month, and next month.

3. Scroll down to the bottom of the page and click **See More** at the bottom of the list to extend it further.

Send a Happy Birthday Greeting

On the day of the birthday, the friend's name will be shown in the right column under the Ticker or on the Events page under Today.

1. Either click **Events** and find and click the friend's name under Today, or click the friend's name in the right column beneath the Ticker callouts.

2. To send him or her a happy birthday message, on their Timeline, click in the **Write On His/Her Timeline** text box, type your message, and press ENTER or click **Share**.

You may also find that someone else has already initiated a birthday greeting. In that case, you can simply click **Comment** and type your message inline with the rest of the messages.

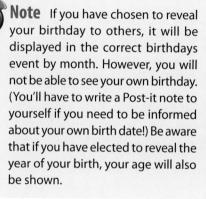

Note If you have chosen to reveal your birthday to others, it will be displayed in the correct birthdays event by month. However, you will not be able to see your own birthday. (You'll have to write a Post-it note to yourself if you need to be informed about your own birth date!) Be aware that if you have elected to reveal the year of your birth, your age will also be shown.

Tag a Friend

When you tag a friend, you notify them that they are mentioned in a comment or posting. You might do this if you wanted a specific person to respond to something you have said, or if you wanted her or him to be aware of your posting, while allowing the comment to be public. It can make your posts more personal. You can tag confirmed friends, Pages, photos, events, and so on. When you tag someone, their name appears as a link in your posting. Others can then click the link and view the tagged person's Timeline. You can tag more than one person in a single item.

1. Click in the **What's On Your Mind** or **Write A Comment** text box on your Home page or Timeline page, or on a friend's Timeline. Type your message.

2. When you want to type the name of your friend, type @ and begin typing the name of the friend you want. A list of candidates will be displayed as you type.

3. Click the name of the person you want to tag. The tagged person will appear as a link in your post. Repeat steps 2 and 3 to tag additional people.

Add a Note

To Facebook, notes are a form of *blogs,* or online journals. Blogs, which is short for "web logs," are webpages dedicated to discussions, journals, presentations, and other written material. You can find blogs created by teenagers, businesses, political pundits, and vacation-goers. If you know the website address for a blog, you can read it and sometimes contribute to the discussion with your own comments and opinions.

Facebook Notes are very much the same; they provide a place for you to create a discussion or diary, such as a journal, and share it with your friends, depending on your privacy settings. As with other comments, you can enhance the notes with photos. If your notes contain references to others, such as a shared experience, you can tag specific people to be notified. Your notes can be shared with everyone or no one, depending on your privacy settings.

Notes are posted to your News Feed on the Home page, your Timeline, and, of course, on your Notes page.

> **QuickQuotes**

Helen Has Fun Writing Notes

I started using Facebook just after I turned 94. Entering the world of Facebook has brought more fun and fulfillment than I could have dreamed of at this stage in life. It's like joining a club that allows me to meet new people every day from all over the world. I enjoy being part of this ever-growing family of friends.

I like using Notes to communicate because I can formulate longer thoughts in Notes. I think writing and conversations are much more interesting when one can take the time to build an argument and reach a conclusion. When Facebook asks me "What's on your mind?" on the News Feed, it doesn't offer as much room to share my thoughts as the Notes feature does. Notes offers an opportunity to engage in a more meaningful discussion.

Using Notes is like keeping a diary and sharing it with friends. It's also easy in Notes to find older writings and review people's comments. Older comments on the News Feed fall off the page as new ones are added at the top, and topics get jumbled. With Notes, I just open the Notes link and can quickly look at what I've written and see people's comments. It's much more convenient and a lot of fun.

Thanks, Mark, for creating Facebook.

Helen S., 95, Oregon

Write a Note

To write your note on Facebook:

1. On the Home page, click **Notes** in the left column under Apps. (You may have to click **More** to extend the available links and then click it on the Apps page.)

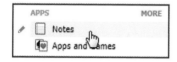

2. Click **+Write A Note** on the top of the center column. The form shown in Figure 4-4 is displayed.

3. Click in the **Title** text box, and type a name for the note.

4. Click in the **Body** text box, and type your note text. You have formatting options for boldface, italics, underlining, numbered lists, bulleted lists, and quote blocks. Select the text to be formatted, and click the appropriate formatting button.

5. If you want to notify specific people about your note, click **Tags** and type the name of the person. A menu of friends matching your typing is displayed. Click the one you want.

6. To add a photo, click **Browse**, navigate to your hard disk to locate the photo file, and double-click it to upload a photo from your disk onto your note. If you have already created an album, you may also select that (see Chapter 6 for how to create albums).

7. When the photo appears on the note, enter a caption for it and select a layout, which determines how the photo will be placed within the text.

8. Click the **Privacy** down arrow, and select who will have access to this note.

9. When you're finished, you'll have these options:

   - **Publish**   Places the note on your Timeline and on your friends' News Feeds.

   - **Preview**   Lets you see how your note is going to look when it is published. If you're satisfied, click **Publish**; if you'd like to refine it, click **Edit**.

   - **Save Draft**   Saves the note so you can come back to it later for further editing. To continue to refine the note, save it, display it again by clicking **My Drafts**, and then click **Edit** beneath the note title.

   - **Discard**   Deletes the note and does not publish it.

Edit or Delete a Note

1. To display your note, on the Home page, click **Notes** beneath Apps in the left column, and then click **My Notes**.

2. Find the note you want to edit.

3. To place the note in Edit mode, click **View Full Note**. Your note will be displayed with all of its text and photos. An example is shown in Figure 4-5.

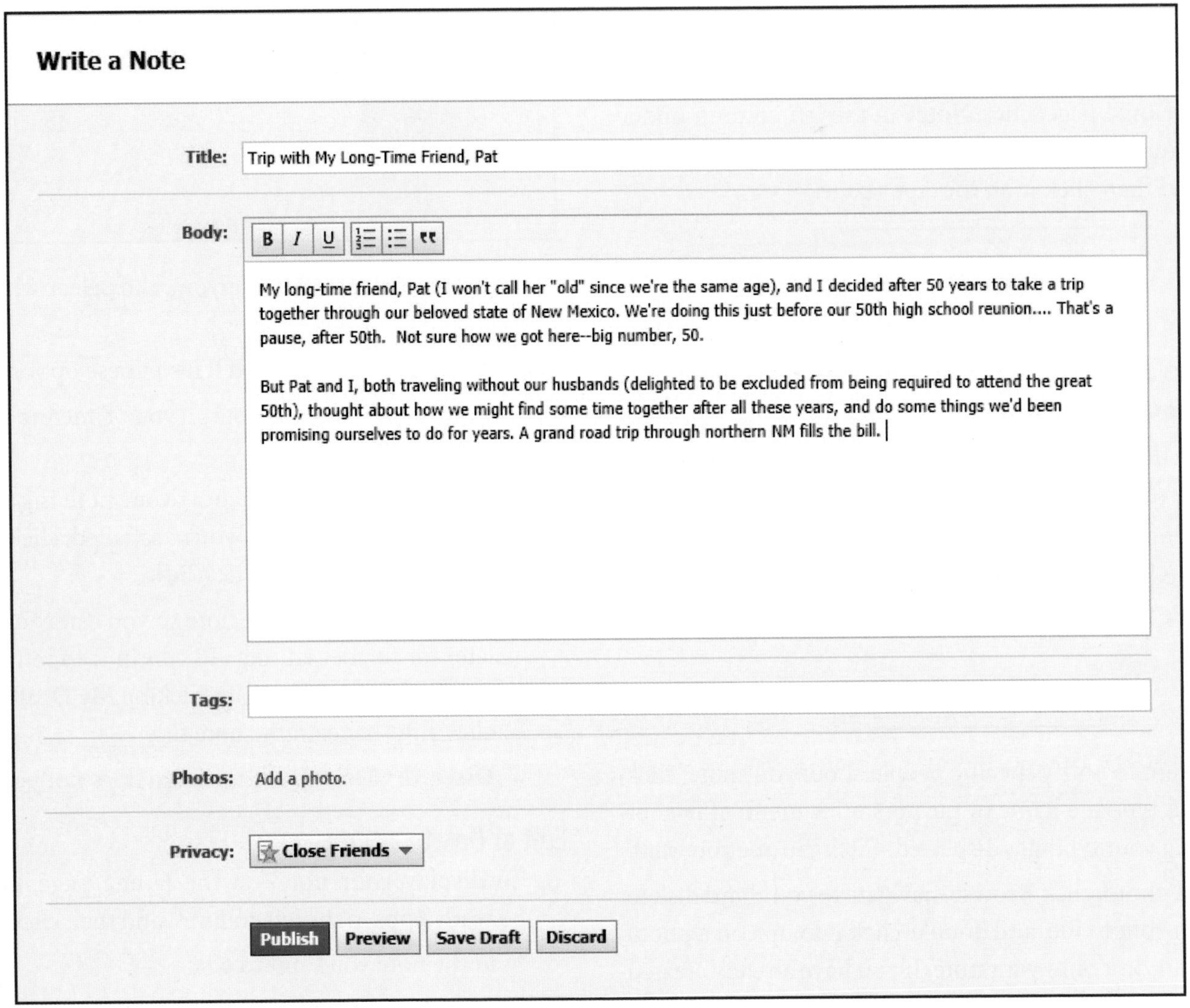

Write a Note

Title: Trip with My Long-Time Friend, Pat

Body:

| B | *I* | U̲ | ☰ | ☰ | ❝❝ |

My long-time friend, Pat (I won't call her "old" since we're the same age), and I decided after 50 years to take a trip together through our beloved state of New Mexico. We're doing this just before our 50th high school reunion.... That's a pause, after 50th. Not sure how we got here--big number, 50.

But Pat and I, both traveling without our husbands (delighted to be excluded from being required to attend the great 50th), thought about how we might find some time together after all these years, and do some things we'd been promising ourselves to do for years. A grand road trip through northern NM fills the bill. |

Tags:

Photos: Add a photo.

Privacy: ⭐ **Close Friends** ▼

Publish | Preview | Save Draft | Discard |

Figure 4-4: You can create a type of Facebook blog using the Notes feature.

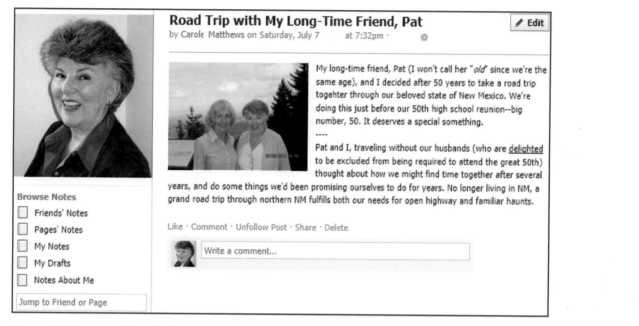

Road Trip with My Long-Time Friend, Pat
by Carole Matthews on Saturday, July 7   at 7:32pm ·   ✻

✎ Edit

My long-time friend, Pat (I won't call her "*old*" since we're the same age), and I decided after 50 years to take a road trip togehter through our beloved state of New Mexico. We're doing this just before our 50th high school reunion--big number, 50. It deserves a special something.

Pat and I, traveling without our husbands (who are <u>delighted</u> to be excluded from being required to attend the great 50th) thought about how we might find time together after several years, and do some things we'd been promising ourselves to do for years. No longer living in NM, a grand road trip through northern NM fulfills both our needs for open highway and familiar haunts.

Like · Comment · Unfollow Post · Share · Delete

Write a comment...

Browse Notes
☐ Friends' Notes
☐ Pages' Notes
☐ My Notes
☐ My Drafts
☐ Notes About Me

Jump to Friend or Page

Figure 4-5: Your note, when displayed fully, can be edited or deleted.

4. You have these options:

- To edit the note, click **Edit** to the right of the note title. Click **Save** to save your changes.

- To delete the note, click **Delete** beneath the note.

▷▷ Adjust Your Audience for a Note

You can change the audience for individual notes—perhaps you write a note sequence just for a specific list of friends.

1. To display your note, on the Home page, click **Notes** in the left column beneath Apps, and then click **My Notes**. You'll see a list of your notes.

2. Find the note for which you want to change the audience, mouse over the title, and click the Audience Selector icon that appears on the right.

3. Click your desired setting. If you click **Custom**, you can choose between making the note visible to selected persons or groups and hiding the note from them.

 Tip If you do not see the Audience Selector icon to the right of the note title (it is the gear icon), click the note's title and click **Edit** on the right of the title. Then click the **Privacy** down arrow beneath the note.

Ask a Question

There may be times when you want to take a poll or ask a question of your friends. Perhaps you're trying to organize something and you need to know what dates are best for your friends. Perhaps you want to take a political poll to find out which of your friends vote Democratic and which vote Republican. (I'm stretching it here, I know—that can be risky!) You can restrict whether anyone else can add options, or let others add options. Figure 4-6 shows an example.

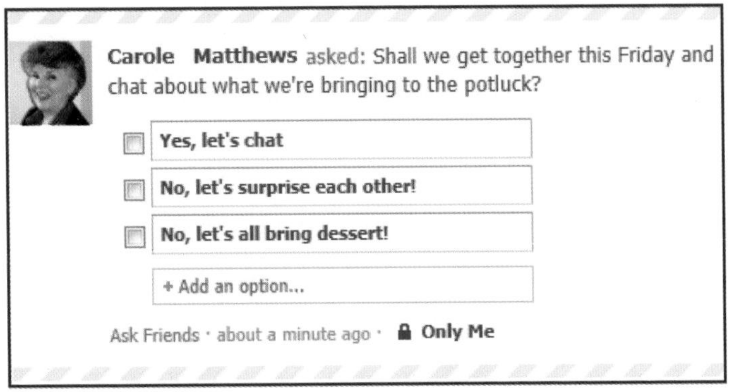

Carole Matthews asked: Shall we get together this Friday and chat about what we're bringing to the potluck?

Yes, let's chat

No, let's surprise each other!

No, let's all bring dessert!

+ Add an option...

Ask Friends · about a minute ago · 🔒 Only Me

Figure 4-6: This is an example of how you can poll your friends for their opinions about various concerns.

Here is how you can do it:

1. On your Home page, click **Ask Question** on the top of the center column. A text box is displayed.

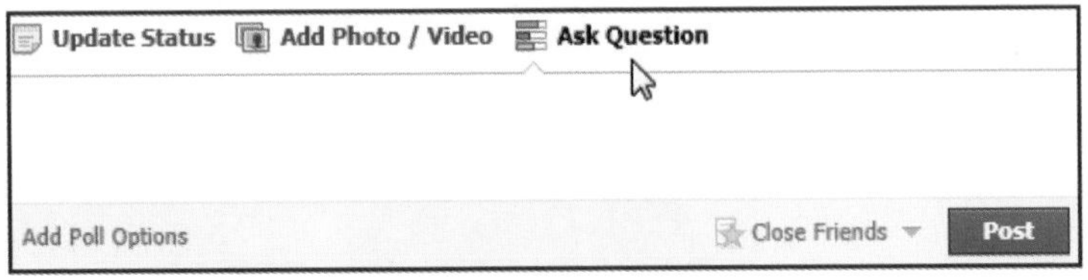

Update Status Add Photo / Video Ask Question

Add Poll Options   Close Friends ▼   Post

2. In the text box, type your question.

3. Click **Add Poll Options** on the left of the question text box if you want the group to vote on various possibilities.

4. Click in the first **Add An Option** text box, and type the polling possibilities. A list of possible options is displayed. Click to the side of the list to remove it. Continue this process with each of the possible answers.

5. Click the **Audience Selector** icon and set your audience. (In Figure 4-6, I restricted the audience to Only Me, since I really don't have a potluck planned this Friday!)

6. Click **Post** to post it.

Add a Subscribe Button or Be a Subscriber

You can choose whether to install a Subscribe button on your Timeline. This enables others, friends or not, to follow your posts. When you post something, it shows up on their News Feed. The Subscribe button is placed in your Timeline along with other buttons on the top of your page. And you can subscribe to others who have chosen to display a Subscribe button on their Timeline.

Let Others Subscribe to You

To let others subscribe to your posts, you must first choose to display a Subscribe button on your Timeline.

1. Click the down arrow to the right of Home, and click **Account Settings | Subscribers**.

2. Click the **Allow Subscribers** check box to place a check mark in it. You will see other settings, as shown in Figure 4-7.

3. You have these options:

   - **Subscriber Search** Your Timeline will show up in Internet searches. This gives you a wider visibility to potential subscribers.

   - **Subscriber Comments** Set the conditions for who can add comments to your public posts. You can allow anyone to post, in which case you really need to watch it.

Or you can restrict comments to people you know or trust to use common sense.

- **Subscriber Notifications** Set the conditions for when you will be notified about subscribers' comments, resharing, and new subscribers. This allows you to judge how successful your posts are.

- **Username** Displays the setting for how your username is displayed.

- **Twitter** Connect the Facebook subscription to a Twitter account, giving you wider visibility and more ways to reach subscribers.

- **Want To Know What Subscribers Can See? View Your Public Timeline** View your Timeline as it will display with the new button.

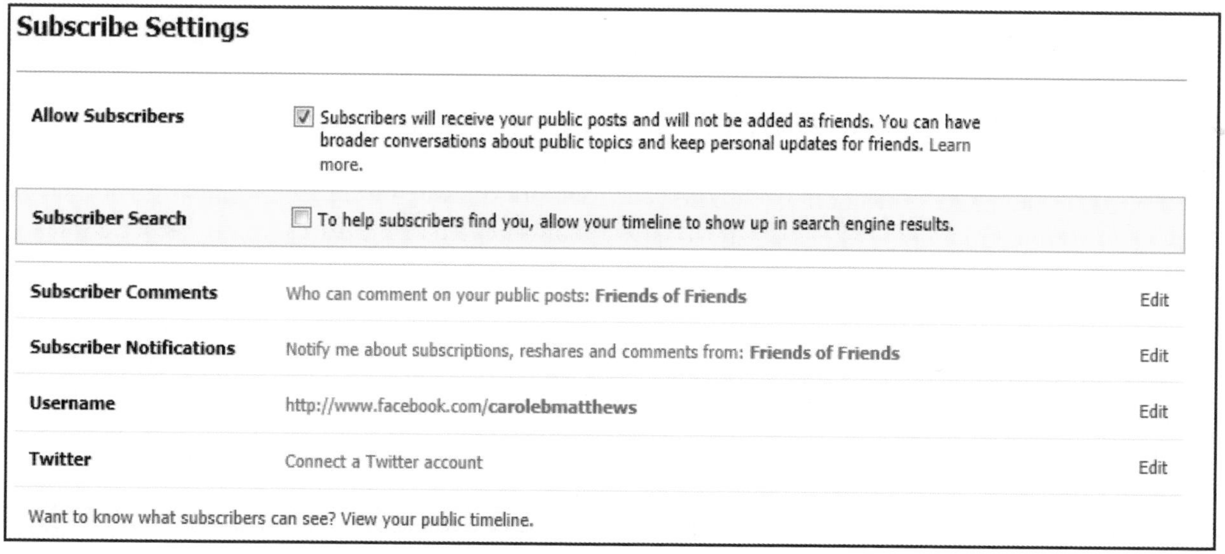

Subscribe Settings

Allow Subscribers	☑ Subscribers will receive your public posts and will not be added as friends. You can have broader conversations about public topics and keep personal updates for friends. Learn more.
Subscriber Search	☐ To help subscribers find you, allow your timeline to show up in search engine results.
Subscriber Comments	Who can comment on your public posts: **Friends of Friends** Edit
Subscriber Notifications	Notify me about subscriptions, reshares and comments from: **Friends of Friends** Edit
Username	http://www.facebook.com/**carolebmatthews** Edit
Twitter	Connect a Twitter account Edit
	Want to know what subscribers can see? View your public timeline.

Figure 4-7: When you choose to display a Subscribe button, friends and not-friends who choose to subscribe to you will see your posts in their News Feeds.

4. Click **Return To Timeline** and the Subscribe button will be displayed on your Timeline.

Post to Your Subscribers

To post something to your subscribers, create the post you want, and then set the privacy settings to Public, so everyone can view it. That will ensure that your subscribers get your posts on their News Feeds.

Find Interesting People to Subscribe to

You can only subscribe to people who have chosen to put a Subscribe button on their site. You can find some of these people through a special website within Facebook.

1. To get to a Facebook suggestion list of candidates, type www.facebook.com/subscriptions/suggestions/ into your browser address text box. You'll see some famous people you may be interested in following.

2. Click their thumbnail image to preview their Facebook page.

3. Click **Subscribe** to follow their posts. Their public posts will be posted in your News Feed.

4. To unsubscribe, go to their Facebook page and click **Subscribe | Unsubscribe**.

Subscribe to Others

Find someone's page you would like to follow, click **Subscribe**. You'll see their public posts in your News Feed. See Figure 4-8

for an example. If later you change your mind, find the page again and click **Subscribed | Unsubscribe**.

▷▷ Work with Networks

The early days of Facebook were primarily about networks, college networks to be specific. A network is another way of grouping people using common email addresses. For instance, a workplace, high school, or college might have a common email address provided for those who work there or attend it. In some way, networks seem to be a diminishing capability on Facebook. For instance, regional networks are no longer available. Facebook has removed them from the system. Also, at the time of this writing, there is no easy way to create a new network. Facebook does not openly provide a way to create new networks, and the links available that might work seem to be inconsistent.

In any case, to join existing networks, you must have a common email address provided by the organization. If you are an alumna of a college or high school, you may be able to join a network if the organization provides official email addresses for alumna. You'll have to get such an address for yourself before you can join. If your school or workplace does not have common email addresses, you will not be able to join or create such a network.

You can join up to five networks, and if you have more than one, you'll have to identify one as being your "primary" network. This is simply the network that is listed on your profile information.

Tip If you do have an official email address for your workplace or school and yet are not receiving a confirmation email to join a network, check your spam filters.

Figure 4-8: *Find someone you admire or are interested in following and click Subscribe.*

Find and Join a Network

1. On a Facebook page, click the down arrow to the right of Home, and then click **Account Settings | General**. General will be the default setting. You probably will not need to click it.

2. Click **Edit** to the right of Networks. The Networks edit box will open.

Networks	Your primary network will appear next to your name.
	Join a network
	Save Changes Cancel

3. Click **Join A Network** and the text box will open. Type the name of the organization or school for which you want to find a network. A list of possibilities will display as you type.

4. Scroll through the list, and click the name you want.

5. Type your network email address into the text box.

6. Click **Save Changes**.

You will see either a confirmation message or an error. If you receive a confirmation message, check your email and click the link to activate your membership in the network. If you receive an error message, double-check your email address and organization name and try again. There is not much you can do without a valid email address. Click **Cancel** to abort and try again another time.

| Network name: | Arizona | ✕ |
| Network email: | cbm@ua.edu | ✖ Email is not valid for this network. |

Leave a Network

1. Click the down arrow to the right of Home, and click **Account Settings | General** (you probably won't have to click General, as it is the default).

2. Click **Edit** to the right of Networks. Your network memberships are listed.

3. Click the **Leave Network** button associated with the network name.

> **Note** You may not be able to leave the first network you join. At the time of this writing, there seems to be a bug associated with leaving the first network assigned to your Facebook account.

⏵⏵ Add a Location

You can let people know when you're out and about by posting a location of where you are. I don't recommend this, but if you want to identify places you've been after the fact, that seems fine. Also, if you do enter a location at the time, don't enter the exact location—just enter a nearby city, for instance. This protects you against others who would take advantage of the fact that you are gone from your home and how far away you are.

To activate your location:

1. Click in the **What's On Your Mind** text box and click the location icon ▣. Then type the name of the place or the name of an event. As you type, you'll see a list of possibilities; click the one you want.

2. If you want to identify who you are with, click the person icon ▣ and type the name. As you type, a list of matching names will be displayed. Click the one you want.

3. Click the **Audience Selector** button, and click who you want to be able to see this post.

4. Type the post and click **Post**.

   On your Home page and Timeline, you'll see the post. You'll see the map location on the Timeline as well.

5. Click the map thumbnail and it will be enlarged to show all the pointers you have identified—a record of your journeys.

Map 3

Remove a Location

To remove a location before a post is shared, click the **X** on the location name to delete it. You can also retype the name, making it less personal.

Chapter 5

Communicating Using Email and a Mobile Device

I don't think we (humanity in general) understand the enormity of how cell phones are impacting our lives. I certainly don't. Mobile phones are very present in Facebook, and allow you to keep track of what is going on, regardless of whether your computer is handy. They enable you to alert your friends immediately about what you're doing and what you're seeing—all armed with your smart cell phone (smartphones) and the ability to text or connect using Facebook. As mentioned in Chapter 1, we have been able to learn and see through text messages and photos uploaded from cell phones to Facebook about revolution, earthquake, fires, flooding, and more. Electronic sources, including smartphones connected to Facebook, have changed the way we understand our world. It boggles the mind.

You can get connected, too, whether you have a regular cell phone or one connected to the Internet, or whether you're simply looking for free email. Facebook can widen your reach.

USE FACEBOOK FOR EMAIL

Facebook has an email feature that allows you to send and receive email messages using a Facebook email address. The email feature is free, and the email address assigned to you will not change as long as you have a Facebook account since it is derived from your username, which you normally set up at the time you register with Facebook.

When you adopt this new feature, Facebook emails are sent to your Messages page. You can see your messages and chats along with your Facebook email, all in one place.

> **Note** We use the term *smartphone* when describing mobile devices that function as telephones (for example, the iPhone and Motorola's Droid line), as well as those mobile devices that can use the Facebook app but lack a telephone component, such as the iPad, Samsung's Galaxy, and Motorola's Zoom. If your mobile device doesn't have a telephonic component, the features in the chapter that pertain to telephone and texting will not apply.

Set Your Username

When you sign up for a Facebook account, you are assigned a username—using your public name appearing on your Timeline—usually all names run together in lowercase with a unique number attached. Your username is used both for a Facebook URL to find your page **https://www.facebook.com/*username***, and as part of your email address, like this: ***username*@facebook.com**. You can change your default username to another.

Here are some guidelines around customizing your username:

- The username must be unique within the Facebook community. If someone else has the username you want, you'll have to find another.

- The username can contain letters and numbers or a period (which doesn't count in making the name unique; that is jane.smith and janesmith are the same).

- The username has to be close to your own name—it cannot be something unrelated.

- You must have a mobile phone registered to verify your username before you can change it. If you have already registered a phone, you might have already been verified. If not, first see "Verify Your Account" and then return here.

Username	Your account must be verified before you can set a username.
	If you have a mobile phone that can receive SMS messages, you can verify via mobile phone. If not, please try to register your username at a later time.

- You can only change your username once, so make sure it is what you want.

Here is how to do it:

1. On any Facebook page, click the down arrow to the right of Home, and then click **Account Settings**.

2. With the General link selected on the left, you'll see your assigned username. Click **Edit**.

Username	http://www.facebook.com/carole.matthews	Edit

3. In the Username text box, type the name you'd like to use for your Facebook username. As you type Facebook will verify whether the name is available. If not, type another until you find one that is available. You are reminded that you can only change the name one time, so you need to

find a name that reflects how you want to be seen in your email address.

http://www.facebook.com/ somename2012 ✓ **Username is available**

You can only change your username once.

[Save Changes] [Cancel]

4. Click **Save Changes**. Note that you may be told that you need to verify your account. If so, you'll have to click **Cancel** and refer to "Verify Your Account."

5. If you have previously registered a phone, you'll be asked to re-enter your password. Type it in and click **Save Changes**. You'll now see your username reflected in the Username option.

▷▷ Verify Your Account

If you are trying to create a Facebook email account and cannot do so because you need to verify your account, you'll have to enter a mobile phone number and receive a confirmation code by text message. Facebook is trying to verify that everyone on Facebook is a valid person. Although this is a bit of a hassle, it is worthwhile. Note that if you have not registered your mobile phone, you'll need to enter a valid phone number to verify your account. Upon verifying your phone, you'll very likely not have to register your phone in the "Register Your Mobile Phone" section.

1. Click the down arrow to the right of Home, and then click **Account Settings**.

2. On the left, click **Mobile**, and then click **Add A Phone**. After re-entering your password, and clicking **Submit**, the Activate Facebook Texts (Step 1 of 2) dialog box is displayed.

3. Beneath the text boxes will be the message "If you need to verify your account…." Click **Add Your Phone Number Here**. This will divert you to a quicker way to verify your account. A Confirm Your Number dialog box is displayed.

Activate Facebook Texts (Step 1 of 2)

Facebook Texts are supported in the following countries/regions. Please select your country/region and mobile service provider to receive activation instructions.

Country/Region: United States ▾

Mobile Carrier: Choose a carrier ▾

If you just need to verify your account or your operator isn't listed above, add your phone number here.

[Next] [Cancel]

4. Click the **Country/Region** down arrow and select your country name.

5. Click in the **Phone Number** text box and type your phone number.

6. The Confirm Number By Sending Me A Text default cannot be cleared. You'll have to receive a text message from the phone number you entered.

7. Click **Continue**. A message or call will be sent to your mobile phone.

8. When you've received the code on your mobile phone, type it into the Facebook dialog box, and click **Confirm**. You'll get a message saying that your code was correctly received. If not, click **Resend Code**.

Enter Your Confirmation Code

You should receive a text at +1 360-929-5170 with your confirmation code soon.

typecodehere|

Resend Code   Confirm   Cancel

9. Click **Turn On Text Notifications** to enable your phone to receive texts when you get certain notifications.

10. Click **Let My Friends See My Number** if you want to hide your phone number to your friends. It is set to reveal your number by default.

Tip You might want to disable the default to show your phone number to your friends until you have a better understanding of some privacy issues. You can elect to show it later.

11. Click **Save Settings**.

If you have been unsuccessful with creating a username because you needed to verify your account, you can now retry it again.

USE YOUR MOBILE PHONE WITH FACEBOOK

Your mobile phone provides an extension of Facebook so that you can be contacted about notifications and messages wherever you are within a cell phone coverage area. In addition, if you have a smartphone or tablet that uses the Facebook Mobile app, you can enjoy the most important aspects of your Facebook experience whenever you have an Internet connection.

QuickQuotes

John Digs His Mobile Phone

I resisted the move to a smartphone until my carrier, Verizon, came out with a single device that could act as a phone, camera, contact manager, browser, and substitute for a laptop on trips. Also, since I write books in the QuickSteps series, I felt it was time to get plugged into this new tidal wave of apps and mobile communication that was sweeping everyone off their feet. In December 2009 the Motorola Droid was introduced, and I took the bait; I haven't regretted it a single minute. To be able to pull up any information that is available on the Web; to communicate with people via phone, email, and applications such as Skype and Facebook; and all the other features and cool things you can do, all within a single device I can carry around in my pocket … priceless!

I've also resisted joining the Facebook party, but since having the Facebook Mobile app on my Droid, I've found it, like so many other features of the phone, so convenient and omnipresent that I'm becoming a fan. Just the other day I was lamenting not including a visit to Montevideo on a recent trip to Buenos Aires. Well, not to worry, a friend of mine posted 40 pictures of his trip there on Facebook—problem solved!

By John C., 57, Washington

Register Your Mobile Phone

To use your mobile phone, whether it is Internet connected or not, you must first sign it up with Facebook. This also verifies your account so you can create a username and get a Facebook email address. If you have already verified your account, you may not need to register it. Registering involves identifying your phone number, carrier, and optionally, setting a few options.

1. Click the down arrow to the right of Home on the menu bar, and select **Account Settings**.

2. On the left, click **Mobile**. (Note if you see your phone number here, you'll know that your phone is already registered.)

3. In the Mobile Settings panel, click **Add A Phone**. After you re-enter your password, a two-step Activate Facebook Texts dialog box will display.

Mobile Settings

Activating allows Facebook Mobile to send text messages to your phone. You can receive notifications for friend requests, messages, Wall posts, and status updates from your friends.

You can also update your status, search for phone numbers, or upload photos and videos from your phone.

+ Add a Phone

4. If the default United States is not your country, click the **Country** down arrow and select your country.

5. Click the **Mobile Carrier** down arrow and select your mobile phone carrier. Click **Next**. You'll see the second-step text box.

Activate Facebook Texts (Step 2 of 2)

1 Text the letter F to **32665 (FBOOK)**

2 When you receive a confirmation code, enter it here:

Facebook doesn't charge for this service. Standard messaging rates apply.

☑ Share my phone number with my friends
☑ Allow friends to text me from Facebook

Next **Cancel**

6. I suggest deselecting the **Share My Phone Number With My Friends** check box. This prevents your cell phone number from being revealed to your Facebook friends. If you keep **Allow Friends To Text Me** selected, you'll still be able to hear from your friends who already know your number.

7. Using the mobile phone you want to register, send as a text message the letter **F** and type in the number 32665. (This code is for the United States, and is FBOOK alphabetically. If you are from another country, your code will differ.) Press **Send**.

8. You'll immediately receive a confirmation code. Type it into the confirmation message text box and click **Next**. You'll receive a confirmation text message on your phone, and you'll see a page similar to that displayed in Figure 5-1 (it may not be exactly the same, but the features will be similar).

Set Options for Text Messaging Notifications

You can get text messages about the status of your Facebook account and send messages to friends, whether you have an

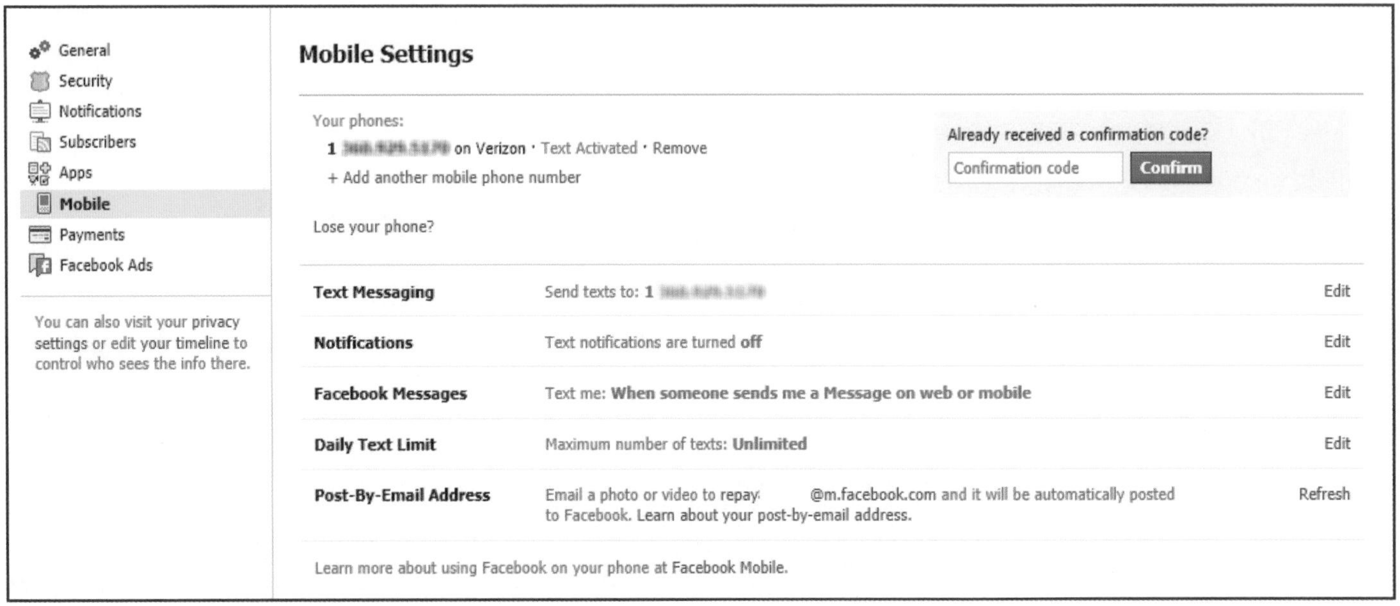

Mobile Settings

Your phones:

1 ▓▓▓ ▓▓▓ ▓▓▓ on Verizon · Text Activated · Remove

+ Add another mobile phone number

Lose your phone?

Already received a confirmation code?

[Confirmation code] **Confirm**

General		
Security		
Notifications		
Subscribers		
Apps		
Mobile		
Payments		
Facebook Ads		

You can also visit your privacy settings or edit your timeline to control who sees the info there.

Text Messaging	Send texts to: 1 ▓▓▓ ▓▓▓ ▓▓▓	Edit
Notifications	Text notifications are turned **off**	Edit
Facebook Messages	Text me: **When someone sends me a Message on web or mobile**	Edit
Daily Text Limit	Maximum number of texts: **Unlimited**	Edit
Post-By-Email Address	Email a photo or video to repay ▓▓▓ @m.facebook.com and it will be automatically posted to Facebook. Learn about your post-by-email address.	Refresh

Learn more about using Facebook on your phone at Facebook Mobile.

Figure 5-1: You can set notification and texting options after your phone is registered in Facebook.

Internet-activated cell phone or not. All you need is a registered regular cell phone with text messaging. After you have set up your mobile phone for text messaging, you may want to be notified about your Facebook activities via text messaging. You'll need to establish some Notification settings.

1. Click the down arrow to the right of Home, and click **Account Settings**.

2. On the left, click **Mobile**. The panel shown earlier in Figure 5-1 is displayed. (If your mobile phone is not set up for text messaging, you will not see this exact panel.)

3. Click **Edit** to the right of Notifications to change several ways you can restrict text notifications. The panel shown in Figure 5-2 is displayed.

- Click **On** or **Off** to enable or disable your phone to send and receive text messages for Facebook notifications.

- Under Send A Text Message When Someone, click the check boxes that apply: when you receive a comment on your Wall, when you are added or confirmed as a friend, or for all other notifications.

- To restrict those from whom you are notified about activities on Facebook, click the **Receive Text Notifications From Friends Only** text box.

- To define the times of day when you want to receive notifications, click **Only From**, click the down arrows next to the times, and select the to and from hours you wish to receive text notifications.

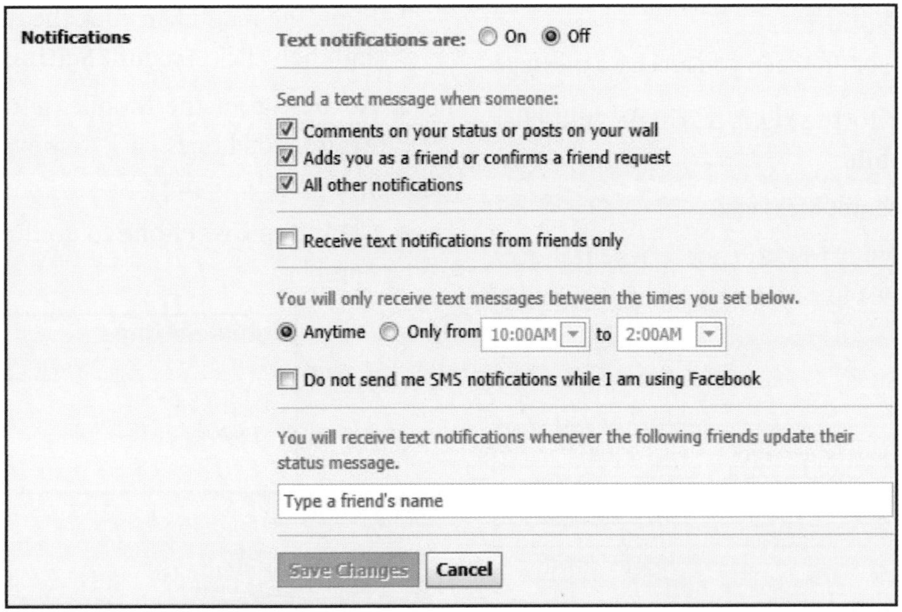

Notifications

Text notifications are: ◯ On ◉ Off

Send a text message when someone:
- ☑ Comments on your status or posts on your wall
- ☑ Adds you as a friend or confirms a friend request
- ☑ All other notifications

☐ Receive text notifications from friends only

You will only receive text messages between the times you set below.

◉ Anytime   ◯ Only from 10:00AM ▼ to 2:00AM ▼

☐ Do not send me SMS notifications while I am using Facebook

You will receive text notifications whenever the following friends update their status message.

Type a friend's name

[Save Changes] [Cancel]

*Figure 5-2: **Notification Settings allows you to control your text messaging transactions.***

- To avoid getting duplicate notifications while on Facebook, click **Do Not Send Me SMS Notifications While I Am Using Facebook**.
- To ensure that you are notified when specific friends update their statuses, click in the **Enter Name** text box and begin to type the friend's name. As you type, a selection will be displayed. Click the friend you want, and repeat as needed.

4. Click **Save Changes** or click **Cancel**.

Limit Text Volume

To make sure your phone is not inundated with tons of text messages, you can set a limit.

1. Click the down arrow to the right of Home, and click **Account Settings | Mobile**.

2. Click **Edit** next to Daily Text Limit.

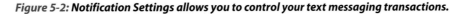

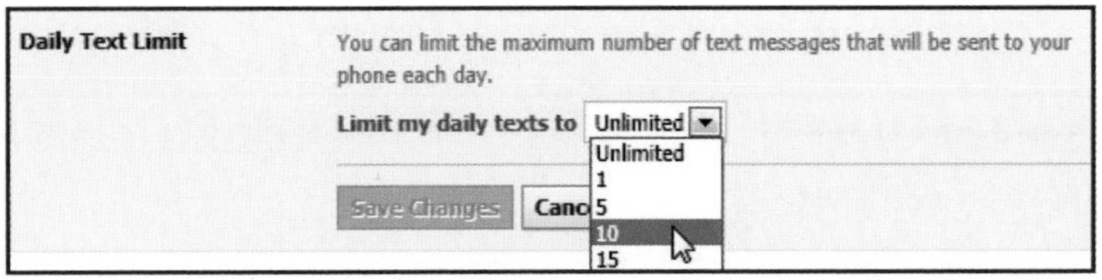

Daily Text Limit   You can limit the maximum number of text messages that will be sent to your phone each day.

Limit my daily texts to Unlimited ▼
- Unlimited
- 1
[Save Changes] [Canc 5]
- 10
- 15

3. Click the **Limit My Daily Text To** down arrow, and click the number you want.

4. Click **Save Changes**.

Turn Text Notifications On or Off

To turn text notifications on or off when you receive a message:

1. Click the down arrow to the right of Home, and click **Account Settings | Mobile**.

2. Click **Edit** next to Facebook Messages.

3. Click the **Text Me** down arrow to choose when, if ever, you should be notified via text messages when you should receive a message.

4. Click **Close**.

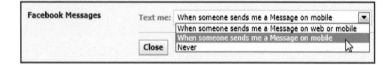

Find Your Post-By-Email Address

You can email photos or videos from your mobile device to your Facebook account by sending them to a unique post-by-email address.

1. Click the down arrow to the right of Home, and click **Account Settings | Mobile**.

2. To the right of Post-By-Email Address, click **Refresh**. Your current post-by-email address is shown.

Post-By-Email Address	Your new post-by-email address is apollc@m.facebook.com
	Close

3. Click **Close**.

⏩ Remove a Phone from Facebook

Once you have registered a phone number, you can easily remove it.

1. From the menu bar, click the down arrow next to Home, and then click **Account Settings | Mobile**.

2. At the top of the Mobile Settings panel, beneath Your Registered Phones, click **Remove** next to the phone number you want to remove.

3. Click **Remove Phone** to confirm you want to delete the number.

Mobile Settings

Your phones:

1 ▓▓▓▓▓▓▓▓ on Verizon · Text Activated · Remove

+ Add another mobile phone number

🗨 QuickQuotes

Daniel Prefers Computer to iPhone

A Facebook user for four years, I appreciate the real-time connection to friends, the amazing window into what is happening in their lives. Being pervasive, it's also a way to locate lost friends.

I enjoy the News Feed, but some postings can be a bit boring with "too much information." Fortunately, Facebook allows limits on those who tend to be glib.

I had lost contact with old friends, international and domestic—we didn't write or they may have moved and didn't update me. Using Facebook, I was able to locate them and reconnect. Without Facebook, they would have been lost forever.

(continued)

When I first got my iPhone, Facebook was one of my first apps. My use has been infrequent, however, due to the small screen. When notified by iPhone email of a friend contact, I will bring up the app, read the message, and respond. Occasionally I will upload iPhone photos. I've found browsing mobile Facebook to be much less satisfying than on the computer with its larger screen.

My caution about Facebook: it can be seductive and will absorb your time. Witness those who feel compelled to be "on the scene" reporters of their lives, relating every event, no matter how trivial.

Daniel M., "a senior," Washington

Send Text Messages from Facebook

You can send a text message in the same way you send an ordinary message, with one small change.

1. Click **Messages | Send A New Message** on the menu bar. The New Message dialog box is displayed.

2. Begin typing the name of your friend in the **To** text box. Select the correct name from the displayed list.

3. Click in the **Message** text box, and type your message.

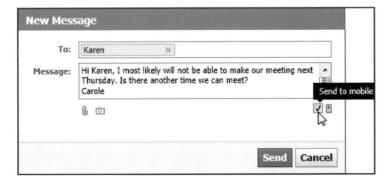

4. Click the **Send To Mobile** icon on the right.

5. Click **Send**.

Note The illustrations, figures, and steps in the next several sections were taken using an Android smartphone (Motorola Droid Bionic). The Facebook app on your mobile device may not appear or function exactly the same, but it should offer similar options.

Use the Facebook Mobile App

The Facebook app available on mobile devices provides a great way to stay in contact with your Facebook life. The features and options that are offered rival those you can use in a browser, and are available from the app's toolbars and your Home page's left column. After logging in, the Facebook app opens, ready to view your recent posts and share new ones, as shown in Figure 5-3.

Find Facebook Pages

When you log in to Facebook, you are in Facebook land! You have access to your Facebook Home, profile, Find Friends, Messages, Notifications, Accounts, and other pages, including your friends' profiles. Your Facebook email address is already in your phone, as are those of your friends. You'll recognize these common icons that help you navigate the Facebook app:

- **Friend Requests** Shows Friend Requests and a list of People You May Know.
- **Messages** Displays your outstanding messages.
- **Notifications** Displays your outstanding notifications.
- **Home Menu** Displays your Home page, left column.

- **Status** ⊟ Status Displays the Update Status screen where you can post an update.
- **Photo** ⎙ Photo Allows you to shoot a photo or video and attach it to a post.
- **Check In** ⎙ Check In Displays a list of nearby places that you can choose to post to your location.
- **Events** ⎙ Displays upcoming events on your Facebook page.
- **Location** ⎙ Lets you select your location.
- **Photos/Videos** ⎙ Lets you replace the photo/video in your post.
- **Audience Selector** ⎙ Presents options for who you want to see this post. (The icon can change depending on who you choose; for instance, the world icon is a Public audience; two people, Friends only.)

Change Notifications

You can determine which notifications you receive, as well as how you are notified.

1. With the Facebook app open (log in using your Facebook email and password), tap your device's **Home Menu** icon ⎙, and tap **Settings** (or **Account Settings**).
2. Under Notifications Settings, choose which of the several features you want. Features include ways to be notified, such as vibrating the device and setting a ringtone, as well as selecting which notifications you want to be alerted to, such as Wall posts and friend requests.

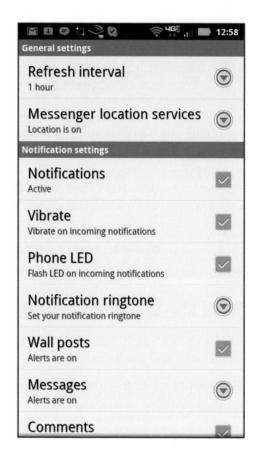

Save Bytes and Battery Life

You can change the interval at which your device requests updates from Facebook in order to conserve consumables, such as the amount of data you use (bytes used equals money paid to data providers) and the drain on your battery.

1. With the Facebook app open, tap your device's **Home Menu** icon, and tap **Settings** on the pop-up menu.

2. Under General Settings, tap **Refresh Interval** and select a longer internal than the default interval, or select **Never**. You can always perform a manual refresh to update notifications when you want them by tapping your device's **Home Menu** icon and tapping **Refresh**.

Change Account Settings

You can easily view and change how you interact with Facebook.

1. From the Facebook toolbar, tap the **Home Menu** icon [≡] .
2. Swipe to the bottom of the three-lines, and tap **Account | Account Settings**.
3. Tap the category whose settings you want to view or change.

▷▷ Send Photos and Videos from Your Mobile Device to Facebook

From the mobile Facebook app on your device, you can send the photo or video you're currently shooting and attach it to a post, or you can send one from your phone's photo gallery.

Send from the Facebook App

You don't have to leave your Facebook app to snap and send a photo or record a video.

1. From your Facebook app, tap **Photo**. Your device's camera app will open. Choose between shooting photos or video [📷] (if shooting photos, whether you want to use the front or rear camera [↻]), make any settings adjustments, and then take your photo or record your video.
2. Tap your completed photo or video in order to tag friends. Tap **Done** when finished, and then tap to cancel or accept the photo or video.

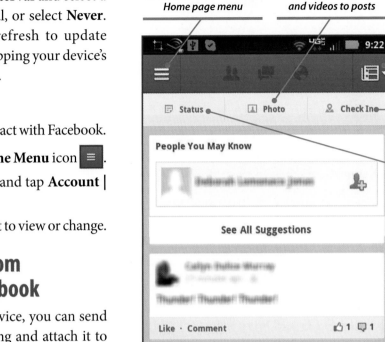

Open/close the Facebook's Home page menu

Take and attach photos and videos to posts

View recent and popular stories

View and post your location to close-by locales

Send posts and update your status

Figure 5-3: The Facebook app looks and behaves very much like the Facebook browser version.

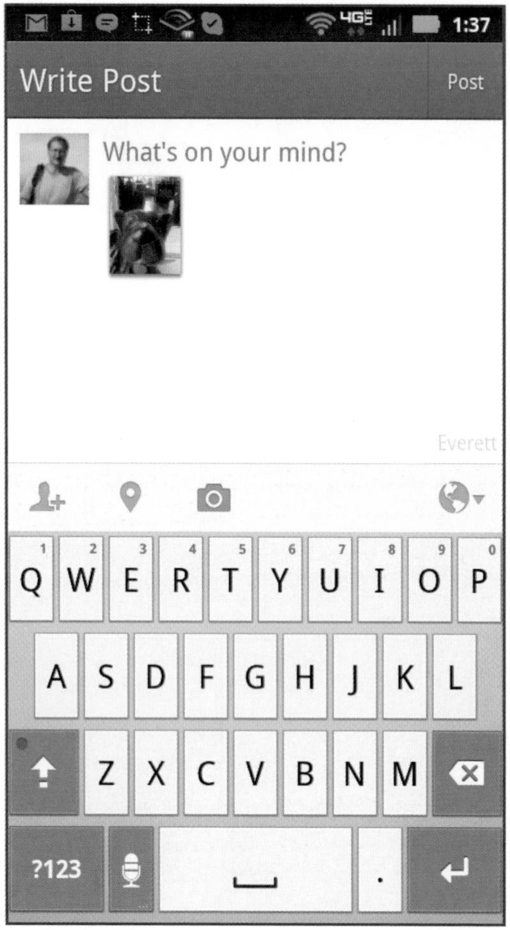

Figure 5-4: *Attaching photos and videos to a post from the Facebook app is as easy as tapping a few buttons to tag friends and typing a post.*

3. For accepted photos/videos, on the Write Post screen shown in Figure 5-4, you'll see a thumbnail of your photo/video. Click the **What's On Your Mind** text box, type your post, and select common features such as choosing an audience setting to selecting friends and the audience you want view the post. Tap the **Camera** icon if you decide to reshoot your video or photo.

4. Tap **Post** to send it to your Facebook page.

Send from Your Gallery

Photos and video you have taken and stored on your mobile device can be uploaded to your Facebook page from your gallery.

1. From the Facebook app, tap **Photo**. On your camera screen, tap the **Gallery** icon ▦ to open it.

   –Or–

   Open your device's Gallery app directly from a shortcut on your device.

2. Navigate through your gallery until you find the photo or video you want to attach to your Facebook page.

3. Tap the photo/video to open its context menu, tap **Share**, and then tap **Facebook** from the list of possible places you can share with.

4. On the Write Post screen (see Figure 5-4), write a comment, and tap **Post**.

Chapter 6

Adding Photos and Videos

Photos and videos lend a personal touch to your Facebook pages. They give you a way to visually add beauty, humor, and impact. Often you can say so much more with a carefully chosen photo or video than you can in words. This chapter explains how to view, upload, edit, and tag photos and videos.

UPLOAD AND USE PHOTOS

Adding photos is a way to share experiences—a vacation, wedding, birth of a grandchild, or a severe winter storm. You can download images from a digital camera onto your computer and then upload them onto Facebook. You can share images from friends' pages and place them on your own Timeline. You can upload photos from a mobile phone directly into Facebook. You can upload photos one at a time or arrange them in albums so that people can view them together.

1 2 3 4 5 6 7 8 9 10

Understanding the Photo Arena

You can view photos from your primary Facebook pages. Your Home and Timeline pages are the best places to upload photos:

- On your Home page, click **Add Photo/Video** in the top middle column (this is how we recommend you upload photos in this chapter) or, on the left column, click **Apps | Photos | Upload Photos** (you may have to click **More** under Apps to see Photos).

- On your Timeline, click **Photo** beneath your photo, or beneath your name click **Photos | Add Photos**.

- If you have not installed Timeline yet, you can get to the upload command from your Profile page. Click **Photos** on the left column and then click **Upload Photos**.

Photos are organized into albums. Even when you upload a single photo, such as your profile picture, it is inserted into a default photo album. However, you can create an album and place your photos into it according to the criteria you select—your last vacation, grandchildren, birthday parties, and so on.

You upload your photos and determine at that time whether to share them or not. If you do not share them, that is, you indicate the audience is only you, they remain available to be edited, deleted, added to, or rearranged until you are ready to put them out to the world.

▷▷ Scan Your News Feed Photos

You can filter your News Feed so that you only see postings with photos. You might remember a photo, but not exactly when you saw it or who posted it. This is a good way to find it.

On your Home page, click **Photos** (under Apps) in the left column. The center column will be populated with postings only containing photos.

When you click a photo, album, or video, you display the Photo Viewer view with options for working with the photo. See "Edit Using the Photo Viewer" later in the chapter.

▷▷ Upload a Photo from Your Computer

An album is automatically created for you when you upload single photos. Your photos must be at least 180 pixels large in order to be uploaded; you will receive a warning message if your photo is too small. To upload a photo from your computer to add to your Timeline or News Feed:

1. On your Home page, click **Add Photo/Video**. On the Timeline, click **Photo** (beneath your profile picture, not beneath your name).

📝 Update Status	📷 Add Photo / Video	❓ Ask Question
Upload Photo / Video	Use Webcam	Create Photo Album

2. Click **Upload Photo/Video**.

3. Click **Browse**. When Windows Explorer opens, find your photo file, click it to select it, and click **Open**. This will place the photo location in your dialog box.

4. You have these options:

   - To add a caption for the photo, click in the text box and type your comment.

   - To select your audience for the photo, click the **Audience Selector** 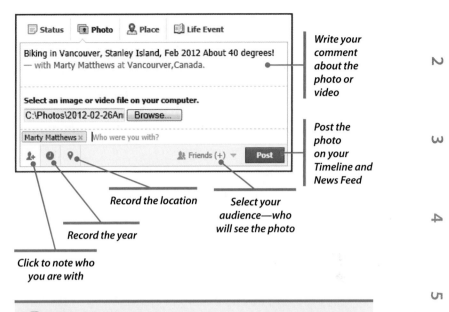 (yours may be different depending on your default) and select your setting.

   - To record who you are with in the photo or video, click the **Who Were You With "Tag"** icon and type a name starting with "@," such as @Marty. A list of matching friends will be displayed from which you can select the correct one.

   - To record the year for your Timeline, click the **clock** icon and choose a year. This is a way you can place photos in previous years for your Timeline.

   - To record the location where the photo was taken, click the **pin** icon and type the location.

5. Click **Post** to upload the photo to your News Feed stream and Timeline, or to a friend's Timeline.

Write your comment about the photo or video

Post the photo on your Timeline and News Feed

Record the location

Select your audience—who will see the photo

Record the year

Click to note who you are with

Tip You can upload a photo to a friend's Wall/Timeline as well as to your own. Display your friend's Timeline, and click **Add Photos/Videos** beneath their name. Note that if you post a photo to a friend's page, it will not appear in the photos on your own Timeline. Also, it will be visible to all viewing your friend's Wall/Timeline.

Upload a Photo Using Email

Facebook enables you to use a unique email, assigned just to you, to send photos or videos to your page. You need to protect it so that others do not send information to your page as if they were you.

Find Your Post-by-Email Address

You can email photos or videos from your mobile device to your Facebook account by sending them to a unique post-by-email address.

1. Click the down arrow to the right of Home, and click **Account Settings | Mobile**.

2. To the right of Post-By-Email Address, click **Refresh**. Your current post-by-email address is shown. It will be a name followed by "@m.facebook.com." If you don't have a post-by-email address, you most likely do not have an active mobile device registered.

Post-By-Email Address   Email a photo or video to   tablet@m.facebook.com and it will be automatically   Refresh
                          posted to Facebook. Learn about your post-by-email address.

3. Click the unique email address ending in "@m.facebook .com" to create an email that will be sent directly from your computer to your page. When you click this, an empty email message will appear, an example of which is shown in Figure 6-1.

4. Insert your photo or video file into the email. Type the caption into the Subject text box.

5. Click **Send**. After a bit, the photo will appear on both your Timeline and News Feed.

Note When sending a photo to your Facebook page using the unique Facebook address, use the Subject line as the caption. If you don't attach a photo, the Subject line will be used to update your status on your Wall.

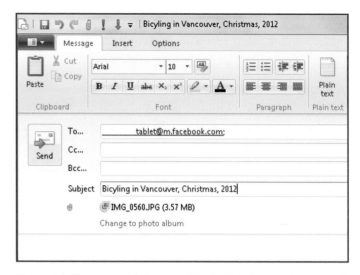

Figure 6-1: *You can send photos to Facebook using a unique email address that is just for your Facebook page.*

Note It's a bit rude to attach large photo and video files to emails sent to friends and family. It slows down the recipient's response time, and is annoying. When sharing graphics and videos, you should consider using links and file formats that don't create an unnecessary burden on the Internet. Still photos and other images look great if you use the JPEG file format, which can compress an original image to easily one-tenth its size while maintaining fidelity and clarity. For videos, the MPEG 4 file format is popular because the file size is small, but fidelity is good and can be read by Windows, Mac, and Linux users.

Upload Photos into a New Album

You can upload at least 1,000 pictures into an album, and there are no limits to the number of albums you may have. To create an album of photos grouped together by event, relationship, time, or other organizational approach, you simply name the album and select the photos you want included.

1. Click **Add Photo/Video** at the top of the Home page or click **Photo** beneath your profile picture (not beneath your name) on the Timeline. Click **Create Photo Album**. You'll see a Windows Explorer or other dialog box. (If you have not installed Timeline yet, on your Profile page, click **Photos** on the left column and then click **Upload Photos**.)

2. Find the photos you want in your album. Hold down CTRL while you click each photo that you want in the album. When you're finished, click **Open**. It will take a moment, but the Untitled Album dialog box will open. You will be asked for certain identifying information, which is visible to friends with permission to see these photos.

3. The dialog box displays these options, as shown in Figure 6-2:

   - **Name Your Album** Click in the **Untitled Album** text box, and type the name of the album itself.
   - **Identifying Info** Click in the **Say Something** text box beneath the title to add a description of the album.
   - **Location** Click in the **Where Were These Taken** text box, and type the location or other identifying information for the album. The album may be about an overall location, with individual locations for some of the photos.

- **Date** Click **Add Date** and set the month, year, and day, if you want.
- **Photo ID** Click the **Say Something About This Photo** link beneath the photo and type a description about the individual photo itself.
- **Set Privacy** Click the **audience selector** icon beneath each photo and click who you want to see it—essentially the level of privacy you want.
- **Tag People** Click the **tag** icon, click the spot in the image, and type the name of the person or other identifying info in the text box.
- **Photo Date** If your photos have different dates, click the clock icon and select the month, day, and year when the photo was taken.
- **Photo Location** If your photos have different locations, click the **location** icon and type the location. You may need to delete the current location before you can enter a new one.
- **Audience Selector** To set your privacy, click the **Audience Selector** and select the audience you want for the album. This can be changed later if you want.
- **High Quality** Click the **High Quality** check box to make the photos high resolution. Unless there is some reason for high resolution, keep the default setting, which is no check mark. High-resolution photos take much longer to load.
- **Add More Photos** You may want to add more photos at this point, but you can also do it later.

Figure 6-2: *Uploading photos is easily done, along with entering identifying information.*

4. Click **Post Album**. The photos are uploaded to your Facebook site. You can either change or edit the photos. See "Edit Your Photo Albums" for more information.

Tip You may also see a dialog box, shown in Figure 6-3, titled "Who's In These Photos?" You can either type a name in the text box beneath each image and click **Save Tags**, or click **Skip Tagging Friends**.

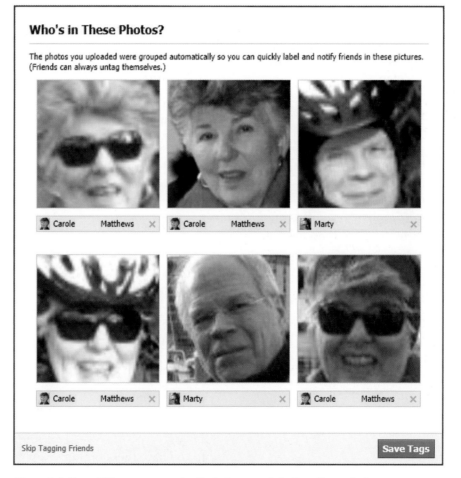

Figure 6-3: **You will have an opportunity to tag people in the album photos.**

Download a Photo on Your Wall

If you see a photo on someone else's posting that you would like to download onto your own computer, you can do it this way:

1. Click the photo to enlarge it.
2. Beneath the photo click **Options | Download**.

3. You may be asked if you want to open or save the image. Click **Save | Save As**. The Save As dialog will appear.
4. Type a name you prefer for the photo if you don't like the original, and then select the image type. You will probably want to retain the .jpg file type.
5. Click **Save**.

Find Your Albums

You may find that you want to return to your album to edit at a later date. First, you need to find it.

1. Click your name on the menu bar for your Timeline.
2. Click **Photos** beneath your name. You'll see a list of albums. You may have to click **See More** beneath the thumbnails of the Your Albums rows.
3. Click the album you want to work with.
4. To edit the photos in the album, click **Edit Album**.

Edit Your Photo Albums

Once you have uploaded photos, you can reorganize them; delete them; change or add captions, dates, or locations; change your audience; and so on.

1. Click **Home | Photos** (in the left column under Apps) | **My Albums**.
2. Find the photo album you want to edit and click it.
3. Click **Edit Album** beneath the album title.

4. You have these options, as seen in Figure 6-4:
   - Click the title to open the text box and type a new name.

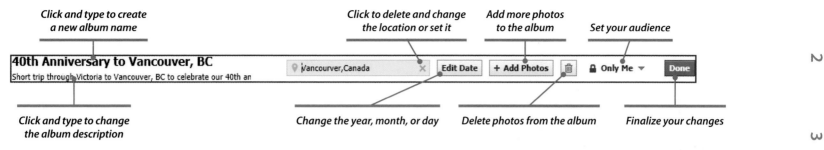

Click and type to create a new album name

Click to delete and change the location or set it

Add more photos to the album

Set your audience

40th Anniversary to Vancouver, BC
Short trip through Victoria to Vancouver, BC to celebrate our 40th an

📍 Vancouver, Canada ✕ | **Edit Date** | **+ Add Photos** | 🗑 | 🔒 **Only Me** ▾ | **Done**

Click and type to change the album description

Change the year, month, or day

Delete photos from the album

Finalize your changes

Figure 6-4: **You can edit the overall specifications of the photo album.**

- Click in the **Description** text box to enter a new description for the album itself.

- If you already have a description, delete it and begin typing a new one. If you don't have one, click the **location** icon and begin typing. As you type, a list of locations will display. Click the one that matches.

- Click **Edit Date** to change the year, month, and day.

- Click **Add Photos** to add new photos to the album.

- Click **Delete Album** (the trashcan icon) to delete a photo from the album.

- Click the **Audience Selector** to set who may see your photos.

5. Click **Done** to finish.

Change the Order of Photos in an Album

To move photos in an album or re-sort the order:

1. On your Home page, click **Photos** on the leftmost column under Apps.

2. Click **My Albums** at the top of the page.

3. Click the album you want. The photos in the album will be displayed.

4. Click and drag the photo to the location you want it.

Edit Individual Photos

There are at least two ways to edit your photos. In one case you edit photos within albums, and in the other, you edit photos with the Photo Viewer, the enlarged image that appears when you click a photo.

Edit Album Photos

1. Click **Home | Photos** (in the left column under Apps) | **My Albums**.

2. Find the photo album you want to edit and click it.

3. Click **Edit Album** beneath the album title. You see the rows of photos in the selected album.

4. At the bottom of each photo, you'll find a way to edit the photo's data:

- To change or add a description, click in the text box beneath the photo and type.

- To tag someone, click the **tag** icon, click in the photo to place the tag, and type the name you want in the photo.

- To record the year, month, or day, click the **clock** icon and choose what you want.

- To record or change the location, click the **pin** icon and type the name, choosing the match when it appears.

5. When you are finished with each photo, click **Done** at the top.

⏩ Edit Using the Photo Viewer

This technique is easy and accessible. It uses the Photo Viewer feature in Facebook, which enlarges photos on a black background. If it is a photo you have posted rather than a friend's photo, you'll find additional commands available (you can't edit a friend's photo other than to share or download it). Although you might want to search for a photo in the My Albums section of your photos (because sometimes we forget where a photo is), you can also just click a photo of your own on your Timeline or Home page.

1. On your Timeline or News Feed, click your picture you want to edit. Or, click **Home | Photos | My Albums**.

2. Find the photo album you want to edit and click it. (Do not click Edit Album.) The contents of the album will be displayed.

3. Simply click the photo—it will be enlarged. Click **Edit** in the right sidebar. The sidebar will open with the data you can change, as seen in Figure 6-5.

- Click in the **Description**, **Who Were You With**, or **Where Was This Photo Taken** text box and type what you want.

- Click the down arrows to set the year, month, and day.

- Click the **Audience Selector**, and an Edit Album Privacy option is displayed. Click it and set your privacy. When you change the privacy here, it is for the whole album.

- Add a comment if you like, or share or like the photo.

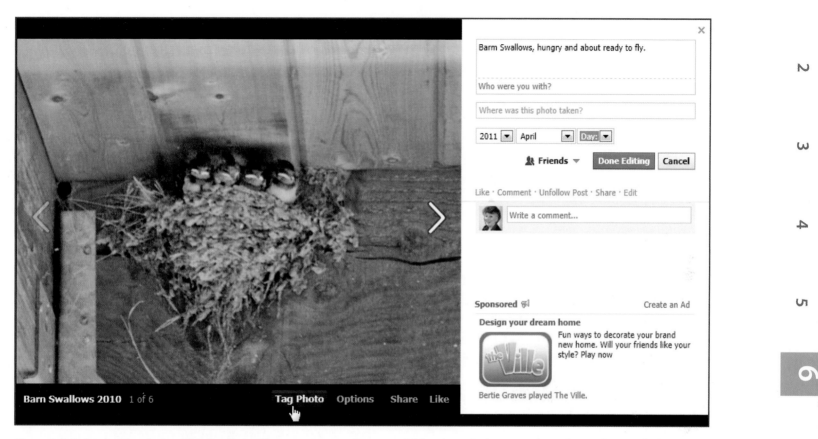

*Figure 6-5: **Enlarging the photo within its album allows you to record many variables about the image—what, where, when, and who are just starters.***

- Beneath the photo, you can tag a photo or find another way to like or share the photo. (See "Tag a Photo" for details.)

- Click **Options** for a menu of more options: you can again add or change a location or date, rotate the photo right or left, download the

♦ Add Location
⊘ Change Date

Rotate Left
Rotate Right

Download
Make Profile Picture
Make Cover
Delete This Photo

photo, make this photo your profile or Timeline cover, or delete it.

- Click the left and right arrows to scroll to the previous and next photos, respectively.

4. Click **Done Editing** to finalize your changes.

5. Click **X** to close the photo and return to the previous page.

Tag a Photo

Tagging allows you to identify someone in a photo of yours and notify them that they are tagged in a photo. To bring up the Photo Viewer so you can work with a photo, follow the steps in "Edit Using the Photo Viewer." With the photo open in the Photo Viewer:

1. Click **Tag Photo**. Your cursor will turn into a crosshair.

2. Click the spot on the photo where you want the tag. A text box will open.

3. Type your tag. A list of your friends will appear. You can select a name or type another. If you find a name on the list is similar to the one you typed, but not identical or not the one you want, unselect the name by mousing over the list so that the selection goes away before you press ENTER to finalize the typed name. In this way you can add a name that is not a friend, not in your list names, and will not be assigned erroneously to be the tagged name.

4. When you're done, click **Done Tagging**.

Delete a Tag

To get rid of a tag, you must first delete it and then retype a new tag.

1. In the Photo Viewer, find the tagged name on the right, and mouse over it (it will follow the word "with.") When you have several tags, you'll see the box surrounding the point on the photo that contains the selected tag.

2. When you have the pointer over the correct tag, click **Remove Tag**.

Rotate a Photo

Sometimes a photo is sideways and you want to straighten it. From the Photo Viewer, click **Options** beneath the photo. A list of options is displayed:

- Click **Rotate Left** to rotate your photo 90 degrees counterclockwise.

- Click **Rotate Right** to rotate your photo 90 degrees clockwise.

Delete a Photo

Perhaps you want to get rid of a photo.

1. From the Photo Viewer, click **Options** beneath the photo.
2. Click **Delete This Photo**. A Delete Photo dialog box will appear.
3. Click **Confirm** to verify that this is what you want.

Make a Photo Your Profile Picture

Depending on whether you want to upload or take a new photo, or whether you want to make an existing uploaded photo into your profile picture, you have a couple of ways to create your profile photo.

1. On your Timeline, mouse over your current Timeline profile picture, and click **Edit Profile Picture**. (Yours could also say Edit Picture.) A menu is displayed:

- To upload a new photo from your computer, click **Upload Photo** and follow the steps.
- To take a photo of yourself using a webcam, assuming you have a webcam on or in your computer, click **Take Photo**. The Take A Profile Photo window will open and display the Adobe Flash Player Settings dialog box.

Click **Allow**, click **Close** to remove the Flash Player, and click the **camera** icon to take the picture. If you don't like the picture, delete it and click the camera icon again (remember to look at the camera, not the screen, and that there is a 3-2-1 countdown). If you like the picture, click the **padlock** icon to set the privacy, and then click **Save Picture** to save the photo. (Refer to Chapter 2 for the details of this approach.)

–Or–

1. To use a photo for your profile picture that is already uploaded onto Facebook, click **Choose From Photos**. The dialog box will be displayed showing all the photos of you.
2. If you want one that is displayed, click it. If not, click **View Albums** to see a display of all your photos. Click through the albums until you find the one you want. Click **Make Profile Picture**. A page will be displayed allowing you to crop the photo.

3. Click in the center of the highlight box, and drag the box so the object you want to use for your profile photo is centered in the box the way you want it.

4. Click one of the four corners to enlarge or reduce the size of the box as you wish. Your photo will be cropped so that only the area within the box will left and used for your profile picture.

5. When you are ready, click **Done Cropping** to finalize the profile picture replacement. Click **Cancel** to stop the process.

Save a Photo to Disk

You may want to save your changed photo or another one to your computer disk.

1. To save a photo, first follow the steps in "Edit Using the Photo Viewer" to find and display the photo. Essentially, find it and click it.

2. Mouse over the bottom of the enlarged image for the menu bar.

3. Below the image, click **Options | Download**. At the bottom of the page a dialog box will open.

> Rotate Left
> Rotate Right
>
> Download
> Make Profile Picture
> Delete This Photo
>
> **Options**   Share

4. Click the **Save** down arrow, and click **Save As**.

5. Find the folder where you want to save the file, change the name to something you'll recognize, and click **Save**.

Share Your Photos

You may find that you want to share your photos with others. You may be looking at a photo on your News Feed or Timeline, or you may have just finished editing it in the Photo Viewer.

- To share a photo on your News Feed or Timeline, click **Share** beneath the photo.

- To share an edited photo displayed in Photo Viewer, mouse over the bottom of the enlarged image for the menu bar, and then click **Share**.

> **Tip** The pencil icon ⟨✎⟩ indicates that something can be edited. Click the icon, and a text box or other format will be presented that enables you to edit or change the information.

⟩⟩ Share Photos or Albums with Non-Facebook Friends

To share your photos or albums with people who are not on Facebook:

1. On the Timeline, click **Photos** beneath your name.

2. Click the album you want to share.

3. On the bottom of the page, as seen in Figure 6-6, click **Want To Share Your Album? You Can Give Friends Or Relatives This Link**. A blank email with the link will be displayed.

4. Type the email address, change the subject line if you don't like the default listed, add anything you want in the body of the message, and click **Send**.

Photos
By Carole Boggs Matthews (Albums) · Updated on Friday · ✎ Edit Album

These photos as taken in   NM   ✎
Like · Share

[Write a comment...]

Want to share your album? You can give friends or relatives this link:
https://www.facebook.com/media/set/?set=a⌐⁰28405644388.

Figure 6-6: *You can send photos or albums to people not on Facebook or to people who are not your Facebook friends.*

▷▷ Make Your Facebook App Photos Private

For the most part, you set your privacy, your audience, at the time a photo is posted. It will have the same audience as the post. However, some Facebook Apps do not have audience selectors to use when uploading photos from your cell, for instance. You can set an overall default for these types of photos and status updates sent from your mobile phone or other Facebook app. To set your default security for these posts:

1. Click the right arrow to the right of Home, and click **Privacy Settings**.

2. Under For Mobile Apps Without The Inline Audience Selector, you have these options:

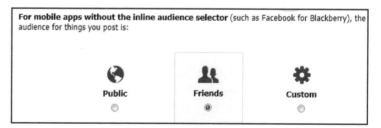

- **Public**   Allows anyone to see this photo or album.
- **Friends**   Allows your friends to view the photo or album.
- **Custom**   Allows you to select specific people, lists, or groups to see or not see a post.

3. When you have selected the audience you want, click **Home** or **<*your name*>** on the menu bar to leave the Privacy Settings page.

USE VIDEOS

Using videos is a delight—especially when you don't have to watch a lead-in advertisement first! You can share your own family videos or links to those on YouTube or other visual networking sites. You can set your audience intentions for each video as well, making them available for both group and individual viewing.

Upload a Video

You can upload videos from your own computer, from another website (such as YouTube), or from your mobile phone (see Chapter 5 for how to work with your mobile phone).

> **CAUTION!** The video must have been created by you or your friends—that is, you have the right to upload it. In addition, because of storage requirements, you are asked to restrict your videos to those that are under 1MB in size and run under 20 minutes in length.

Upload a Video from Your Computer

1. On your Home page in the top-center column, click **Add Photo/Video | Upload Photo/Video**, or on your Timeline beneath your photo, click **Photo | Upload Photo/Video**.

> **Tip** To find your videos if you don't have Timeline, click your name on the menu bar for your Profile page. Then click **Photos** on the left column, and then click **Videos** to the right of the Your Photos title.

2. Click **Browse**. When Windows Explorer comes up, find your video file, click it to select it, and click **Open**. This will place the file location in your dialog box.

3. To comment on the video, click in the text box and type your comment.

4. To set your privacy settings for the video, click the **Audience Selector** icon, as shown in Figure 6-7, and select your setting.

5. Click **Post** to upload the video to your News Feed stream and Wall:

   - The first time you upload a video, you may see a message about allowing a pop-up blocker on your computer to permit this upload; if so, click **Okay** and then **Allow Once**.

Figure 6-7: **When uploading your video, add a comment explaining what it is and select your privacy intentions before clicking Post.**

- Also, you may have to click **Agree To The Terms Of Service** before you can proceed. This is a legally binding agreement verifying that you know the creator of the video, that it is an original work, and that you have the right to share it with others—that there is no copyright violation.

- You'll have to wait for a few minutes while the video is uploaded.

6. When you see the Upload Complete message (you may also get an email), click **Close And Edit Video**. See the following "Edit the Video Title" section.

Edit the Video Title

If you select to edit the video immediately upon uploading it, you'll see the screen shown in Figure 6-8. This allows you to tag people, add comments, a title, the when and where of the video, a description, and set your privacy, if you have not already done so.

1. Click **In This Video** to tag any friends who appear in this video.

2. Click **Title** and type a name for the video.

3. Click **Where** and type the location. Select a location from the list of possibilities if it is correct.

4. Click the **When** fields as they are displayed to add the date—year, month, and day.

Edit Video

| In this video: | |
| Tag people who appear in this video. |

Choose a Thumbnail:

Title:	
Where:	Where was this video taken?
When:	+ Add year
Description:	Video by Gary Bouton of TheBoutons.com

◄ ► Thumb 1 of 3

| Privacy: | 👥 Friends ▾ |

Save   Delete   Cancel

*Figure 6-8: **The first editing opportunity allows you to enter a title and description for the video and tag friends connected with it.***

5. Click **Description** and type a description of what the video is about.

6. Click the **Privacy** down arrow, and select your desired audience.

7. Click **Save**. When you click Save you'll see an additional editing screen, as described in "Make Further Video Edits."

Make Further Video Edits

When you first upload a video, click **Edit Video**, and save the title editing page, the page shown in Figure 6-9 is displayed. It contains additional functions you can perform with videos:

- **Write A Comment**   Adds a comment that will be seen beneath the video on your Timeline or News Feed.

- **Tag This Video**   Enables you to identify people or objects in the video.

- **Change Date**   Allows you to change the date or set it so it is positioned correctly on your Timeline.

- **Edit This Video**   Redisplays the Edit Video page shown in Figure 6-8, allowing you to do several editing functions, such as adding a title and tagging individuals.

- **Delete Video**   Allows you to delete the video from Facebook.

- **Embed This Video**   Provides Hypertext Markup Language (HTML) code so that you can embed the video on any site on the Web.

Embed your video

You can use this code to display your video "Polly Wants a Cracker!" on any site on the web. The video will respect privacy settings applied by you on Facebook.

Embed code: `<object width="400" hei`

Okay

- **Rotate Video**   Click **Rotate Right** or **Rotate Left** to rotate the video 90 degrees to the right or left.

Find and Edit a Video Using the Video Viewer

You can also access this screen in a different way, from your Timeline, as described here.

1. From your Timeline, click **Photos** beneath your name.

2. On the top of the Your Albums page, on the left, click **Videos**. You'll see a list of your videos.

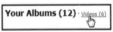

3. Click the video you want to edit. Figure 6-10 shows the edit screen for the uploaded video. You have these options:

- Mouse over the bottom of the video to reveal the Options menu, which enables you to rotate the video, change the date, edit the video, delete, or embed it. You also see Share and Like options.

- To the right of the video, you have the option to tag the video, comment, or edit it again.

4. Click **X** on the upper right of the white space to return to the previous page.

Polly Wants a Cracker!
Back to Album   Previous · Next

0:03 / 0:09 HQ

Carole Boggs Matthews
Video by Gary Bouton of TheBoutons.com — at New York.
Like · Comment · Unfollow Post · Share · Edit · 2011 · ⊘

Write a comment...

Title: Polly Wants a Cracker!
Share with: 🔒 Only Me ▾

Tag This Video
Change Date
Edit This Video
Delete Video
Embed this Video

*Figure 6-9: **After uploading a video, you'll be presented with ways to edit it.***

Upload a Video from a Video Site

1. Find the Uniform Resource Locator (URL) of the video you want to upload to Facebook. Copy the address by clicking in the URL of the page to select it and pressing **CTRL+C**.

2. On your Timeline, click **What's On Your Mind** and paste the copied address by pressing **CTRL+V** or type the link you want from the other site into the text box, and click **Attach**. An example of what you'll see will be displayed.

Figure 6-10: *Using the Video Viewer allows you additional ways to edit your video.*

3. Click in the text box in front of the URL, and add comments to let people know what the video is about.

4. Click the **Audience Selector** to set your privacy desires if the default is not correct.

5. Click **Post** to place the video link on your Timeline and News Feed.

Gary Is a Pro with Photos and Videos

As an author, illustrator, video editor, and special effects artist, I connect with friends by uploading images I've photographed or drawn and videos I've either created or edited—with little text. My friends know me as a graphics sort of person, and I try not to disappoint!

Facebook lets you post an image on your Wall as a spontaneous gesture, a visual augmentation of a chat, or as part of an album. My advice is not to post all your family photos—once you've uploaded something, it is fair game for copying—and abuse!

⬛️ve to upload media directly to Facebook. You can ⬛️ high-resolution images to *lots* of galleries online. ⬛️reen and think of ways to post images or videos ⬛️ Web, and use links to distribute and advertise ⬛️. I have a repository for most of my work and ⬛️ks to make it accessible. For example, YouTube ⬛️e logged in as a director) can link videos directly ⬛️k or other social networks. So if you upload, say, a 7MB video to YouTube, you've uploaded it onto the Internet only once—but it can be viewed often using links to different social networks.

Gary B., 68, New York

⏩ Record a Video with a Webcam

Recording your own video is a way to personalize your Facebook page dramatically. To record a video you'll need a webcam and microphone. You should also think about background lighting and appearance. First, you set some options, then you record, and then you review the video.

1. On your Timeline, click **Photos** beneath your name, and click **Add Videos | Record Video**. The Create A New Video dialog box will appear. You'll see a red rectangle with a white spot at the bottom with a small dialog box above it. (If you don't see the dialog box, click your right mouse button and select **Settings**.)

💡 **Tip** To record a video if you don't have Timeline, click your name on the menu bar for your Profile page. Then click **Photos** on the left column, and then click **Videos** to the right of the Your Photos title. Click **Record** on the upper right of the page.

2. In the Adobe Flash Player Settings dialog box, click **Allow**.

3. Click each of the icons along the bottom of the dialog box, and consider whether the settings are correct for what you want to do. From left to right, the icons and their meanings are as follows:

- **Enable Hardware Acceleration** This is selected by default and is most likely what you want.

- **Privacy** Allows Facebook to use the camera and microphone. Clicking **Remember** allows you to change the defaults.

- **Local Storage** Determines the amount of storage a video can use. You probably want to limit this to 10MB, which is a fairly short video.

- **Microphone** Lets you set the volume being recorded by the microphone. You can test it by talking and looking at the meter on the left. You want the fewest possible red spikes.

- **Camera** Lets you select the camera you want to use. You probably only have one.

4. When the settings are the way you want them, click **Close** to close the Flash dialog box.

5. To start capturing the video, click the **Start** button (white dot) at the bottom center of the window. Record the video and sound. When you are done, click the **Stop** (white square) button at the bottom center of the window.

6. Click **Play** on the bottom-right corner to preview your video. If you are not happy with it, click **Reset** to erase the video so you can re-record it.

7. When the video is the way you want it, Click **Save**. Then, on the Edit Video page, click the **Audience Selector** to set the privacy to your liking, and then click **Save** to save the video and post it to your Timeline and News Feed.

You should be able to return to your Timeline and see your video. See "View a Video" to understand how to play the video.

After playing the video, you can click **Go To Video**, where you can tag, edit (add titles and descriptions), and delete the video.

▶▶ View a Video

You can access a video either from your Home page or Timeline. It may start playing immediately, or if you need to start it, you must first click the **Play** icon ▶ . As it plays, if you move your cursor over the video, the video commands appear on the screen.

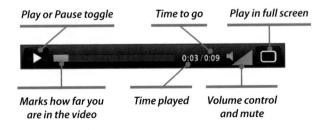

Play or Pause toggle   Time to go   Play in full screen

Marks how far you are in the video   Time played   Volume control and mute

1. From the Home page, click **Photos** (under Apps) in the leftmost column—you may have to click **More** to expand the list. Click **My Albums** and then click **Videos** to the right of Your Albums. You'll see a list of your videos. Scroll through the list until you see the one you want. Click the video you want to play. It may begin to play immediately.

2. Mouse over the bottom of the video to see the option bar.

3. After it finishes, or before it starts, you'll find these options:

   - Click the **Play** icon to start the video. The Play button toggles into a Pause button.
   - Click **Pause** to stop the video.
   - Click the **Mute** icon to suppress the sound.
   - Click and drag the **Volume Control** triangle to control the volume.
   - Click the **Play In Full Screen** icon to display the video in a full-screen mode. Press ESC to return to regular viewing.

Chapter 7

Administering and Participating in a Group

Groups are specialized pages created to support people who share a common interest. Examples include people organizing a class reunion, an investing club, a hunting and fishing club, or carpools. Anything that draws people together can be turned into a group. Groups enable members to communicate with each other, post photos or videos, chat, and edit shared documents. But the real fun of groups is simply the ability to share a common conversation about common interests.

Group Administrators (called "Admins" by Facebook) are those who create and maintain the Group page for participating members. The groups can be open to anyone interested, closed for posting but visible to all, or secret—invisible to all but members. Closed and secret groups require candidates to be invited or to request membership. This chapter discusses how you can create a group, find and join an existing one, and what you can do in a group.

ACTING AS ADMIN FOR A GROUP

The creator of a Facebook group becomes its Admin. An Admin has commands and abilities to control the site that its members will not. Admins can enter and change information describing the group, remove members, add other Admins—and then remove them—and send messages to the group as a whole.

Having additional Admins has several advantages and disadvantages. As the creator of a site, you can ask others to help shoulder the load of maintaining it. They can help keep the group voice going when the members are not engaging fully. On the other hand, Admins can remove members, change group settings, and add even more Admins. So you'll want to add someone who you trust and who will maintain the site in a nonthreatening way. (Adding people inappropriate to the group, adding new Admins for the wrong reasons, or deleting people from the group for personal reasons are some examples of abusive actions by an Admin.)

▷▷ Create a Group

To create a group, follow these steps:

1. On the leftmost column of your Home page, click **Create Group**. If you don't see that option, click **More** (displayed when you hover your mouse over the Groups title) to expand the list of options, and then click **+ Create Group** on the top of the middle column. The Create Group dialog box opens, as shown in Figure 7-1.

2. You have these options:

   • **Group Name**   Click in the **Group Name** text box, and type the name of the new group.

   • **Members**   Click in the text box, and start typing the name of a friend you want to include in the group. A list will appear with the name and thumbnail of the name being typed. Click the person you want to include in the group. Their name will appear in the text box.

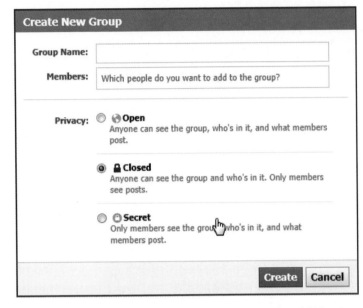

Figure 7-1: *When creating a group, you simply name it, add friends, and set your privacy.*

Type the next name, and so on. Beneath the text box is a list of suggested members. Click names if they fit; otherwise, just ignore them. Don't worry if you can't think of all you want to add to the group. You'll have another opportunity to select names for membership. If you change your mind about someone, click **X** next to the name to delete it.

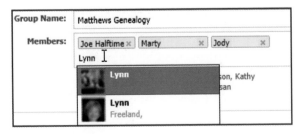

- **Privacy** Click the radio button for the privacy setting you want:
  - **Open** The public can see everything, including the group's posts.
  - **Closed** The group and group members are visible to the public, but only members can read the posts.
  - **Secret** The public is unaware of the group. It is invisible except to invited members.

3. Click **Create**.

4. Click an icon to represent your new group, and click **Okay**. (You can click **Skip** if you don't want an icon.) The new Group page is displayed.

▷▷ Add and Remove Admins

Admins have tenure. The primary advantage of tenure is that the oldest Admin can add or delete everyone else. Newer Admins can only delete those with less tenure than they have. Older Admins need to leave the group before newer Admins have total control of it.

Add More Admins

An Admin must, of course, be a member of the group.

1. Click *no*. **Members** below the members' thumbnails in the right column of the group's page.

2. Click the **gear** icon beneath the member's name and information, and click **Make Admin** from the menu. You'll see a dialog box confirming that your new administrator will be able to perform important tasks.

Add Group Admin

As a group admin, Marty Matthews will be able to edit group settings, remove members and give other members admin status.

Make Admin **Cancel**

3. Click **Make Admin** in the dialog box.

Remove Admins

You can only remove those who became Admins after you did.

1. Display the Group page and click *no*. **Members** in the right column, beneath the thumbnails and menu bar. The list of members is displayed.

2. Click the **gear** icon and then click **Remove Admin** from the menu. The Remove Group Admin dialog box will be displayed.

3. Click **Okay** to confirm you want to remove the Admin.

▷▷ Add Friends to a Group

When you are first creating a group, you may not be sure which of your friends might belong. You can add friends after the fact. Also, you may get new members who need to be added after the group is organized. When you add someone to a group, they receive a message in their Messages that they have been invited to join, and the group name appears in their Groups list. All they have to do is click the name to see the Groups page.

1. If you have a large number of friends you're trying to add to the group and can't remember each name, open two windows: one for viewing the list of friends eligible to be

members, and the other for entering names into the dialog box. To do this, open Facebook in two windows (start a second copy of Internet Explorer by right-clicking the icon in the taskbar and selecting **Internet Explorer**, and then open your Facebook page):

- Open the window on the left with your **Timeline | Friends** view.

- Open the window on the right with your **Home | *newgroupname***. On the Group page, click *no*. **Members | Add People**, both found in the right column, under the header of current member thumbnails. The Add People To Group dialog box is displayed, also seen in Figure 7-2.

+ Add People

2. Scroll through the friends list in the first window, and begin to type appropriate names in the Add People To Group dialog box in the second window.

3. As you begin typing a name, a list will be displayed. Click the person you want to include. You can add all the names you want in the dialog box.

4. When you have added all the names you can find or think of, click **Add**. You can always come back to this process and resume adding new friends.

Control Who Approves Members

As the creator and Admin of a group, you can solely control who is admitted into it. As Admin, you can approve all new members or allow the group to add and approve members. If an Admin approves all new members, the prospective member will not be notified about the group until they are approved by an Admin.

1. In the Group page, click the gear icon [⚙] at the top right, and click **Edit Group Settings**. The basic information page is displayed.

2. Beside Membership Approval place a check mark in the appropriate check box for controlling membership in your group.

3. At the bottom, click **Save** and then click the group name under Groups on the left column to return to the Group page.

Add or Change a Group Description

You can add a description to the Group page to clarify your intent for the group, or its mission.

1. Click **About** to the right of the group name.

2. Click **Add A Description** and type your intent, mission, or other information.

3. Click **Save**.

Figure 7-2: *To remember who might belong in a group, display two Facebook windows—one with a list of your friends, and another with the Add Friends dialog box.*

Set Up Group Email

You will most likely want to set up an email address that will send email to all your members with one email. For instance, you may want to notify everyone in your group of your group site, or have some other reason to notify all members via email. Facebook has a special email address for your group.

1. On the Group page, click the gear icon in the menu bar beneath the member thumbnail strip, and then click **Edit Group Settings**.

> ✓ Notifications ❋
> Send Message
> Create Event
>
> Add to Favorites
> Edit Group Settings
> Report Group
> Leave Group

2. Beside Group Address, click **Set Up Group Email**. The Set Up Group Web And Email Address dialog box is displayed.

3. Click in the text box, and type the ID for the email address. Click **Set Address**. You may have to try out a few names until you find one that is available. When you do, you'll see the new email address displayed next to Email Address instead of the Set Up Group Email button.

4. Click **Save**. Then click the group name again to return to its main page.

Set Basic Group Information

You can edit or change some of the group's basic information, such as its name, description, and privacy settings.

1. On the Group page, click the gear icon in the menu bar (beneath the thumbnails), and then click **Edit Group Settings**. The edit panel is displayed, as shown in Figure 7-3.

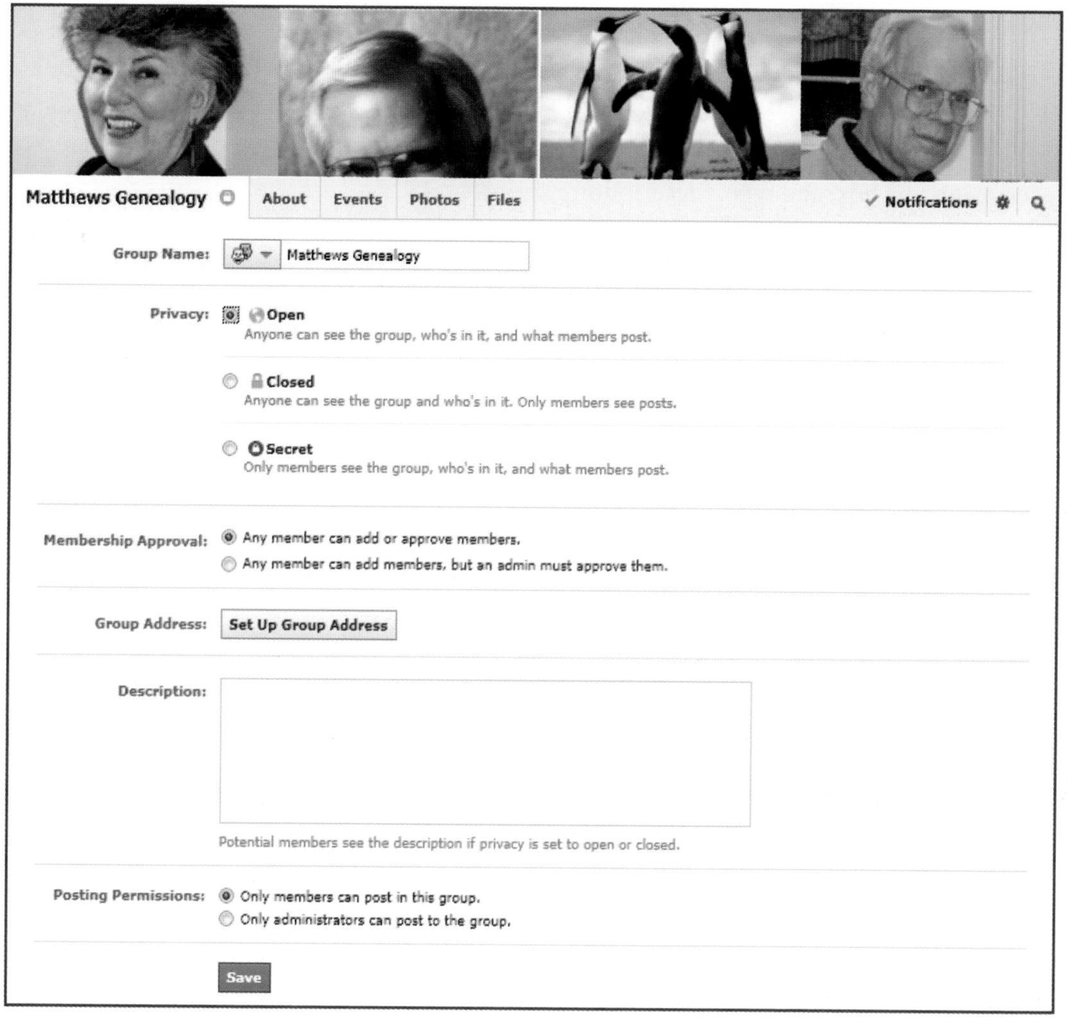

*Figure 7-3: **The Admin of a group can edit its basic information.***

2. On the basic information page, as you've seen earlier, you have these options:

   • Click in the **Group Name** text box, and type a new name.

   • Click a **Privacy** button to change the group security settings:

     • **Open**   The public can see everything, including the group's posts.

- **Closed**   The group and group members are visible to the public, but only members can read the posts.
- **Secret**   The public is unaware of the group. It is invisible except to invited members.
- Click in the **Description** text box, and type a description of the group. This description is visible to nonmembers if the privacy is set to Open or Closed. It is not visible when the privacy is Secret.
- Click one of the **Posting Permissions** buttons to determine whether only members or only the Admin can post in the group's Wall.

3. Click **Save** when your basic information is the way you want it.

⏩ Remove or Ban a Group Member

Removing a member from a group enables the ex-member to again request membership in the group. In other words, being removed from a group can be a temporary status. However, banning a group member not only removes the membership from the group, but also disables the member's ability to find the group so that a request to be reinstated can be made.

Remove a Member
1. Beneath the group menu bar on the right column, click *no*. **Members** to display the list of members.
2. Click the **gear** icon beneath the member information, and click **Remove From Group**.
3. Click **Confirm** when you are asked if you are sure.

Ban a Member
1. Remove the member from the group as described in the previous section.

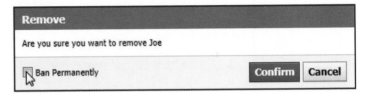

2. Click the **Ban Permanently** check box.
3. Click **Confirm**.

⏩ Remove Abusive Comments

You may have a member who does not post comments you want to encourage or retain. An Admin can delete a member's comments.

Place your cursor over the offensive comment. A down arrow in the top-left corner of the comment will appear. Click it and a menu will open. You have these options:

- **Delete Post**   Deletes the comment.
- **Delete Post And Remove User**   Gets rid of both the post and the person who posted it.
- **Report/Mark As Spam**   Signals to Facebook that the member is posting illegal or irresponsible comments, or that spam is getting through the filter. The member could be removed from Facebook if the comments and history of the individual are serious enough. There is no delay or confirming message for this—when you click the option, notice is immediately sent to Facebook, so use this carefully.

Suzanne Reconnects with Childhood Friends

I use Facebook to reconnect with childhood friends where I grew up on a lightly populated, remote tropical island. My friends, both living on the island and not, enjoy gathering online to reminisce about our days in this small edenic place. One man posts a weekly picture from "olden days" for us to guess where it is. We have great fun guessing the location, as the island has changed over the years. This prompts sharing of stories and memories of playing together and getting into mischief. Sometimes it can take a half hour to read entries about one picture! Many comments make me laugh out loud and remind me that even after all these years, we are still the same people deep down in our hearts.

Through Facebook many of us have reconnected and even made plans to meet. An annual picnic weekend has been organized for a few years now. It's a blessing to reconnect with folks who have known you in your formative years and who still find you worth spending time with. Without Facebook, I doubt it would have happened.

Suzanne F., 62, Washington

HAVE FUN WITH A GROUP

Using a group is similar to using a regular Facebook page, except that you'll find some of the instructions in a different place.

▷▷ Add Friends to a Group

All members of a group can suggest friends to add to it. Some groups allow members to add others without interference. Others require an Admin to first approve of the submitted name. If you don't have permission to approve new members of a group, you will see a message to the effect that the person you suggested will be added pending approval.

1. On the Group page, click **Add Friends To Group** on the right column, under the thumbnails of current members. The Add Friends To Group dialog box will open.

2. Begin typing a name, and a list will be displayed as you type. Click the person you want to include. If you don't have permission to approve the person, you'll see a "pending" message.

> 5 members · Chat
>
> +
>
> Ann Morrow has been added, pending admin approval. Undo

3. If your Admin needs to approve the person, he or she will add or remove the person when the request is received. If the person is added to the group, the group name will appear on their Facebook Home page under Groups.

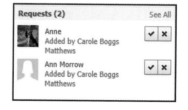

View All Members of a Group

To see thumbnails of all members in the group displayed in a full-page spread:

- Click *no.* **Members** below the menu bar and members' thumbnails in the right column.

- When you're finished with the member display, click the group name on the left column under Groups to return to the normal Group page.

Chat with the Group

A chat including all members of a group can be scheduled. One approach is to ask the Admin to send an email to all members announcing a time and date for the chat. Then at that time, each member must be available in order to be included.

1. In your Group page, at the top of the third column, click **Message**. A Chat box will open.

2. Click the thumbnails of those you want to include in the Chat and click **Start Chat**.

3. Click and type your message in the text box at the bottom. When you are ready, press **ENTER**. All chat responses from the group will be reflected in the larger text box above.

4. Click **X** to remove the chat from the page.

Create a Document

If your group is working together to create a document, or if you want to create a document for the group to read, the process is easy.

1. On the menu bar beneath the member thumbnails, click **Files | Create Doc**. The document page will open, as seen in Figure 7-4.

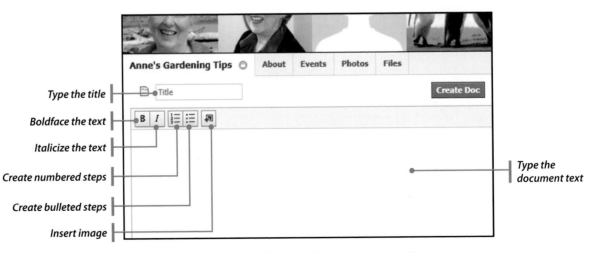

Figure 7-4: *You can create a document in Facebook to be shared or worked on together.*

2. Click in the **Title** text box, and type a title for the document.

3. Click in the main text box, and type your document. Figure 7-4 shows the formatting options available to you as you create the document.

4. When your document is finished, click **Create Doc**.

Ask Questions and Take Polls

Suppose you want to ask a question of the group or take a poll of how they feel about a group experience or desire.

1. In the menu bar beneath the member thumbnails on the Group page, click **Ask Question**.

2. In the text box, type your question.

3. Click **Add Poll Options** on the left of the question text box if you want the group to vote on various possibilities.

4. Click in the first Poll Options text box, and type the polling possibilities. A list of possible options is displayed. If they are not what you want, click to the side of the list to remove it. Continue this process with each of the possible answers.

5. Click **Post** to post it. Figure 7-5 shows an example.

Post a Link

Posting a link requires that you copy and paste the Uniform Resource Locator (URL) to the Status Update text box.

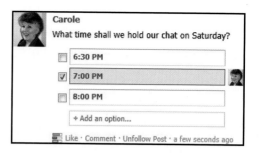

*Figure 7-5: **You can poll the members for their opinions about various concerns of the group.***

Information from the website will be displayed automatically. To post a link suggesting to your group that they view another website or page:

1. Find and copy the URL of the website you want to include for the group.

2. Click in the **Write Something** text box and paste the URL of the website. A thumbnail image of the page will display.

3. Click **Post** to post it for others.

Tip To see how to upload photos, create albums, and upload videos for your group site, refer to Chapter 6.

 Tip To share links with others outside the group, click **Share** beneath the posting and then click the **Share** down arrow. You'll be able to choose where you want the link displayed, for example, on your Timeline.

▷▷ Create an Event

To create an event for your group members:

1. On your Group page in the menu bar beneath the member thumbnails, click **Events | Create Event**. A Create New Event page is displayed, as shown as a completed form in Figure 7-6.

2. Set the parameters of the event:
   - Click in the **Name** text box and type a name for the event.
   - Click in the **Details** text box to describe the event more fully.
   - Click in the **Where** text box to set the location or other identifying information (optionally, you may enter an address). If you enter a location, it will be pinned to the map.
   - Click the **When** calendar, and find the date you want. Click in the **Time** text box, and type the time. You may want to enter an **End Time** by clicking that option.

Create New Event for Anne's Gardening Tips

Name	Garden Party!
Details	Come to our July Garden Party--celebrate summer!
Where	⦿ Joy's Secret Garden
From	7/12/2013 🗓 1:00 pm PDT
To	7/12/2013 🗓 5:00 pm ✕
Privacy	🔢 Anne's Gardening Tips ▾

☑ Invite all members   Create   Cancel

*Figure 7-6: **Setting up an event for a group is easy and can help support group programs or meetings.***

- The default privacy will be your group name. Who sees the details of the event depends on the group membership (Open, everyone can see details; Closed or Secret, only members can see). To invite others, click **Privacy** for a menu of other possibilities. You can choose **Public** for an open invitation to everyone—everyone on Facebook sees the event details, even if not specifically invited. Choose **Friends** to invite only your own friends as the host (the host is automatically determined to be the one who creates the Facebook event). In this case, friends can see the event information, but are not sent an invitation. Also, if a friend joins the event, their friends will see the details of the event in their News Feed. Click **Invite Only** to invite specific people. In this case, only the invited people (plus their guests, if that option is set) will see the event.

- If you choose Invite Only, click a check box to remove the check mark, thereby deselecting whether a guest can invite friends, and whether you want to show the guest list on the Events page.

- Clear the **Invite All Members** check mark if you don't want an invitation sent to all invitees immediately.

3. Click **Create** to make it final. You'll see the Events page.

Invite Friends to an Event

You can invite friends at the time you create the event by selecting the Invite All Members option at the bottom of the dialog box. However, if you want to do it later (Invite All Members is deselected), or if you remember someone afterward, you can invite members from the Group page. The invitees must be within the defined "privacy" of the group—for instance, if your group is the privacy setting, all invitees must be members in the group.

1. On the Group page, click **Events** on the menu bar beneath the members' thumbnails to view the events. If you have more than one, click the event name you want to view.

2. On the Events page, click **Invite Members** on the event menu bar at the upper right. The Invite Members dialog box is displayed, as seen in Figure 7-7.

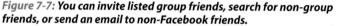

3. You can use these three methods to find friends to invite:

- Click the names of those you want to invite.

- Click in the **Search By Name** text box, and select the group or list containing more members you'd like to include.

- Click in the text box, and type a name. A list will be displayed. Click the name you want.

Figure 7-7: *You can invite listed group friends, search for non-group friends, or send an email to non-Facebook friends.*

4. Click **Save**. You'll see a message that the invitations will be sent.

Respond to an Event Invitation

You can receive an invitation in your Messages area. You can also see your invitations in your Events area. To find and respond to an event invitation:

1. In your Notifications area, click the invitation that you want to respond to.

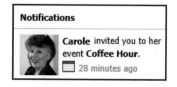

–Or–

1. In your Home page, click **Events** to view your events. Click the response you want.

2. You have these options:

  • Click **Join** to indicate acceptance of the invitation.

  • Click **Maybe** if you're not sure.

  • Click **Decline** to send regrets.

3. The buttons will change to reflect your choice. If you have the option of inviting your friends, a button will be provided to do that. Just click **Invite Friends** and follow the prompts.

View Group Photos

Photos can be wonderful for a group. They can reveal good times together, recapture old memories, and display possibilities for new things to do. To see photos for a group:

1. Click the name of the group on the leftmost column of the Home page.

2. Click **Photos** in the menu bar beneath the member thumbnails.

3. To see the contents of an album, click the top picture on a page.

4. To see the photos in full view, click the photo.

Leave or Delete a Group

You may find yourself in a group that simply doesn't interest you. Or perhaps the group simply serves no purpose any longer. You can leave a group you no longer are attached to, and you can delete a group.

Leave a Group

Be aware that if you choose to leave a group, you'll have to display the Group page again and click **Ask To Join Group** if you ever change your mind. Note that if you are the Admin of the group, someone else will be asked to act as Admin.

1. In the Home page, mouse over the group name on the leftmost column.

2. Click **Edit** (pencil icon) and click **Leave Group**. The Leave *groupname* Group dialog box is displayed.

3. Confirm that you want to leave by clicking **Leave Group**.

Delete a Group

Facebook automatically gets rid of groups with no remaining members. So to get rid of a group, all members must be deleted. Remember, however, that in order to delete members, you have to be the Admin with the most tenure—the originating Admin, or at least the one remaining the longest. To delete members:

1. Click the group name from the Home page.

2. Click **About** in the menu bar beneath the members' thumbnails.

3. Click the **gear** icon below each member's name and information, and click **Remove From Group** to delete them from the group. A confirmation message will inform you that you are about to delete the group.

4. Click **Delete Group**.

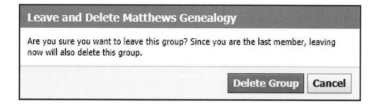

⟫ Share a Comment

Comments are how communications are enabled among the group. The quality and frequency of the communications are what vitalize and stimulate group spirit. No comments, no group.

To share a comment with the members of a group:

1. Display the Group page by clicking its name on the Home page.
2. Click in the **Write Something** text box, and type your comment.
3. Click **Post**.

WORKING WITH AN EXISTING GROUP

Thousands, perhaps millions, of groups already exist within Facebook. You may want to find an existing group rather than create a new one. Facebook Groups support both groups that meet physically, such as clubs, and those that only meet online.

⟫ Find a Group

There are several ways to find groups. If you know what group you want to join, you can just search for the name. You can accept an invitation from a friend, or you can ask friends for the names of groups they belong to.

Search for Groups

The most common way to find groups is to search for them. Searching for groups is a bit tricky. You search by keyword, unless you know the exact name of the group. When you get a list of matches, you'll need to filter it for groups. Then, if the group is open, you can immediately join the group, or if the group is closed, you can request to join. Figure 7-8 shows an example of a keyword search narrowed to groups.

1. On your Home page, click in the **Search** text box, and type the keyword describing the group you want to join. You'll see a list matching your keyword.
2. When you get the initial search result, scroll down the list, and at the bottom click **See More Results for *keyword*** to see additional results. Facebook often displays a regular search result instead of a list of possibilities, and you want a list—asking for more results allows you to take the next step in accomplishing this.

3. Click **Groups** in the leftmost column to filter the list so that only groups are available, as was done in Figure 7-8.
4. Scroll through the list and mouse over those you want to investigate. You will be able to see certain information for the group, giving you a sense of what it is about and who its members are. If the group is open to the public, you can even see posts for a group.
5. When you find a group you're interested in joining, click **Join Group**.

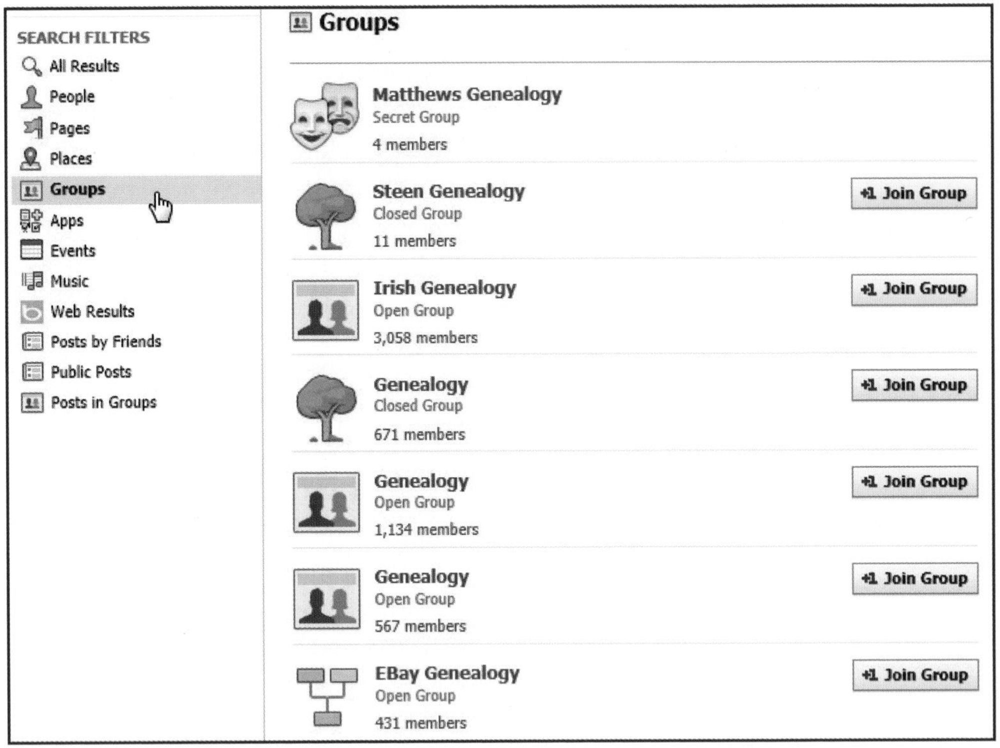

SEARCH FILTERS

- All Results
- People
- Pages
- Places
- **Groups**
- Apps
- Events
- Music
- Web Results
- Posts by Friends
- Public Posts
- Posts in Groups

Groups

Matthews Genealogy
Secret Group
4 members

Steen Genealogy
Closed Group
11 members
+1 Join Group

Irish Genealogy
Open Group
3,058 members
+1 Join Group

Genealogy
Closed Group
671 members
+1 Join Group

Genealogy
Open Group
1,134 members
+1 Join Group

Genealogy
Open Group
567 members
+1 Join Group

EBay Genealogy
Open Group
431 members
+1 Join Group

Figure 7-8: You can find groups by searching for its name or by using keywords.

Note As of the writing of this book, Facebook is reformatting the Groups feature—the conversion is called "archiving." Old groups are being converted to the new group formats. Certain aspects will be lost, such as the discussion threads, which are being converted into regular posts; officer names; group networks; and the Information box beneath the group photo. Newly formatted groups can chat with each other or the entire group, upload photo albums, create group documents to share and co-create, poll members to take votes on issues, and have access to a group email address.

Use Friends to Find Groups

Searches work well if you have an idea what you're looking for, and if the group privacy setting allows it to be seen by the public ("closed" or "open" will be found by searches; "secret" will not be found). But if there is a specific group you'd like to join, you're better off finding someone already in the group who can invite you to join, or ask the Admin to invite you.

> **CAUTION!** If you get an invitation via an email to join a group with which you're unacquainted, check out the site before you confirm your interest. Do not click the email link, but go to the group site on Facebook. Links can contain hidden viruses.

Join a Group

Groups, as you know, can be open or closed. If they are open, or public, anyone can join. If they are closed, you'll need an invitation. The first step is to find a group you want to join and open the group site, as described earlier. Then you simply either join or ask to join:

- Click **Join Group** to become a member immediately—this can be done if the group is open or closed.
- If the group is closed, you must be approved for membership. Your confirmation will come to you via email and a Facebook Messages notice.

> **Tip** You may join as many as 300 groups. After that, in order to join additional groups, you'll have to remove some from your Facebook site. See "Leave a Group."

View Group Requests and Memberships

Facebook makes it easy to keep track of your existing memberships and outstanding requests:

- On your Home page, in the leftmost column, click **Groups** to see your group activity. If you do not see Groups, click **More** to expand the list. If you belong to more than one group, click the name of the group you want.

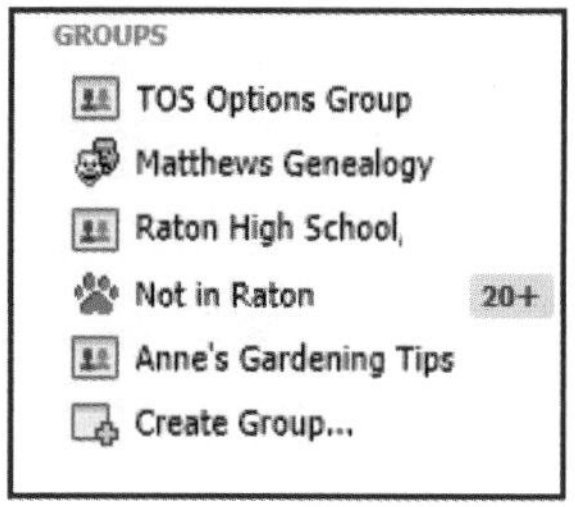

GROUPS
TOS Options Group
Matthews Genealogy
Raton High School,
Not in Raton
20+
Anne's Gardening Tips
Create Group...

- As you hover your cursor over the Groups title, you'll see More. Click **More** to see all your group requests and memberships. Click a group name to see its activity.

Figure 7-9 shows an example of a Groups page with outstanding groups.

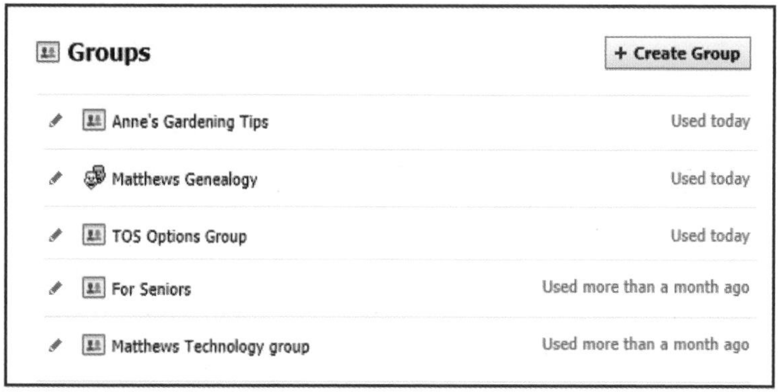

Groups
+ Create Group
Anne's Gardening Tips
Used today
Matthews Genealogy
Used today
TOS Options Group
Used today
For Seniors
Used more than a month ago
Matthews Technology group
Used more than a month ago

***Figure 7-9:* From your Home page you can view your Groups page showing recent activity.**

1 2 3 4 5 6 7 8 9 10

Chapter 8

Using Facebook Apps and Games

Apps, which is short for "applications," are computer programs or software that cause a computer to perform some function. Facebook apps are programs that perform some function ancillary to Facebook and are accessed from Facebook as well. There are many different kinds of Facebook apps, some developed by Facebook that are a standard part of the product, like Events, Notes, Photos, Videos, and Music; and a great many more developed by people and organizations other than Facebook (called "third-party apps") that must be added by the user from sources both inside and outside Facebook. Games are just apps in which you play a game, either alone or against other Facebook users, whether currently or soon to become your friends.

In this chapter we'll discuss apps and games; how to locate, start, and briefly use them; how to respond to requests to join a game and be secure in your use of them; and how to edit and manage them.

LOCATE AND USE APPS

Most of the Facebook-created apps appear as options on the top and left of your Home and Timeline pages. They are started by clicking those options, as discussed elsewhere in this book. Many other apps from both Facebook and other developers are available. In this section we'll look at how you locate, start, and use the apps you are interested in.

Note The entries that you have on your lists of apps and games are probably different from those shown in Figure 8-1 and elsewhere in this chapter. This is because Facebook often changes what it displays and new ones are constantly being developed. If you don't see the app you are looking for, do a specific search on its name.

1. From your Home page, click **App Center** and review the apps your friends are using on the right and the suggested apps on the left.

2. Scroll down and review the long list of top-rated apps. Follow this by clicking **Trending** and look at a list of the apps that are growing the fastest, and then click **Top Grossing** to see the apps that are earning the most for their creators.

3. Select an app to use as an example and click its logo or name. Here we'll look at Pinterest (found under Suggested), an online board on which you can pin items you find on the Internet.

Locate Apps

When you click **Apps** (or More which is displayed when you hover over the Apps title), a list of some Facebook apps is displayed. These may also be listed beneath the Apps title in the left column. You can explore any of these links, but the best place to get started is with the App Center shown in Figure 8-1.

4. In most instances the app's Facebook page will open, seen in Figure 8-2. Here you can see information about the app and some of your friends who use it.

5. It is a good idea to read the description of the app and read the ways that the app will use your information and post what you are doing to give yourself a good understanding of the app before trying it out.

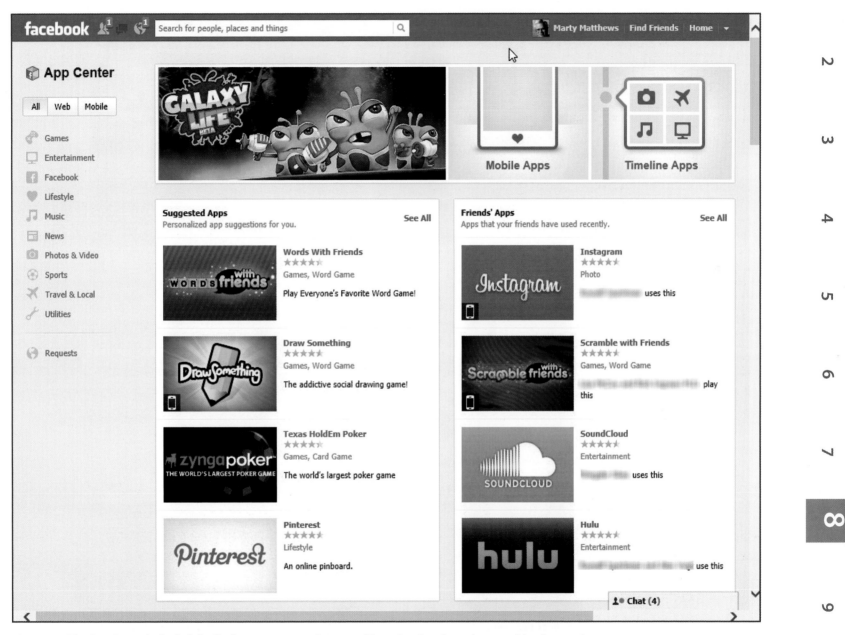

Figure 8-1: *The App Center is the hub for finding ones you are interested in and seeing those that your friends are using.*

Figure 8-2: The initial page that opens when you click an app is a standard Facebook page for that app, which has a look similar to other Facebook pages.

6. When you are ready to go ahead and use the app, click **Visit Website**. In the case of Pinterest, a Create Your Account dialog box is displayed. Enter a user name, your email address, and a password. Click **Create Account**. You should get an email message that tells you "Thanks" and provides an Explore Pins button. Click it. You are taken back to the Pinterest website where you can click **Login**; choose **Login With Facebook**; enter your ID, email address, and password; and click **Create Account**.

Pinterest

Hi!

Thanks for requesting an invite. We're excited to get you pinning! In the meantime, explore some more **pins**.

Explore pins

©2012 Pinterest, Inc. | All Rights Reserved.
Privacy Policy | Terms and Conditions

Other apps have their own pages and processes they use to sign you up. Follow through it if the app is something you want to use. Be aware that the information you give them or have placed on Facebook can be used by the app.

Once you have begun to use apps, you will see the icons and names of apps you have used in the menu on the left of your Home page beneath the title, Apps.

▷▷ Use Apps

How you use the many apps available on Facebook varies greatly. After you start an app and follow its sign-up procedure, as described previously, you are taken to pages unique to that app.

To explore the way you can use these unique pages, we'll briefly explore three different apps: Pinterest, Birthdays, and TripAdvisor. While looking at how to use these three apps won't show you how to use every app, it will hopefully give you confidence to dive in and follow the directions you find in other apps.

Note The three apps were chosen based upon their popularity and what we judged would be of interest to our audience in three different categories. Being chosen does not constitute an endorsement of these apps, just that they are popular and provide examples of how Facebook apps are used.

Use Pinterest

Pinterest allows you to collect pictures, videos, articles, and blogs that you find on the Internet and

Pinterest

share them with your friends and the Facebook community. When you have completed the sign-up procedure, the app displays a number of categories you can select to see a list of people you can follow who are pinning in that area, as you see in Figure 8-3. From this page you can:

1. Click several of the categories and click **Follow People**. You will see a list of a few of the people who are interested in the categories you have chosen. You will also see a set of photos of your friends who are using Pinterest.

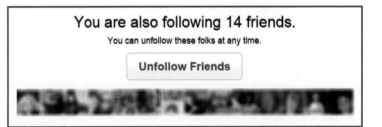

You are also following 14 friends.

You can unfollow these folks at any time.

Unfollow Friends

Figure 8-3: Pinterest gives you a number of categories from which you can get suggestions of people to follow who are also interested in those categories.

2. Just to see where it leads, click **Unfollow Friends**. You'll see your friends' names with buttons to unfollow them individually, or you can click **Unfollow All** to do that.

3. When you are ready, click **Create Boards** to create your own space to collect what you are interested in, as shown in Figure 8-4.

4. Click one of the options in the center or one on the right side, which you then need to click again in the center. You can select several categories for your boards.

5. When you are ready, click **Create**. You are told how to add a "Pin It" button to your browser. Follow those instructions (view the video if you wish). You should see the Add A Favorite dialog box (remember to choose **Favorites Bar**).

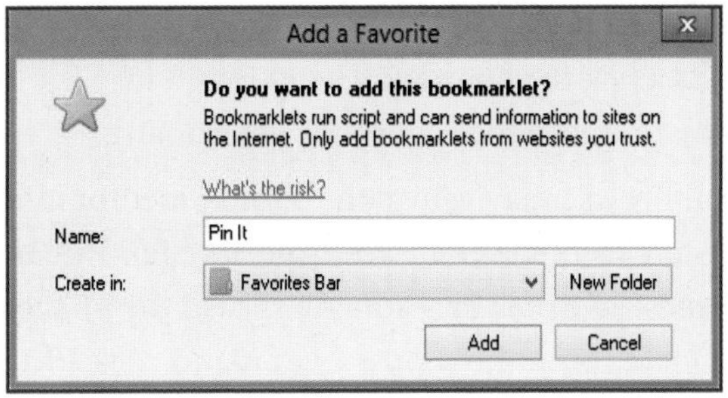

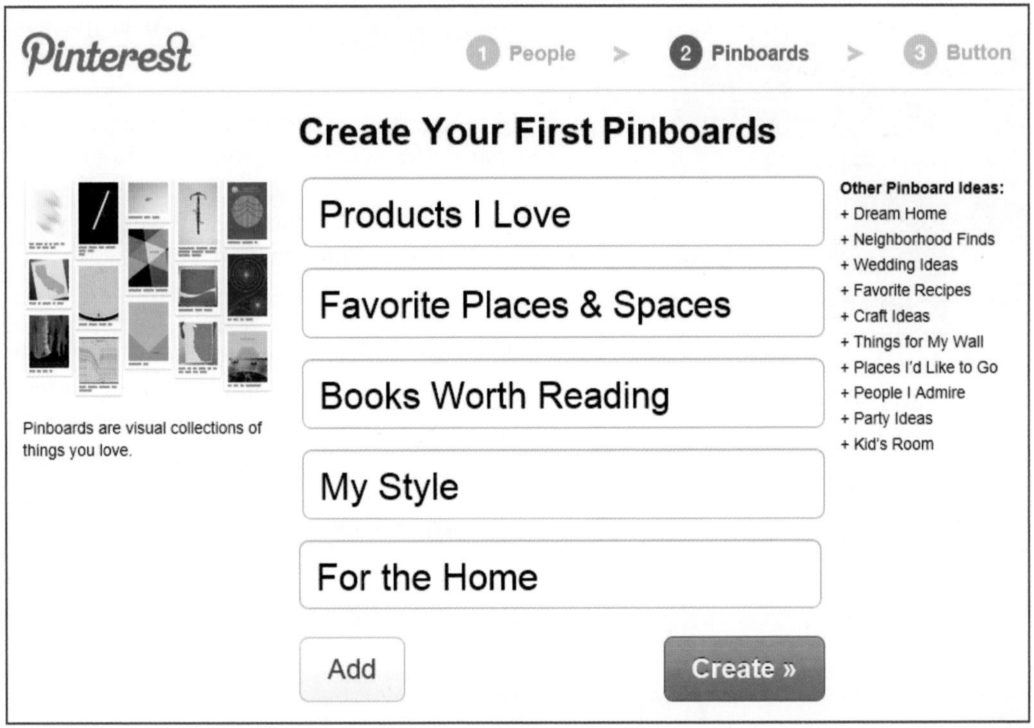

Figure 8-4: *Pinterest uses pinboards to collect items from the Internet you are interested in.*

6. If you don't see your Favorites bar, right-click the top of the Internet Explorer window and click **Favorites Bar**.

7. When you see Pin It on your Favorites bar, click **Start Pinning**. You are taken to the Pinterest site.

8. Click your name in the upper-right corner and click **Boards**, click the board you want to pin to, click the down arrow, and select a category for your board.

9. In your browser navigate to the photo, video, or information you want to pin. When you find it, click **Pin It** in your browser's Favorites bar. You are shown the image that will be pinned; move the mouse over it and click **Pin It**.

10. Click the board you want to pint it to, enter a description, and once again click **Pin It**.

11. Click **See Your Pin**. You are shown your entry enlarged, as you can see in Figure 8-5.

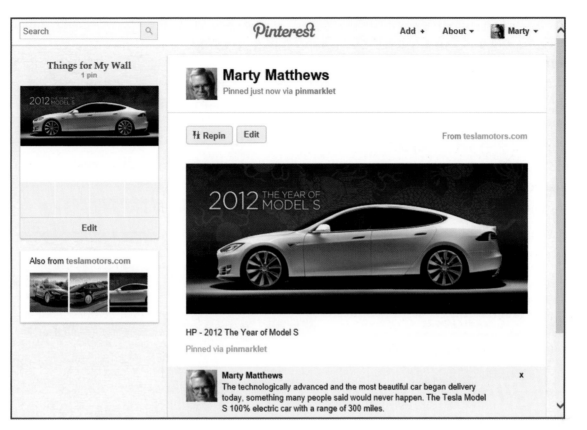

Figure 8-5: *It is amazing how fast people see and repin your pins.*

Use MyCalendar-Birthdays

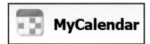

The MyCalendar-Birthdays app calls itself the most popular calendar app on Facebook and has many millions of users. It helps you keep track of friends' birthdays on Facebook.

1. Type <u>MyCalendar-Birthdays</u> (without any spaces) into the Facebook search text box and press **ENTER**. You will select the first Web Results item and then click **Go To App** once or twice before you get to the actual App Welcome page.

2. You will see three checkboxes asking if you want to add birthdays, setup reminders, or accept requests. Clear any checkmarks you do not want and click **Continue**.

3. You are shown a list of your friends whose birthdays aren't already on Facebook and told that a request will be sent to these people saying you want to add their birthday to MyCalendar. If you want to do that, click **Send Requests**. Otherwise, click **Cancel**. If you click **Cancel**, which I would suggest, you are returned to the MyCalendar-Birthdays' home page shown in Figure 8-6.

4. Read about the app and what it will get from you. If you want to go ahead, click **Add To Facebook**.

5. You are asked a series of questions:

   - Do you want to be notified when a friend is having a birthday? (Respond **Yes** or **No**.)

   - Do You want to receive email reminders? (Respond **Yes** or **No**.)

   - If yes, you'll be asked to verify your email address. You will be sent a confirmation email. Open it and click **Confirm Email Address**.

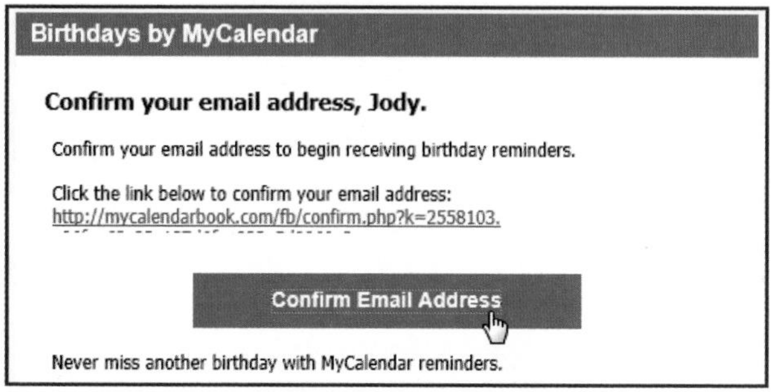

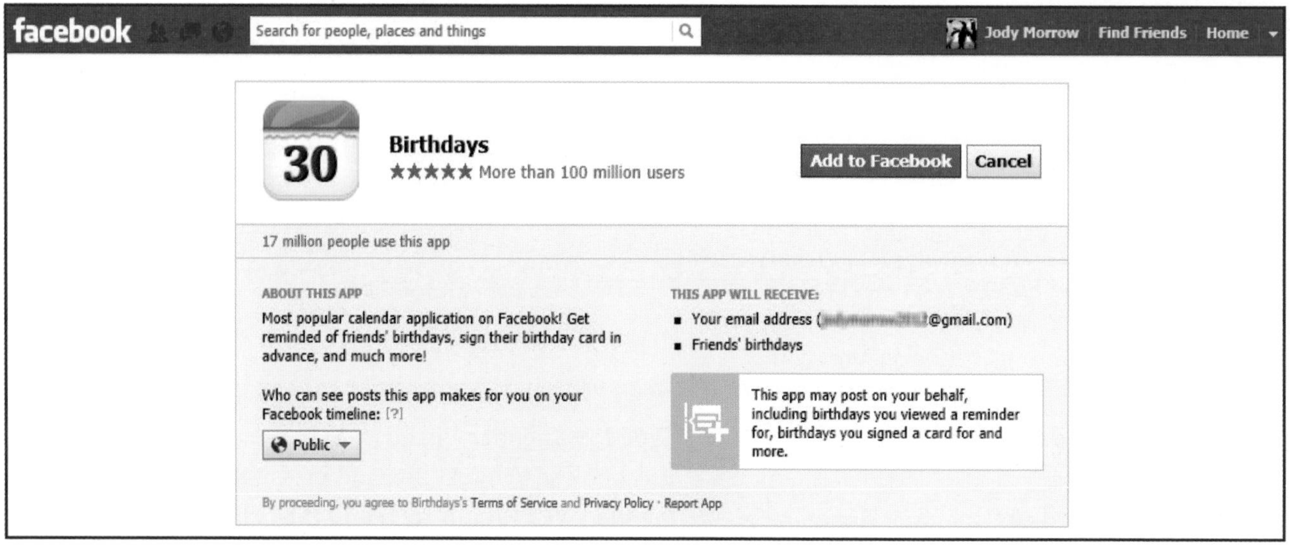

Figure 8-6: *MyCalendar-Birthdays provides a way to remember your friends' birthdays and send them cards, which you can queue up ahead of time.*

6. The MyCalendar-Birthdays calendar page will appear. On the calendar you may see some dates that are highlighted in green. Click one of these dates, and you will see one or more of your friends whose birthdays are in Facebook and have it on the date selected, as you can see in Figure 8-7.

7. In the lower part of the page you are shown a list of your friends. Click in the check box opposite the friends you want to send requests for their birthdays, and click **Add Birthdays**.

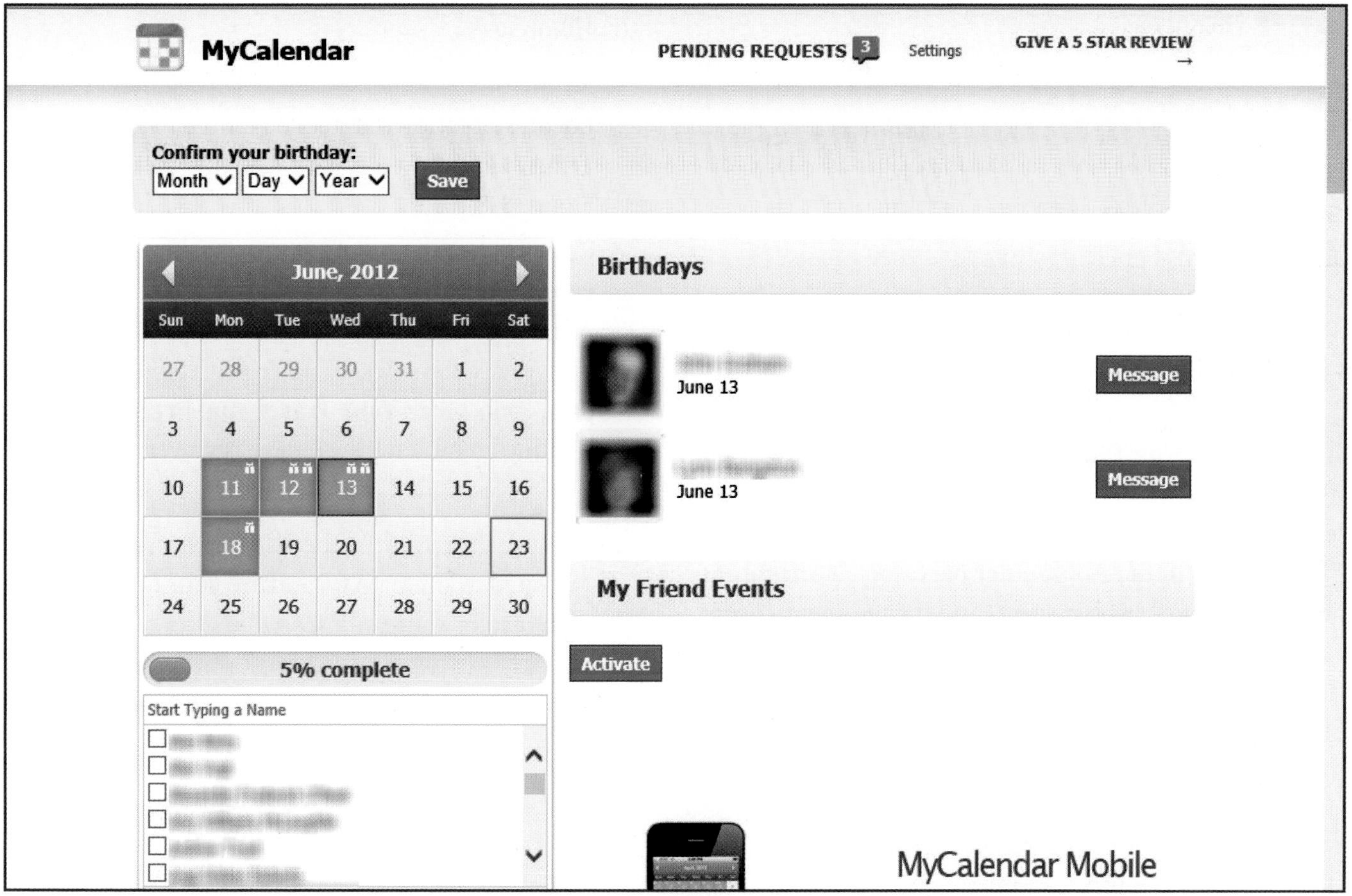

Figure 8-7: **MyCalendar-Birthdays gives you a nice visual picture of your friends' birthdays and lets you easily add others.**

8. You will be asked if you want to send the request and what it will say. If you do, click **Send Request**; otherwise, click **Cancel**.

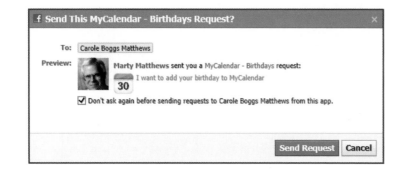

9. When a friend's birthday is displayed, you can click **Message** to send them a greeting.

▷▷ Judge Apps

Most apps are created by organizations other than Facebook, and as a result provide a wide variety of experiences and levels of sophistication. If you find an app in which you might be interested, check out its pages in Facebook *before* using the app itself—type its name in the search text box at the top of the Facebook page. In the App Center page, look at the rating (anything below four stars is suspect) and the number of users or players. Also see if any of your friends are using it. None of those items give you an absolute measure of the app, but they help you get a feel for it. The objective is to determine whether you should use the app. Only you can make that choice. For most apps, your risk can be mitigated by careful, commonsense usage. See "Stay Safe with Games" later in this chapter. Much of the discussion also applies to other apps.

Use TripAdvisor

TripAdvisor allows you to create an interactive travel map you can share with your friends. TripAdvisor is a large online travel community that includes a website (tripadvisor.com) separate from Facebook. On Facebook, TripAdvisor currently has over 10 million users.

1. From your Home page click **App Center**, click **Travel & Local**, scroll down if needed, and click **TripAdvisor**. The TripAdvisor App Center page will open, as you can see in Figure 8-8.

2. Read the description of TripAdvisor and what it will do with your information. When you are ready, click **Go To App**. After choosing friends to invite to participate with you in TripAdvisor, you'll see the TripAdvisor–Cities I've Visited page open. Click **Your Travel Map** in the menu bar to start pinning your own travel map, as you can see in Figure 8-9.

3. Start in one of three ways:
   - Click the cities in the list on the right that you have visited, want to go to, and are your favorites. Click **Next** to display more cities.
   - Begin to type the name of a city, and a list of matching cities will appear. Click the city you want, and click **Add To Map**.

Figure 8-8: **The TripAdvisor app is used to show where you have been and where you want to go.**

Figure 8-9: *You can tell your friends where you have been and help them in their travel plans.*

- Double-click the map several times until you have magnified it to the point you can see the city you want to add. Drag the map using the hand icon to find the country or area you want, and then click the city (or region if you don't see the city), and in the latter case click the city in the list displayed.

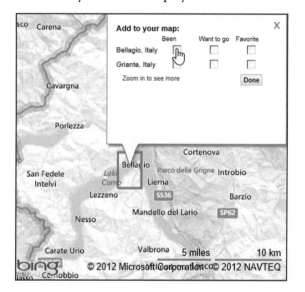

4. When you have added all the cities you want, click **Done** to the right and below the map.

5. You can see your friends' maps and compare them with yours by clicking **Friends** near the top and selecting the friend from the photos. The friend's map will be displayed with their pins next to yours, comparing the number of cities, countries, and ratings each of you have, as shown in Figure 8-10.

⏩ Remove an App

You can hide or remove an app from your Home page's left column and from your Facebook account, and control its settings through its context menu.

1. To hide an app in the left column, hover the mouse over the app icon or name, and click the pencil icon on the left to open a context menu.

2. Click **Add To Favorites** to add the app icon and name to the list of favorites at the top of the left navigational column. Once you've done that, this option becomes Remove From Favorites.

3. Click **Edit Settings** to open the Edit Settings dialog box. The contents of this vary, depending on the app. Generally, you can control the same elements that you could when you originally signed up for the app, as well as control the overall privacy setting.

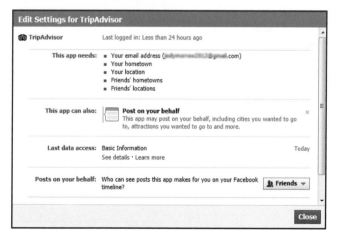

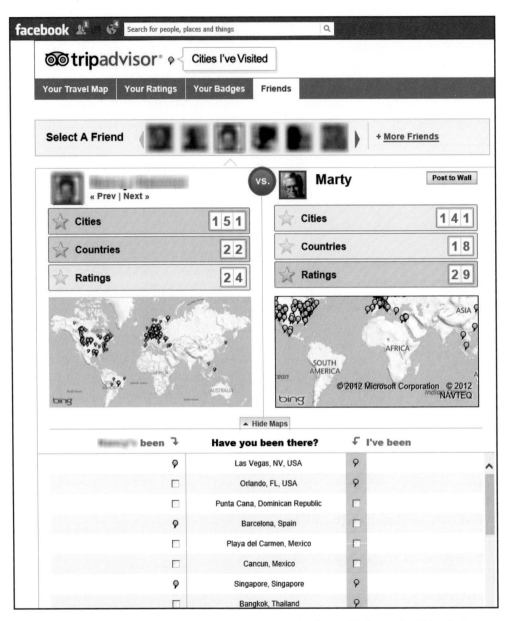

Figure 8-10: Comparing your travels with your friends can be fun and help you find friends that might help you with a trip.

4. To remove an app from your Home page and your Facebook account, click **Remove App** on the bottom of the dialog box. You are told that this will also prevent the app from having access to your profile and other Facebook data. If that is what you want, click **Remove**.

> **Note** You can also delete an app from the Privacy Settings page. Click the **Account** down arrow, and then click **Privacy Settings**. At the bottom, opposite Ads, Apps, And Websites, click **Edit Settings**. Beside Apps You Use, click **Edit Settings**. Next to the app you want to delete or change, click the **X** to remove the app and click **Remove** to confirm it. Click **Edit** to display the app's options in the Edit Settings dialog box shown elsewhere in this chapter.

ENJOY GAMES

We all need to relax occasionally, and playing games is a way that a lot of people like to do that. Games can get competitive juices flowing, and with Facebook games, you can interact with your current friends, meet new friends, and build community around a fun activity. On Facebook you have access to a large number of games, most of which are social games you play with others who are or become your friends. As with any social activity, you need to use good common sense to protect yourself. In this section we'll explore several of the more popular games and then discuss how to stay safe while you play them.

▶▶ Use Games

Facebook games are just Facebook apps that you can start and manage in much the same way as was discussed in the "Use Apps" section.

1. From your Home page click **App Center** on the left of the page to open the App Center shown in Figure 8-1 earlier in this chapter.

2. Click **Games** to review lists of top-rated, recommended, trending, and games your friends play, as shown in Figure 8-11.

3. Click **Friends'** to review the games your friends play and through which you might enjoy connecting with them. Look also at the other tabs (Top Rated, Suggested, and Trending) to see the many games that are available.

4. If you see a game that interests you, click that game. If you don't see something that grabs at you, click the categories on the left under Games that hold possibilities for you, and see if there is anything there you want to try. You can also try searching for games not in the categories listed by typing such queries as <u>war games</u> or <u>fantasy games</u> to search those categories.

5. If you know or have heard of a game on Facebook and don't quickly see it in the lists, type its name in the search text box to see if it can be found.

After selecting and opening the game you want to play, you need to follow a combination of sparse instructions, instinct, and help from your fellow game players to find your way through the game. Here we'll look at several popular games to give a brief look at how they are played.

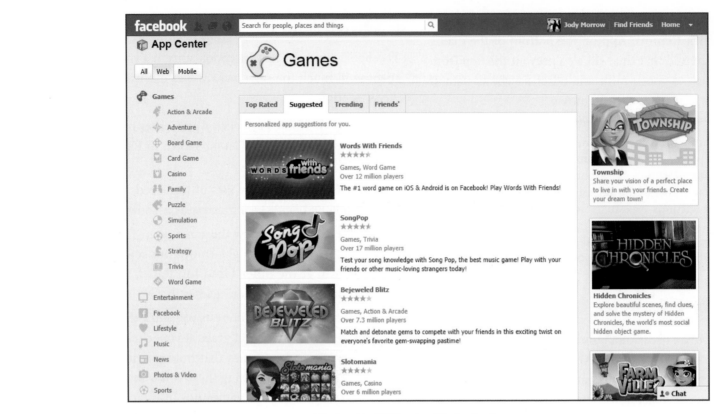

Figure 8-11: **Games are a great way to find and build friends while having fun.**

Use CityVille

CityVille is a very popular Facebook game from Zynga with over 30 million players. CityVille allows you to create a virtual city from scratch by constructing buildings, collecting rent and income, and growing crops to feed your city.

1. In any of the ways just discussed, locate and click **CityVille** to open its Facebook page. Review the description and how the game uses your information.

2. When you are ready to start playing, click **Play Game**. The CityVille game page will open and you can start playing, as you can see in Figure 8-12.

3. Click **OKAY** to start playing. You will see a suggestion such as to become Mayor or build a house.

Figure 8-12: At the beginning of CityVille, you see a lot of suggestions to get you started.

4. Click **Build**, click the little house on the left (not that you have any choice), and follow the remaining suggestions.

5. Soon you will see why the developers build these games. You will see offers to add "coins" and "cash." This will open a page allowing you to buy the fake coins and cash for real money. If you click this, you are taken to the page shown in Figure 8-13, where you can carry out the transaction. You can do this if you wish, but you don't have to.

> **Note** You may see pop-ups appearing on your screen. If you don't want to engage with them, just click **Cancel** or **Close**. They can be confusing and disorienting. Just push them aside (cancel or close them) until you're ready to go forward.

6. There will be many pop-ups suggesting things that you can do. Add houses, businesses, and farms to your city. There are also "gotchas" where you are told you can't do

Figure 8-13: *Many games are a money-making proposition: the developers make it; you pay for it!*

something before you do something else that costs coins, cash, energy, and so on. You have to figure out how to keep moving ahead without running out of resources.

> **Note** You may see offers, like the one shown next, for CityVille cash for free. These are often an excuse to get your name, email address, and your IP address (the Internet address of your computer) and force you to watch several ads that try to sell you things. I would stay away from these offers.

> **Shonta**
> "★★★★★" I just found a legit website that is giving away free 310 cityville cash in less than 5 minutes! CHECK IT OUT HERE!! ENJOY ★♥♥♥♥♥♥
> http://tinyurl.com/G4M3R99 ♥♥♥♥♥★
> 2 hours ago · Like · Comment

Use Texas HoldEm Poker

This game claims to be the world's largest Texas HoldEm poker game. Facebook says there are over 33 million players. You can play with your friends or make new friends while playing. You are periodically given some chips to play with; you can win chips if you are lucky; and you can buy chips, but you cannot cash in chips for money.

1. In any of the ways discussed earlier, locate and click **Texas HoldEm Poker** (or Zynga Poker) to open its Facebook page. Review the description and how the game uses your information.

2. When you are ready to start playing, click **Play Game**. The Texas HoldEm Poker page will open and you can start playing, as you can see in Figure 8-14.

3. If you are new to Texas HoldEm Poker, click **Learn To Play**. A poker table is displayed. Click **Start** and you are led through four lessons on poker hands, betting basics, smart folding, and the game interface. Click **Next** as needed to proceed through the lessons. In the Interface lesson, move your mouse around the poker table, pausing at each question mark to read the comment (see Figure 8-15). When you are ready, click **Done** and then click **Exit Tutorial**.

4. Click **Close** in the Welcome box. You are forced to accept the offer to send you email, and the Request For Permission page opens. If you want to go ahead, click **Allow**.

Figure 8-14: *Texas HoldEm Poker is a real poker game with other players, just not for real money.*

Figure 8-15: **Even if you are an old hand at poker, the tutorial is worth going through.**

5. To start playing, click **Play Now**. A long list of tables will appear. If you are just starting out, look for a table labeled NewUser or Novice with low stakes, like this:

HOLD'EM		TOURNAMENTS		VIP CLUB	
Table Stakes:	All ▼		Normal	Fast	
Room	**Stakes**	**Min/Max Buyin**	**Players**		
⬛ MyAce 1	10 / 20	200 / 4K	- / -	📷	
NewUser 5	1 / 2	20 / 40	4 / 9	📷	
NewUser 6	1 / 2	20 / 40	6 / 9	📷	
NewUser 9	1 / 2	20 / 40	4 / 9	📷	
Novice - Singles 2	1 / 2	20 / 40	3 / 5	📷	
Novice - Social 1	1 / 2	20 / 40	7 / 9	📷	
Novice - Social 3	1 / 2	20 / 40	5 / 9	📷	
Novice - StackEm 2	1 / 2	20 / 40	4 / 5	📷	

Hide Tables: ✔ Empty ✔ Full   REFRESH LIST   JOIN TABLE

6. When you have found such a table, click it and click **Join Table**. You are reminded of the terms of service. Click **Okay** and begin to play.

Tip When you start out playing Texas HoldEm Poker, it is my experience that the game goes rather quickly and you have to fully pay attention to not get left in the dust.

Use Café World

Café World is a role-playing game from Zynga similar to CityVille and FarmVille. In it you run your own restaurant, choosing the dishes to cook and then preparing them. You can invite your friends to help you in a number of ways. Café World has over 3 million monthly active users. You start out with some supplies and will need to buy more with the profits from your business. When you first enter Café World, you open the Play Now page. Explore a bit by looking at the Info, Reviews, and Wall pages.

1. In any of the ways discussed earlier, locate and click **Café World** to open its Facebook page. Review the description and how the game uses your information.

2. When you are ready to start playing, click **Play Game**. The Request For Permission dialog box will open.

3. If you want to play the game, click **Allow**, click **OK** to accept a notice, click **Female** or **Male**, and click **Next**. The Café World page will open. (See Figure 8-16.)

4. Click a stove, and you will be presented with a menu of things you can cook—initially, the selection is pretty limited.

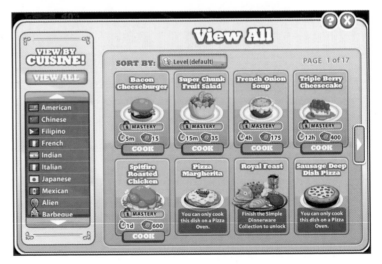

Figure 8-16: *Café World keeps you busy preparing food and upgrading your café.*

5. You need to select items to cook, add stoves to cook more items, add tables to serve more people, and so on. By selling items you make coins to buy more items. You also need to accomplish certain steps, like finishing a spice rack, adding tables and chairs, and so on.

Like all Zynga games, you can spend real money to buy coins and cash, but there is no need to do that if you are patient.

With either type of request, you can accept it by clicking **Accept** or reject it by clicking the **X**. If you reject the request, you can block all requests from a particular game or ignore all requests from a particular person. If you are becoming irritated with requests from either a game or from a person, block or ignore them—there is no need to suffer.

One type of request I often reject are those ostensibly from a friend offering a lot of resources with which to play a game. These often lead to a site where you have to provide your email address as well as other information and have to go through several advertisements to have a *chance* at winning something.

▶▶ Stay Safe with Games

Your safety while playing Facebook games is really not that much different than it is anywhere else in Facebook. The possible exception is that when you are enjoying yourself and you are looking for help or some resource while playing a game, you might let down your guard a bit. Sometimes, exuberance in playing a competitive game can overcome common sense. There are two situations to consider:

- Getting requests to join a friend in playing a game you haven't tried

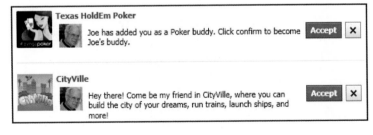

- Getting requests for help and resources from friends while playing games you have signed up for

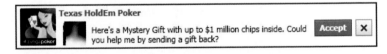

Like Facebook in general, consider who you want for your friends, whether it is friends in general or friends while playing a game. How well do you know them? What are you telling them while in a game? What can they do with the information they are getting about you? It's one thing to be reasonably cautious, but at the same time you don't want to get paranoid.

It is also wise to not invite all your friends to play a game. Some of them might not be your friends for long if you do this. Before asking them, consider if the game you are asking them to join is really their cup of tea. If you don't know, don't ask them, or at the very least, in a regular email ask them if they would like such an invitation.

See the next section "Edit and Manage Apps" and Chapter 10 for a further discussion of apps and Facebook security.

EDIT AND MANAGE APPS

You should closely manage apps, including games that you use within Facebook, to give you what you want from the app and to provide the security you need. There are two areas you should review to edit and manage apps: within the app itself and in Facebook.

▶▶ Edit App Settings

Some apps have settings that you can control to tailor your experience with that app and give the level of security you want. Not all apps have settings, and those that do call them by several names. An example of an app that has controllable settings is TripAdvisor, where you can set member preferences.

On TripAdvisor you can create a profile with your preferences and control subscriptions to online information.

1. From the TripAdvisor home page (www.tripadvisor.com), scroll down to the **Quick Links** section and, under Member Preferences, click **Update Your Profile Or Subscriptions**. You may need to sign in, and then the Profile page opens, as you see in Figure 8-17.

2. Read the note at the top telling you that the information on this page is public, and with that in mind, fill out the information you want to be public by clicking **Edit**, first for your information and then again for your travel preferences.

3. By clicking the options on the left you add or change your photo, change your account information, review the compliments you have received for your reviews, and change the relationship between your Facebook and TripAdvisor accounts.

4. By clicking **Subscriptions** on the left you can control the email information you receive from TripAdvisor, which can be extensive.

5. Similarly, by clicking **Contributions**, you can keep track of your reviews; by clicking **Messages**, you can reference recent email; by clicking **Trips**, you can build and store a detailed plan for a trip; by clicking **Travel Map**, you can maintain the travel maps you have created; and by clicking **Travel Network**, you can enable or disable the following of your friends' travel reviews, as well as the sending and receiving of private messages through TripAdvisor.

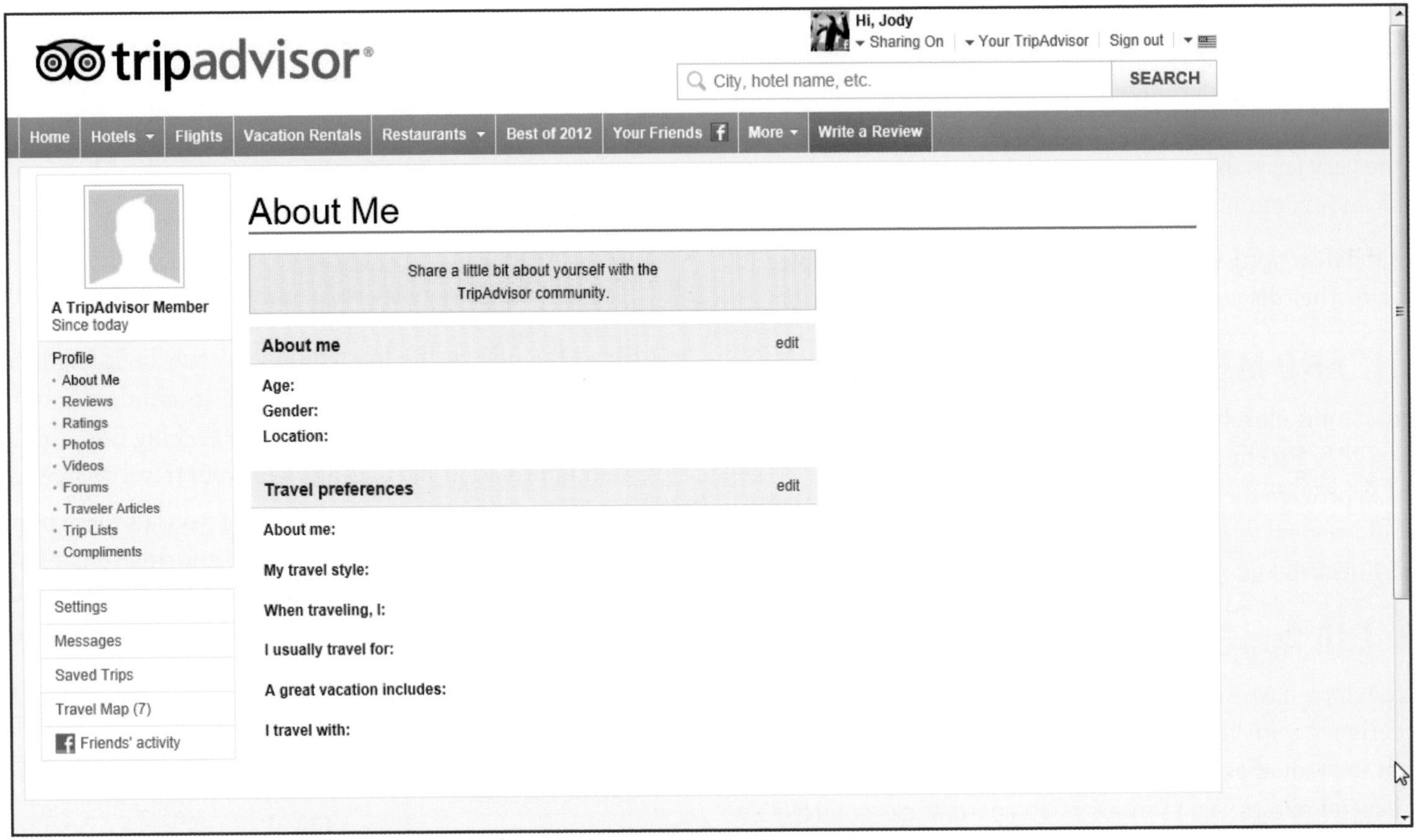

Figure 8-17: *TripAdvisor gives you a moderate degree of control over your experience on its site.*

⫸ Manage Apps in Facebook

Facebook gives you a number of settings to control apps and gives you some degree of protection from them.

1. From your Facebook page, click the **Account** down arrow in the upper-right corner, and click **Privacy Settings**.

2. In the lower part of the page, opposite Ads, Apps, And Websites, click **Edit Settings**. The Choose Your Privacy Settings page will open, as you see in Figure 8-18.

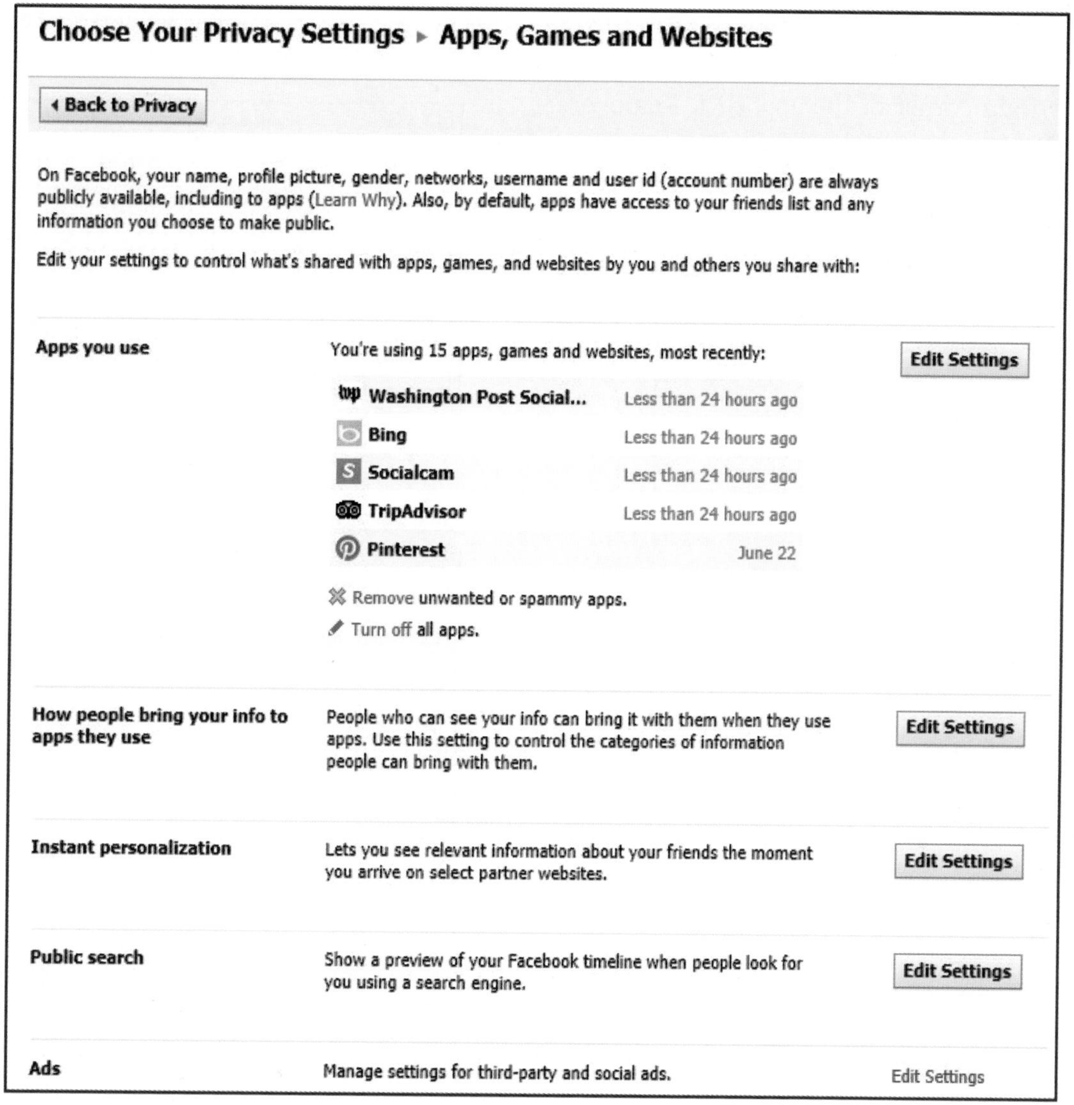
Choose Your Privacy Settings ▸ Apps, Games and Websites
Back to Privacy
On Facebook, your name, profile picture, gender, networks, username and user id (account number) are always publicly available, including to apps (Learn Why). Also, by default, apps have access to your friends list and any information you choose to make public.
Edit your settings to control what's shared with apps, games, and websites by you and others you share with:
Apps you use
You're using 15 apps, games and websites, most recently:
Edit Settings
Washington Post Social... Less than 24 hours ago
Bing Less than 24 hours ago
Socialcam Less than 24 hours ago
TripAdvisor Less than 24 hours ago
Pinterest June 22
Remove unwanted or spammy apps.
Turn off all apps.
How people bring your info to apps they use
People who can see your info can bring it with them when they use apps. Use this setting to control the categories of information people can bring with them.
Edit Settings
Instant personalization
Lets you see relevant information about your friends the moment you arrive on select partner websites.
Edit Settings
Public search
Show a preview of your Facebook timeline when people look for you using a search engine.
Edit Settings
Ads
Manage settings for third-party and social ads.
Edit Settings

Figure 8-18: ***If you will take the time to review your settings, Facebook provides the means to control your information.***

3. Opposite Apps You Use, click **Edit Settings** to open a list of the apps and games you use. For each one, you can click the **X** on the far-right corner of the app, click **Remove**, and then click **Okay** to remove the app from your site and your Profile page. Of course, you also lose any history and accomplishments within the app.

App Settings

You have authorized these apps to interact with your Facebook account:

wp Washington Post Social Reader	October 21	Edit	×
Bing	More than 6 months ago	Edit	×
S Socialcam	More than 6 months ago	Edit	×
TripAdvisor	Less than 24 hours ago	Edit	×
Pinterest	More than 6 months ago	Edit	×
Cities I've Visited	June 12	Edit	×
Yearbook	October 28	Edit	×
We're Related	More than 6 months ago	Edit	×
M Mashable	More than 6 months ago	Edit	×
S Scribd	More than 6 months ago	Edit	×
ShareThis	More than 6 months ago	Edit	×
SSApplication	More than 6 months ago	Edit	×
Socialite (Windows 8 Developer Preview)	More than 6 months ago	Edit	×

4. Also, opposite each app or game you can click **Edit** to expand the app entry to show the original settings you agreed to when signing up for it. For the most part, you cannot change those, but here with Mashable you can change who sees posts the app makes and whether you receive notifications.

M Mashable	Last logged in: February 1	Remove app
This app needs:	• Your email address (marty@whidbey.com)	
Last data access:	No data access recorded Learn more	
Posts on your behal	Who can see posts this app makes for you on your Facebook timeline?	Everyone ▾
Notifications:	When to notify you?	The app sends you a notification ▾

✓ The app sends you a notification
Never

Close

5. You can also remove the app by clicking **Remove App**, and you can see the information that has been mined from your Facebook account by clicking **See Details** opposite Last Data Access. When you have reviewed the information, click **Close**.

Access Log

In the last 90 days, TripAdvisor accessed the following information on your behalf:

Basic Information	Today
Education History, Likes, Music, TV, Movies, Books, Quotes, Current City and Work History	Today
My Friends' Education History, Current Cities and Work History	Today

Learn more about the data shown here   Close

6. Once again click the **Accounts** down arrow in the upper right; click **Privacy Settings**; click **Edit Settings** opposite Ads, Apps, And Websites; and then click **Edit Settings** opposite How People Bring Your Info To Apps They Use to open a dialog box of that name. This is one of the most valuable dialog boxes in Facebook because it allows you to control the information that is available to apps that your friends are using.

How people bring your info to apps they use

People on Facebook who can see your info can bring it with them when they use apps. This makes their experience better and more social. Use the settings below to control the categories of information that people can bring with them when they use apps, games and websites.

- ☐ Bio
- ☐ Birthday
- ☐ Family and relationships
- ☐ Interested in
- ☐ Religious and political views
- ☐ My website
- ☐ If I'm online
- ☐ My status updates
- ☐ My photos
- ☐ My videos
- ☐ My links
- ☐ My notes
- ☐ Hometown
- ☐ Current city
- ☐ Education and work
- ☐ Activities, interests, things I like
- ☐ My app activity

If you don't want apps and websites to access other categories of information (like your friend list, gender or info you've made public), you can turn off all Platform apps. But remember, you will not be able to use any games or apps yourself.

[Save Changes] [Cancel]

7. We recommend that you seriously consider turning off most, if not all, of the check boxes in this dialog box and click **Save Changes**.

8. Click **Edit Settings** opposite Instant Personalization, and consider whether you want apps to personalize their sites for you with your information. In some cases, that is pleasing and worthwhile. Watch the video and click **Close**.

Decide if you want to change the default of enabling instant personalization, and then click **Back To Apps**.

9. Finally, click **Edit Settings** opposite Public Search, and consider if you want your information available to public search engines like Google and Bing from your Facebook site. This is enabled by default. Click the check box to disable it and then click **Confirm**.

10. When you are done, return to your Home page.

Note Seeing the information that was mined from my friends' Facebook sites as the result of my agreeing to give an app access to my site was a little scary, but even worse is the information that is taken off my site when my friends use apps. This is all the more reason to thoroughly check the information you have on Facebook often.

Chapter 9

Creating Pages and Facebook Ads

A Facebook Page (with a capital "P") is oriented toward promoting a person, product, cause, or other entity. It is more official and business-like than your personal page (with a lowercase "p"). Pages are where you present yourself, your products, and your cause to the world, and they are public—that is, they are available to anyone on Facebook. Pages must be created by people who are official representatives of the entity.

Facebook people who "like" the Page, or become its fans, receive any posts created on the Page on their News Feed. If they like the post, they share it with others, just like how a normal Facebook page functions. In addition, you can promote your Page in various ways to get more people to "like" your Page. This is how a business or entity can broadly communicate with its customers, clients, or fans simultaneously.

CREATE A PUBLIC PAGE

Creating a public Page is somewhat of a process. You create the basics, add the photos and other interesting elements, and invite viewers, also called fans. Although the flag for making the Page visible is turned on by default, you can turn it off, making the Page invisible to the world until you're ready to *publish* it, or make it visible again. While it is invisible, the Page is only visible to its Admins. (See "Publish Your Page.")

Set up the Public Page

Setting up a public Page involves first naming the Page, categorizing it, and then adding photos and friends and fans to participate in your Page.

1. If this is the first Page you'll create, scroll to the bottom of the Home page, and on the link bar click **Create A Page**. You'll see the page displayed in Figure 9-1.

 Tip If your Home page is too long to find the bottom easily, click any other page—for example, the Account Settings page—to find the bottom link bar more easily.

Figure 9-1: Facebook has templates from which you can choose for your Page.

–Or–

If this is not your first Page, click any Page name in the left column of the Home page. Click **Create Page** on the top right.

| Create Page |

You have these options describing the type of Page you want to create:

- Local Business Or Place
- Company, Organization, Or Institution
- Brand Or Product
- Artist, Band, Or Public Figure
- Entertainment
- Cause Or Community

2. Click the type of Page that fits your needs. You'll see a group of text boxes, with some differences between the types of Pages. At a minimum:

   - Click the **Category** down arrow, and select the category that matches your entity.
   - Type the **Name** of the business, product, organization, artist, entertainment, or cause.
   - Click **I Agree With Facebook Pages Terms**.

Brand or Product

Choose a category ▼

Brand or Product

☐ I agree to Facebook Pages Terms

Get Started

3. Click **Get Started**. You'll see a three-step process, beginning with inserting an image or photo, as shown in Figure 9-2. Note that you do not have to complete the setup process right now. You can skip these steps and come back to them later.

Set Up Genealogy for Seniors QuickSteps

1 Profile Picture 2 About 3 Facebook Web Address

Upload From Computer | Import From Website

Save Photo | Skip

Figure 9-2: Once you have named your Page, you can begin a three-step process to fill in the details.

Work Through the Entry Form

1. In Step 1 you have the option of uploading an image from your computer or importing it from a website. You can select one of these choices:

   - Click **Upload From Computer** in Step 1, Profile Picture. A browser window will open so you can find the path to your photo or graphic. Double-click the image to upload it. You'll see the image replace the profile photo placeholder, an example of which is shown in Figure 9-3. Click **Next** to go to Step 2.
   - Click **Import From Website** in Step 1. In the Website text box, type the Uniform Resource Locator (URL) of the website where you expect to find the image. Click **Import**. Click the left and right arrows until you find the image you want. Click **Select Image**. You'll see the

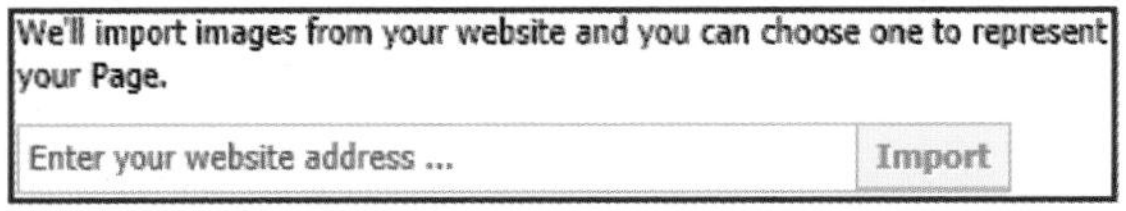

We'll import images from your website and you can choose one to represent your Page.

Enter your website address ... | Import

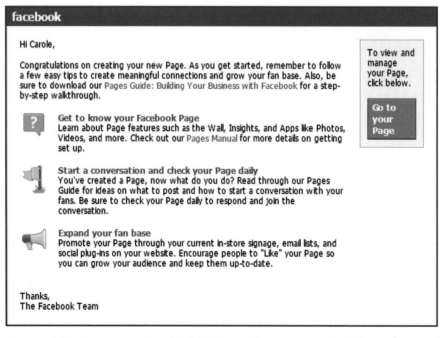

Set Up Genealogy for Seniors QuickSteps

1 Profile Picture   2 About   3 Facebook Web Address

Upload From Computer   Import From Website

Next

Figure 9-3: The uploaded image replaces the Facebook placeholder.

image replace the profile photo placeholder. Click **Next** to go to Step 2.

- Click **Skip** to do this later.

2. Now you will be asked to enter some basic information about your Page. Click in the appropriate text boxes and add a description and then your website page, Twitter, or other website address. Click **Add Another Site** to enter multiple URLs. When you are satisfied, click **Save Info** to save your information. You can also click **Skip** to enter a description later.

3. At this point your new Page will be displayed. You will also receive an email message telling you some basic info on how to proceed with your Page. See Figure 9-4.

An example of your new page is shown in Figure 9-5.

facebook

Hi Carole,

Congratulations on creating your new Page. As you get started, remember to follow a few easy tips to create meaningful connections and grow your fan base. Also, be sure to download our Pages Guide: Building Your Business with Facebook for a step-by-step walkthrough.

? **Get to know your Facebook Page**
Learn about Page features such as the Wall, Insights, and Apps like Photos, Videos, and more. Check out our Pages Manual for more details on getting set up.

Start a conversation and check your Page daily
You've created a Page, now what do you do? Read through our Pages Guide for ideas on what to post and how to start a conversation with your fans. Be sure to check your Page daily to respond and join the conversation.

Expand your fan base
Promote your Page through your current in-store signage, email lists, and social plug-ins on your website. Encourage people to "Like" your Page so you can grow your audience and keep them up-to-date.

Thanks,
The Facebook Team

To view and manage your Page, click below.

Go to your Page

Figure 9-4: You'll get an email with helpful hints of how to proceed building your Page.

Figure 9-5: Once you have entered basic information, your Page is ready to be tailored to your needs.

Note Click **Hide** in the Admin Panel menu bar to switch between seeing what others see, and seeing your Admin Panel. "Hide" hides the Admin Panel; "Show" shows the Admin Panel.

⫸ Understand Facebook Terms for Pages

Before you can create a Page, you must agree to certain terms:

- You must be authorized to represent the product or entity in order to create the Page.

- You cannot solely use a generic name or description, such as "Coffee" or "Hot," unless it is part of the name—for example, "Tucson's Hot Coffee." You cannot use abusive language in your name.

- Names cannot use improper grammar or excessive punctuation, cannot be all capital letters, and cannot use symbols other than alphanumeric characters.

- If you collect information about your users, you must obtain their consent, specify that you are the one collecting the information—not Facebook—and provide a policy statement telling how you are using the information and who else has access to it.

- You cannot identify on the Page which people visit your site.
- Applications and any promotional activities must comply with Facebook's Platform Policies and Promotions Guidelines.
- You cannot have third-party ads on your Page, and your own advertising on your page must comply with Facebook Advertising Guidelines.

Facebook terms are revised periodically, so you must review them yourself to know what is currently required.

Add a Page Image

If you have skipped adding an image during the setup phase, you can still add a logo, a photo, or graphic showing what it is that you are promoting with your Page. Also, once you have added an image, you can change it. The image displays as a square and must be no smaller than 180 × 180 pixels.

1. On your Facebook Home page, find the Pages list in the left column. (You may have to click **More** to see it.) Then click the Page name to be edited.

2. On your Page, click **+Add Profile Picture** located on the image placeholder or click **Edit Profile Picture** to change it. A menu is displayed:

- To take a picture with a webcam, click **Take Photo** (refer to Chapter 1 for further instructions).

- To download a photo or graphic from your computer, click **Upload Photo**. Find the path to your photo or graphic and double-click the image to upload it. You'll see the image replace the profile photo placeholder.
- If you have uploaded other images and the profile picture is among them, click **Choose From Photos**. Then click the image you want.

When you complete installing your profile picture, you'll want to select a cover photo.

Add a Cover Photo

The cover photo is placed as a banner across the top of your Page. Your Profile Photo is set up against it, as seen in Figure 9-6. The best cover photo is one that is not used for sales or promotions, but which represents what your Page is about. In fact, there are some rules about what your cover photo cannot contain:

- Any notation of price, or a cost figure, or promotional figures, such as 25% Discount.
- No instructions about where or how to get the product, such as another webpage or contact or email information, or what to do next to get it.
- No calls to Like or Share the Page.

- No false or untrue information, which can trick others into thinking the product is something other than what it is.

- No violating intellectual properties belonging to others.

- The image should not be smaller than 399 pixels wide.

All cover images are public, so anyone coming to your page will see it. Images are displayed as 851 (wide) × 315 (tall) pixels.

1. To the right of the profile picture, click **Add A Cover**.

2. Click **Okay | Upload Photo** to acknowledge what you're doing and display your computer file manager, such as Windows Explorer.

3. Find the path to your photo and double-click it. The image will be displayed on the top of your Page.

4. If you want to, you can drag the photo at this point to reposition in the banner.

5. Click **Save Changes**.

 Tip To reposition the cover photo after you've saved it, hover your pointer over the photo and click **Change Cover | Reposition**. Then drag the photo as you want it. Click **Save Changes** to finalize it.

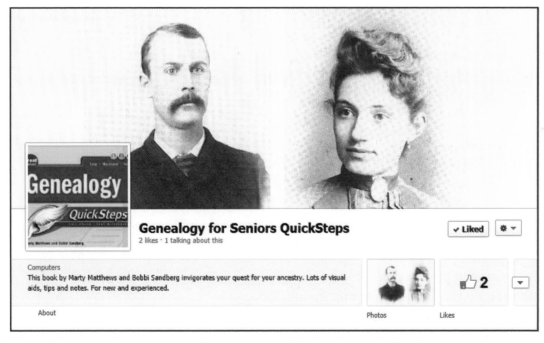

Figure 9-6: A cover photo can personalize your Page, making it unique and tailored to your content.

Freya Builds Face into a Page

The technical setup for my Facebook Page for a nonprofit organization was straightforward and easy to do. Exploring the "face" of our organization has taken more time in learning how to best portray it through Facebook options. A few online classes enabled me to learn how to tailor possible special options. (I attended CharityHowTo.com.)

At first, a central thing to learn was the type of presentation and questions that would successfully engage our "customers." I needed to expand from an *advertising* approach that merely announced a new program or activity, to more *specific types of questions* that invite visitors to engage with our mission and ideas. It's about thinking with a community engagement mindset. This required me to think through what I can do realistically in terms of my time and attention to the Page, and what information is needed and natural to my organization. Facebook is one window for the world to view us, and it is important to be true to our mission and approach.

It's been a slow journey, but the Page and I are coming into alignment with the social-media community.

Freya S., 58, Washington

Build an Audience

Your objective with a Page is to get others to look at it and, perhaps, take an action. If you elected not to invite your friends to look at your Page during the setup, you can still invite them now. You can invite friends in three ways: inviting your email contacts, inviting your Facebook friends, or sharing your page. You can upload a maximum of 5,000 contacts. People who are not Facebook members can still see your Page profile information—the photos and basic information—but they cannot post to your Page or see other posts.

Invite Your Email Contacts

This approach imports contacts from web-based services, such as Yahoo! or Hotmail. (At the time this was written, in order to import from Gmail, you must log into Gmail and create an export file and then upload it into Facebook. The form for enabling you to do this is found under Other Email Service.)

1. In your Admin Panel at the top of your Page, click **Build Audience | Invite Email Contacts**.

2. Next to the email servicer you use, click **Invite Contacts**:

   - Use **Other Email Service** if you don't use the services listed, such as for Gmail.
   - Use **Other Tools** to upload a comma-separated value (CSV) or tab-delimited contact file from specific email programs, such as Microsoft Outlook Express. When you choose this option and click the email service you use, you will be given directions on how to create the contact file. Then you browse for it and upload it into Facebook.

3. Type in your email address and click **Find Contacts**. You may need to enter a password to sign in to your email account. (Note that Facebook does not store your password as one of its security measures.) You may need to negotiate a second sign-in or password entry dialog box for the mail system itself and click **Sign In** to complete the sign-in process. After you have signed in, your contacts will be downloaded and you'll see a list of contacts, such as that seen in Figure 9-7.

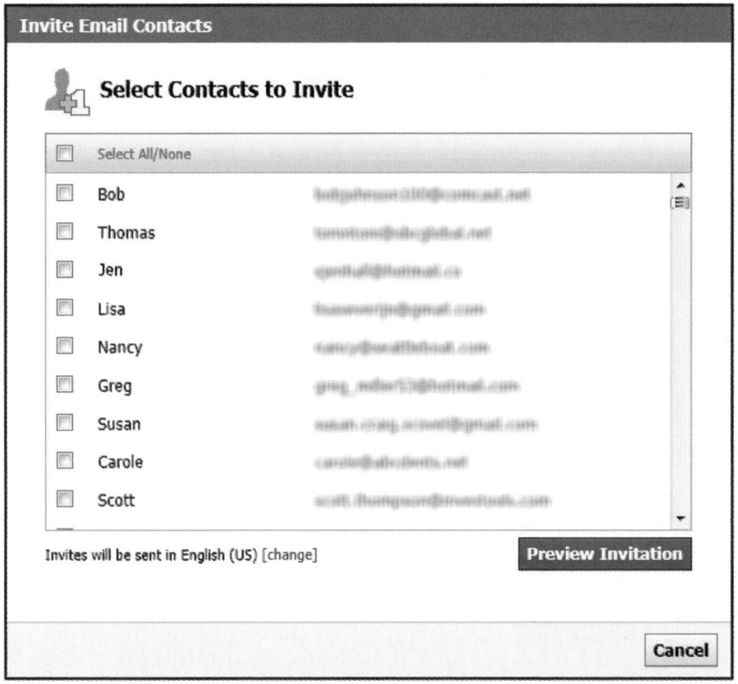

4. Click the names of the contacts you want to invite to view your Page. Click **Preview Invitation** to see the invitation and continue the process. Figure 9-8 shows an example.

5. You must click the check box beneath the invitation to ensure that you have the correct authorization to send invitations to your email addresses.

6. When you are ready, click **Send**. The invitations to join Facebook will be sent to your selected contacts.

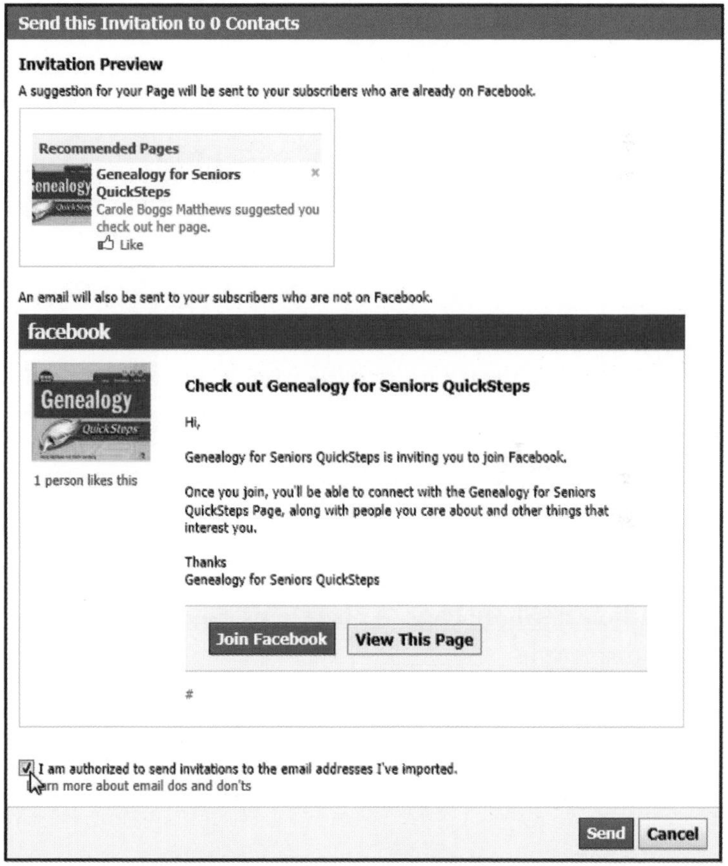

Figure 9-7: Increase the number of fans on your Page by importing contacts from your computer contact list or web email account.

Figure 9-8: An invitation to join Facebook so that non-Facebook friends can view your Page will be sent to contacts from your email service.

Invite Friends

Perhaps your first option to get viewers is to notify your Facebook friends. You have a ready reservoir of people available to become your fans.

1. In your Admin Panel at the top of your Page, click **Build Audience | Invite Friends**. A list of your friends will be displayed.

2. If you wish to filter your list of friends, click **Recent Interactions** and click the group or list you wish to display.

3. Place a check mark next to the friends you wish to invite to view your Page.

4. Click **Submit**.

Share the Page

1. In your Admin Panel at the top of your Page, click **Build Audience | Share Page**. A Share This Page dialog box will be displayed.

Share This Page

Share: On your own timeline ▾   👥 Friends ▾

Write something...

Genealogy for Seniors QuickSteps
Computers
Page · One likes this
◄ ► 1 of 1 Choose a Thumbnail
☐ No Thumbnail

Share Page   **Cancel**

2. Click the **Share** down arrow and choose where to share the page: on your own or a friend's Timeline, in a group, on your page, or in a private message. When you click your sharing destination, you'll be asked for specifics, such as which friend's Timeline.

3. Click in the text box and type a short message introducing your page.

4. Click the **No Thumbnail** check box if you do not want the image to show in the post.

5. Click **Share Page**.

▷▷ Post Status Updates

Posting status updates is how you communicate with your fans or customers. It is the same procedure as when you post a message in your personal Facebook account. If your Page is published, the posts will appear in your Page Wall and on your fans' or supporters' News Feeds. If the Page is unpublished, the Page itself is invisible to all except the Admins, so no one else will see it (see "Publish Your Page").

To post a status update:

1. On your Page, click in the **Write Something** text box and type a post.

2. Click **Post**.

Note You can attach a link on your Page. Find the link you want and copy it. Then on your Page, click in the **Write Something** text box and paste or type in the URL address of the link. A thumbnail and short description will be automatically displayed on the Wall.

Publish Your Page

Your Page can be made invisible, or hidden to the world at large, until you "publish" it, even to those fans you have invited to see your page. For instance, you might want to hide it until your Page is exactly the way you want it or while you update it or make changes. If your Page is unpublished, you'll see a banner across the top of your page.

⚠ This page has not been published. Learn about **unpublished pages** and **publish this page** when you are ready.

Make Your Page Visible

To publish your Page, or make it visible:

Click **Publish This Page** on the banner on the top of the Page screen.

–Or–

On the Page's Admin Panel, click **Edit Page | Manage Permissions**. In the Manage Permissions panel, click the **Page Visibility** check box to clear the check mark. Click **Save Changes**.

Page Visibility: ☐ Unpublish page (only admins can see this page)
What is this?

Unpublish or Hide a Page

You can hide a Page to all fans and supporters by making it invisible. Then, after you have updated the Page, or come back from vacation, for example, you can make it visible again.

1. On the Page's Admin Panel, click **Edit Page | Manage Permissions**.

2. Click the **Page Visibility** check box to place a check mark there.

3. Click **Save Changes** on the bottom of the panel.

Promote the Page with Plugins

You can incorporate several *social plugins*, or Facebook programs that enhance or add to a Page's basic capabilities. The Like box is one of these. You embed code in your website outside of Facebook that allows visitors to "Like" your Facebook Page even if they don't ever see it. You can see an example on the right of Figure 9-9. A Like box is embedded in your website allowing people to click "Like" for your Page. The box tracks the number of people and optionally shows a thumbnail of all who support your Page. (These directions are similar to those you would use for other plugins, such as to link your Page to Twitter.)

1. On the Admin Panel of your Page, click **Edit Page | Update Info**. From the left menu, click **Resources**.

2. Under Connect With People, click **Use Social Plugins**.

Resources	Connect with people
Admin Roles	
Apps	Advertise on Facebook
Mobile	Invite Email Contacts
Insights →	
Help →	Use social plugins

3. Scroll down the list of social plugins and click **Like Box** (ignore the Like Button). A page similar to that shown in Figure 9-9 is displayed. On the left you see the settings for your Like Box, and on the right is an example of what it will look like.

4. Complete the Like Box form (you can click the question mark to the right of each entry to see Facebook's explanation):

- For the Facebook Page URL, go to your Page, select its URL in the browser's address bar at the top of the browser window, and copy it (click the address to highlight it and press **CTRL+C**). Come back to the Like Box page, and paste the address into the text box (click in the text box and press **CTRL+V**). This is used to identify the location when the link in the Like Box to your Facebook Page is clicked.

- Click in the **Width** text box, and type the width in pixels of the box. Do the same with the **Height**.

- Click in the **Color Scheme** text box, and choose between **Light** and **Dark**.

- If you do not want thumbnail images to show of the people who click "Like," click **Show Faces** to remove the check mark. Otherwise, do not change the setting.

- If you do not want to show streaming News Feeds from your Page, click **Stream** to remove the check mark. Otherwise, do not change the setting.

- If you do not want the header "Find Us On Facebook" to show, leave the check mark in the check box. The default is No Header. This header will only be shown when either Show Faces or Stream, or both, are also selected. Otherwise, do not change the setting.

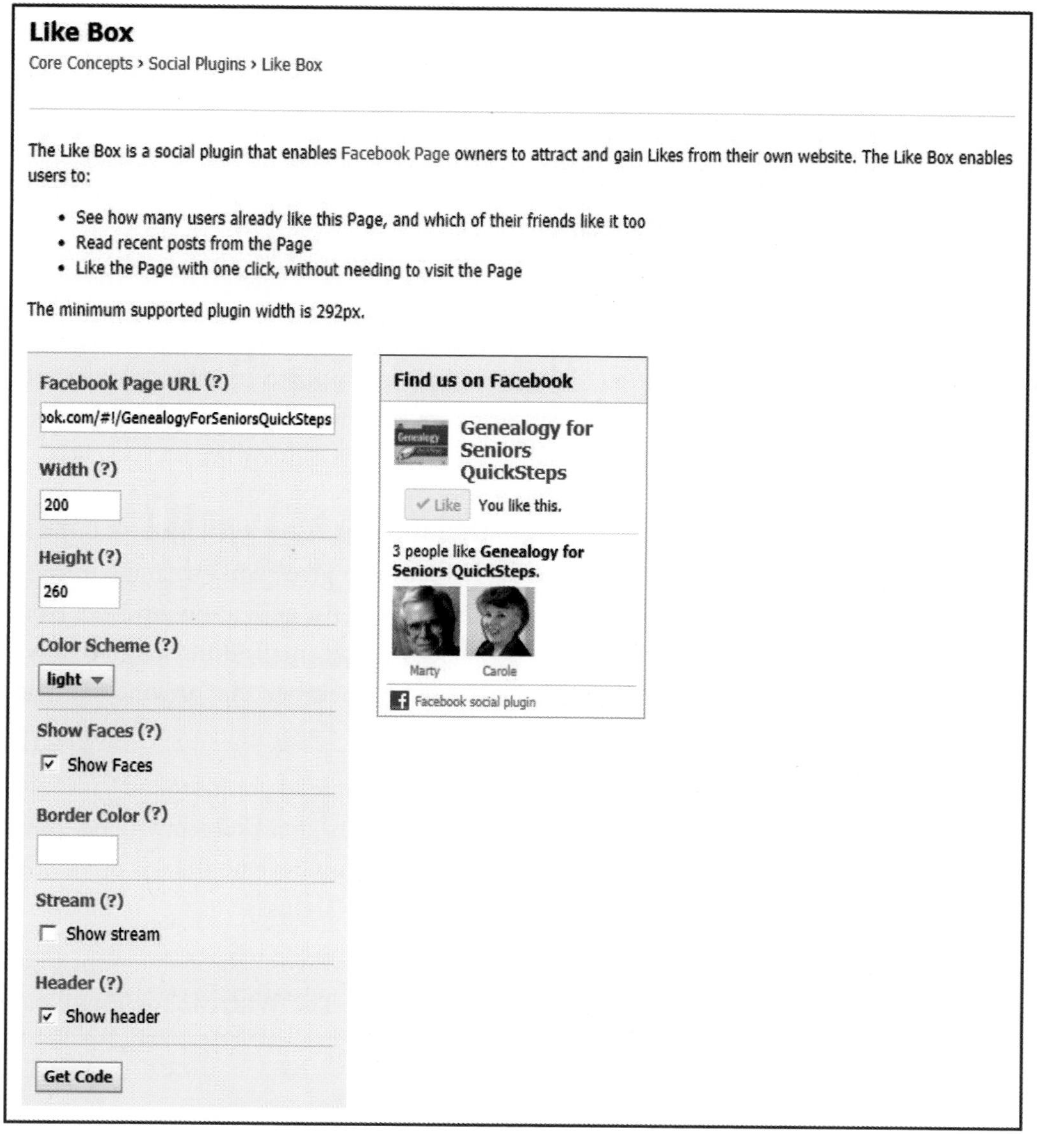

Like Box

Core Concepts › Social Plugins › Like Box

The Like Box is a social plugin that enables Facebook Page owners to attract and gain Likes from their own website. The Like Box enables users to:

- See how many users already like this Page, and which of their friends like it too
- Read recent posts from the Page
- Like the Page with one click, without needing to visit the Page

The minimum supported plugin width is 292px.

Facebook Page URL (?)

ook.com/#!/GenealogyForSeniorsQuickSteps

Width (?)

200

Height (?)

260

Color Scheme (?)

light ▼

Show Faces (?)

☑ Show Faces

Border Color (?)

Stream (?)

☐ Show stream

Header (?)

☑ Show header

Get Code

Find us on Facebook

Genealogy for Seniors QuickSteps

✓ Like   You like this.

3 people like **Genealogy for Seniors QuickSteps**.

Marty   Carole

Facebook social plugin

Figure 9-9: Social plugins, such as the Like box, allow you to promote your Facebook Page on your website rather than within Facebook.

5. Click **Get Code** to get the code needed to embed a Like Box in your website. The Your Like Box Plugin Code dialog box is displayed with two versions. The first, iFrame, uses relatively standard code for websites, while the second, XFBML, uses some Facebook enhancements.

Your Like Box plugin code:

`HTML5`   XFBML   IFRAME   URL

1. Include the JavaScript SDK on your page once, ideally right after the opening <body> tag.

```
<div id="fb-root"></div>
<script>(function(d, s, id) {
  var js, fjs = d.getElementsByTagName(s)[0];
  if (d.getElementById(id)) return;
  js = d.createElement(s); js.id = id;
  js.src = "//connect.facebook.net/en_US/all.js#xfbml=1";
  fjs.parentNode.insertBefore(js, fjs);
}(document, 'script', 'facebook-jssdk'));</script>
```

2. Place the code for your plugin wherever you want the plugin to appear on your page.

```
<div class="fb-like-box" data-
href="https://www.facebook.com/GenealogyForSeniorsQuickSteps" data-
width="292" data-show-faces="false" data-border-color="black" data-
```

Okay

6. Copy the version of the code that you want, and paste it into your website's code, placing the second code grouping where you want to see the Like box. This process will require knowledge of Hypertext Markup Language (HTML) code and where and how to insert this into your own webpage. If you want to change any of the features outside of the dialog box, you will also need knowledge of JavaScript and HTML. An example of what you can expect is shown in the left column in Figure 9-10.

Tip We've found that simply plugging in the Facebook Like Box code all in one spot where you want the Like Box placed is the easiest way to go. You can do this using the iFrame alternative.

Note Social plugins are available to expand and enhance your Page. They require embedding program code into another website outside of Facebook. They require knowledge of web programming and website maintenance to implement.

Set Up a Mobile Phone

You can set up your Facebook Page to accept status updates and photo or video uploads from mobile phones. This allows you to keep tabs on your Page, regardless of whether you have a computer handy or not.

Update Your Page with Mobile Email

This feature gives you an email address where you can send photos, videos, and status updates from your mobile phone. The Facebook email address is saved as a contact in your mobile phone. Remember that anyone can use the email address to update your Page, so protect it and keep it secure.

When you upload photos to the Facebook Page using this email address, your email subject will be used as the photo or video caption. If you have no photos or videos, the subject is used to update your status.

1. On your Page's Admin Panel click **Edit Page | Update Info | Mobile**. The With Mobile Email panel will open.

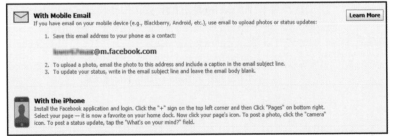

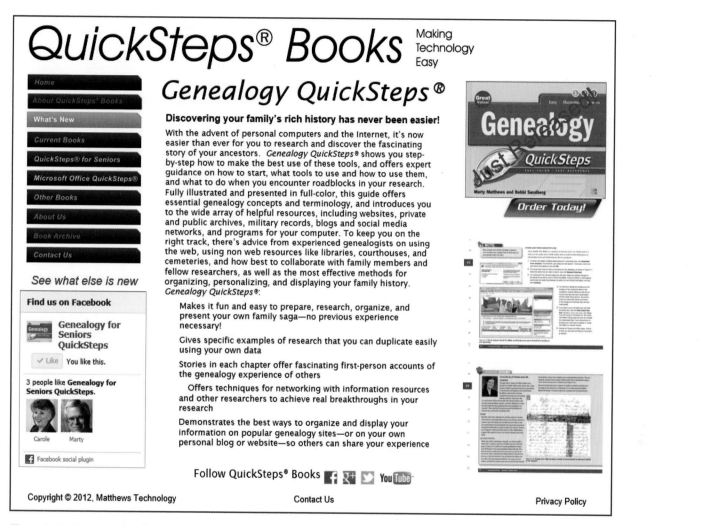

Figure 9-10: **An example of how you might use a completed Like box**

2. Copy the "*someaddress*@m.facebook.com" email address onto your phone as a contact.

3. See Chapter 5 on how to send updates to your Page via email. You'll see that the instructions for the iPhone are different from other devices, such as the Android, etc.

EDIT YOUR PAGE

Once your Page is created, you'll want to make changes. You can change most characteristics of the Page using the Edit Page button. When you click that, you have many options.

Add or Remove Admins

You may find that you want to add or remove Admins for the Page. When you add an Admin, you are giving that person permission to make changes to the Page, including adding other Admins. The only restriction is that someone you add as an Admin cannot remove you. You must first remove yourself to allow someone else to be "first in line."

Add an Admin

You can add an unlimited number of Admins to the Page. Their duties can be specialized so that not all Admins have equal access or ability to change the Page.

1. On your Page's Admin Panel, click **Edit Page | Admin Roles**. You'll see a panel similar to that in Figure 9-11.

2. Click in the **Type A Name** text box, and start typing the name of a confirmed friend of your primary Facebook account who you want to add as Admin. As you type, a list of candidates will appear. Click the name you want, and a thumbnail will be displayed.

3. Click **Manager**. A menu will appear that defines what level of access the Admin will have:

- **Insights Analyst**   Can view Insights.
- **Advertiser**   Can view Insights and create ads.
- **Moderator**   Can do what the Advertiser can do, plus send messages as the Page and manage comments.

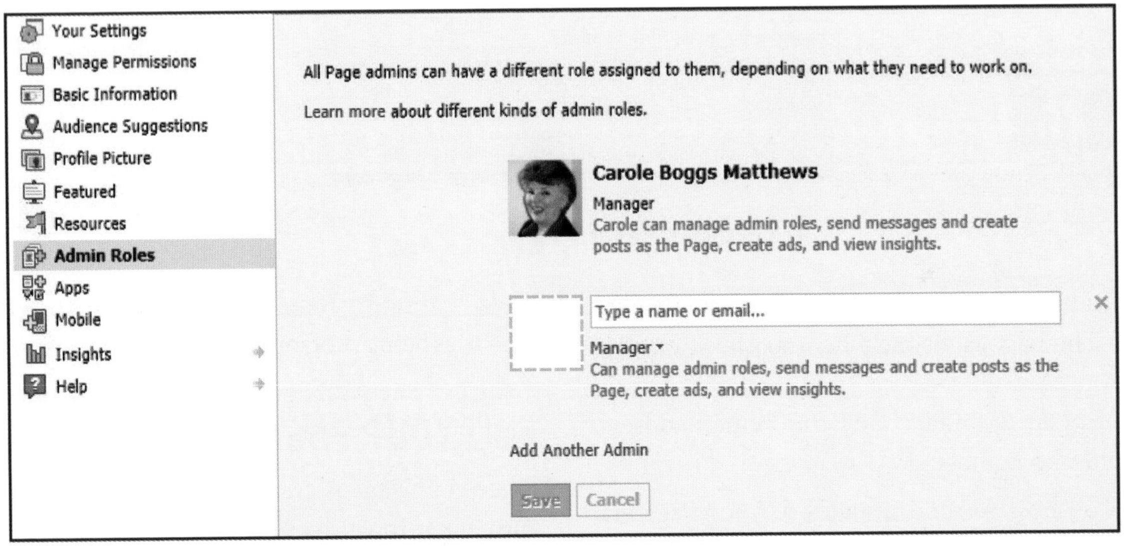

Figure 9-11: *You can add and delete other Admins of the Page, making it easier to maintain and support your fans.*

- **Content Creator** Can do what the Moderator can do, plus create posts and edit the Page and add Apps.

- **Manager** Can do everything on the Page, plus add and delete Admins.

4. If you have another Admin to add, click **Add Another Admin** and do the same as in Step 2.

5. Click **Save**. You see a Change Page Admins dialog box.

6. Type your Facebook password, and click **Confirm**.

Remove an Admin

1. On your Page's Admin Panel, click **Edit Page | Admin Roles**.

2. Click **Remove** (the **x**) to the right of the name you want to remove, and click **Save**.

3. Type your Facebook password, and click **Confirm**.

▷▷ Control Who Sees Your Page

You can tailor your Page to the people most likely to be interested in your product or entity.

1. On your Page's Admin Panel, click **Edit Page | Manage Permissions**. The page displayed in Figure 9-12 is displayed. You have these options:

- **Page Visibility** Makes your Page invisible, even to its supporters. This is a way you can turn its availability on and off. The page is visible when no check mark is present.

- **Country Restrictions** Lists only the countries that are allowed to view or not view your Page. If you do not enter any countries, viewers from all countries can see your Page, which is the default. If you enter a country name,

click one of the options beneath to specify whether the country is able to view or not view the Page.

- **Age Restrictions** Limits the age of viewers. This may be needed for videos, photos, or language that is more appropriate for adults. Over age 13 is the default.

- **Posting Ability** Defines whether users can post content, add videos, or add photos to your Page. If you do not want to allow others to do this, clear the check marks. The default is to allow all viewers to post or add photos and videos.

- **Post Visibility** Allows others to choose to see the most recent posts by others. It is connected with the option **Default Visibility Of Posts By Others**, which sets the default of whether posts by others can be seen on the Page's Timeline or not.

- **Tagging Ability** Determines whether viewers can tag photos on this Page.

- **Messages** Allows others to leave a private message for you by displaying the message button or not.

- **Moderation Blocklist** Allows you to define certain words or phrases, separated by commas, that cannot be posted to your site. If someone uses these, their post will be marked as spam and only you can see it.

- **Profanity Blocklist** Allows you to define certain words as being profane. In this case, the post will not be allowed.

2. Click **Save Changes** to make your permissions permanent.

 Tip To see who "Likes" your page, in the Admin Panel, click **See All** in the New Likes box. If you don't see the New Likes box, click **Show** in the Admin Panel menu bar.

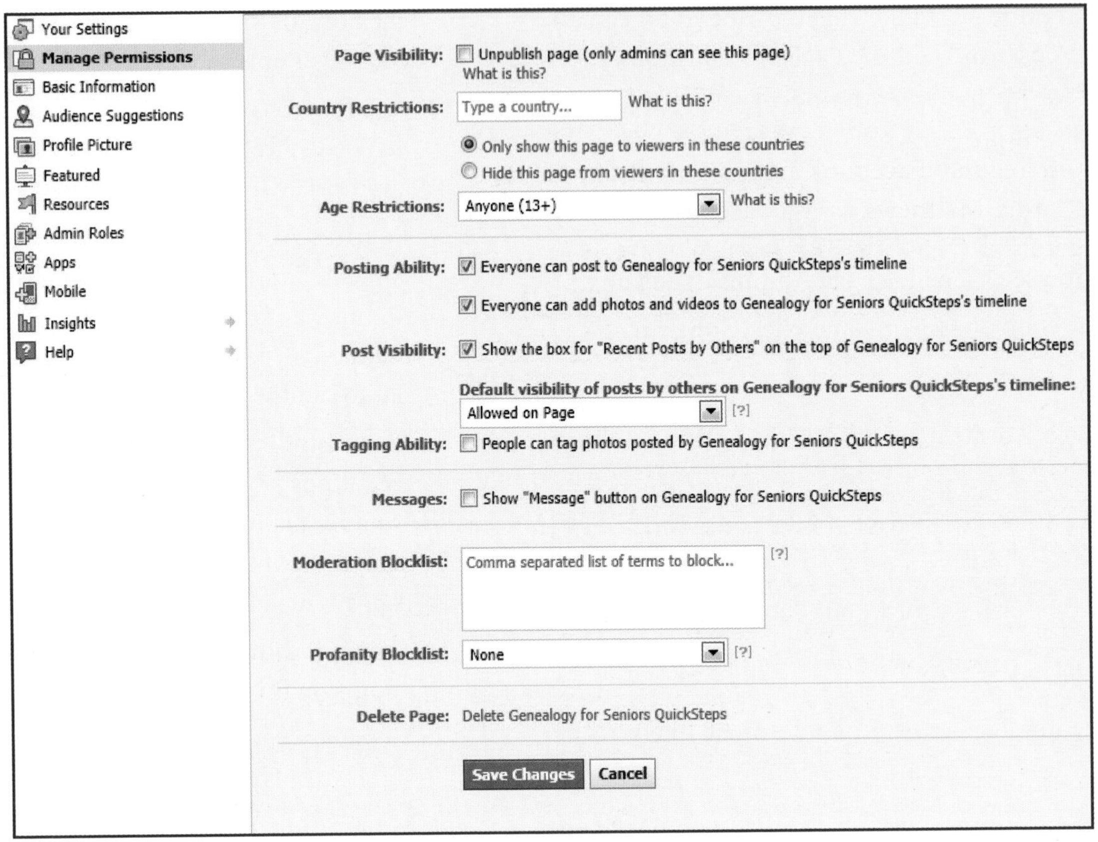

Figure 9-12: *You can define in broad terms who your viewers may be.*

⏩ Delete Your Page

1. On your Page's Admin Panel, click **Edit Page | Manage Permissions**.

2. Click the **Delete Page** link.

3. Confirm you want to delete it by clicking **Delete Page**.

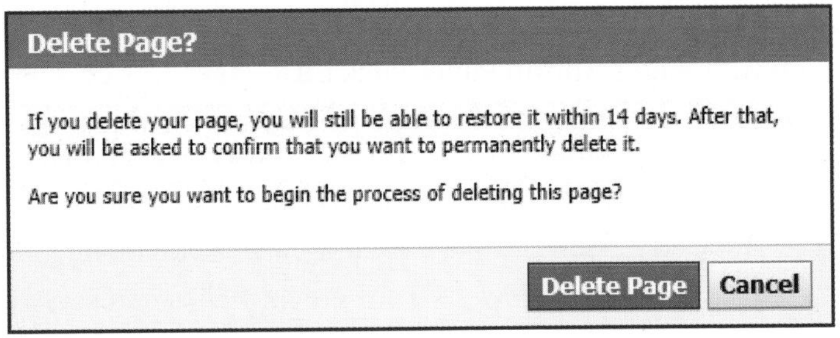

Delete Page?

If you delete your page, you will still be able to restore it within 14 days. After that, you will be asked to confirm that you want to permanently delete it.

Are you sure you want to begin the process of deleting this page?

[Delete Page] [Cancel]

Use Facebook as Your Page

Switching to Facebook as your Page allows you to choose between being identified by your Page name and being identified by your regular Facebook name. For instance, I currently use Carole Matthews as my Facebook identity. When I post to my Page, QuickSteps Books, I am still Carole Matthews. I can switch this if I choose to always be QuickSteps Books. It is important to realize that if you switch, you can immediately switch back.

Switching identities makes your Page the way everyone sees you on Facebook, and the way you see yourself. For instance, you will notice that when you click Home, you see your Page, not your original Facebook pages with all your friends. Your Home page will display a different set of News Feeds, for instance, from other pages you "like." Your Profile shows your Page Wall as others see it. Your original pages are not gone; they are hidden while your Page is being used as your Facebook site. When you reverse the switch, you'll see your original Home and Profile pages again.

To determine which works for you, you need to answer the question: Is my Page the reason I have a Facebook account? Or is my Page something ancillary to my Facebook identity? If you want to use your Page as your primary Facebook identity:

From your Page's Admin Panel, click **Edit Page | Use Facebook As *page***. The identity of the Page will be switched from your name to your Page. This means that your posts from this site will be labeled with your Page name, not your personal name.

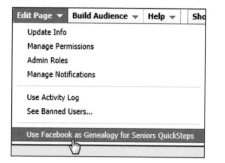

- You will now be notified when others click on or post to your Page, not to your personal Timeline.
- You can now find other Pages to like and comment on using your Page name.
- You'll now have a News Feed just for your Page that is connected to other Pages that you or other Admins have "Liked."
- You can reverse this setting and restore your original Facebook name at any time.

Reverse the Switch

If you want to return to using Facebook as your name:

From your Page's Admin Panel, click **Edit Page | Use Facebook As *yourname***. The identity of the Page will be switched from your Pages to your own name. This means that your posts from this site will be labeled with your own personal name, not that of your Page.

Like Another Page

Featuring other Pages on your own allows you to reach out to a broader community, letting viewers know something more about you. It can be a marketing tool as well, getting your own Page recognized by other Pages. To like or comment on other Pages, you must be switched to Use Facebook As Your Page.

Here is what you need to do to "Like" another Page.

1. Switch your Facebook identity to your Page. To do this, refer to "Use Facebook as Your Page."

2. Search for or otherwise open the Page you want to like.

3. Beneath the cover photo, to the right of the name, click **Like**.

▶▶ Adjust the Page Profile Picture

Your profile photo is used wherever your Page is referenced. It is important—both for personal and professional reasons—to have it be the image you are seeking. If the photo is not exactly what you want, you can delete or replace it or reposition the image to show parts of it more clearly.

1. Hover your pointer over the profile photo. Click **Edit Profile Picture**. A menu will be displayed.

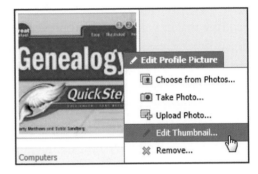

2. You have these options:

- To replace this photo with another one, click **Choose From Photos** to select from uploaded photos, **Take Photo** to use the webcam to take a photo, or **Upload Photo** to upload a new photo, depending on how you want to select your replacement picture.

- To drag your image and reposition it, click **Edit Thumbnail**. Your cursor turns into a crosshair image. Using it, drag the image where you want it placed.

Click **Scale To Fit** to scale the image to fit the space. Click **Save** to retain the new position.

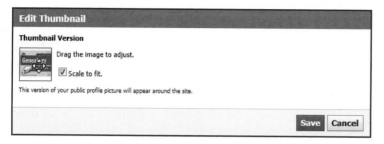

3. To delete the photo, click **Remove**.

Change the Page's Basic Information

Basic information includes everything essential about you. You see it on the Info page—your Page profile—and it gives your fans a way to know about your mission and background. Here is where people will understand who you are and why you are inviting them to look at your Page, so you want the information to be interesting and authentic. To change basic information:

1. From your Page's Admin Panel, click **Edit Page | Update Info**. The Basic Information panel is displayed, as shown in Figure 9-13.

2. The page for editing your basic information is displayed:

   • Click in each text box or click the down arrows, and type or select the contents.

   • Proceed through the form until all the information you want to reveal is entered.

3. Scroll to the bottom, and click **Save Changes** to retain your changes.

4. Click **View Page** in the upper-right corner to return to your Page.

Manage Your Posts

You can manage your posts by placing them in favored positions, deleting them, or pinning them to the top of the post list.

Star a Post

To make a post larger and more prominent on your page:

1. Hover your pointer over the post.

2. Click the **Star**. The post will be expanded to fill both columns, such as seen in Figure 9-14.

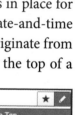

Pin a Post

Pinning a post at the top of a Page displays it more prominently and flags it for readers. The pinned post remains in place for seven days, and then is returned to its posted date-and-time slot. To be pinned at the top, the post needs to originate from the Page (not by a reader). To place a post near the top of a Timeline:

1. Hover your pointer over the post.

2. Click **Edit** (the pencil icon) | **Pin To Top**. The post will be moved to the top of the post list, and a bookmark displayed on the upper right.

Hide a Post

When you hide a post, it is removed from being seen by others. However, any photos will still be visible in the Photos view. Some posts cannot be hidden.

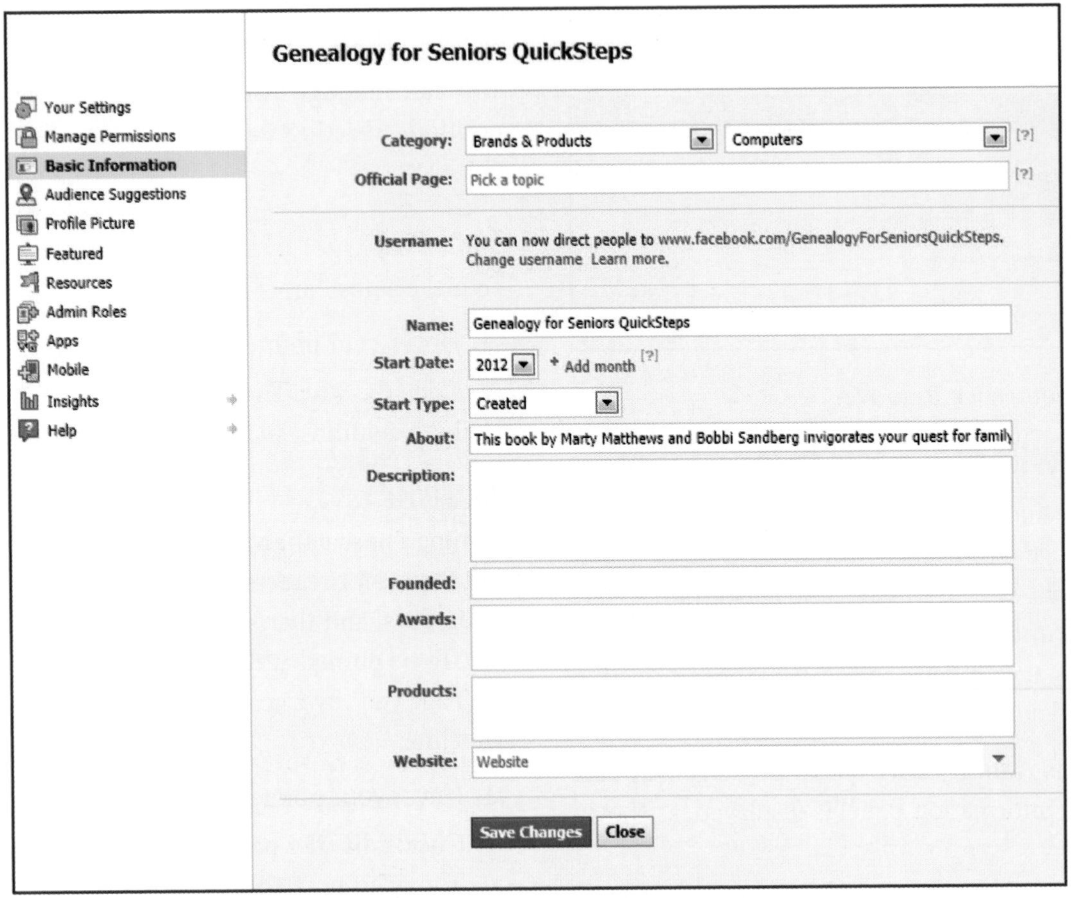

Figure 9-13: *Your basic information is displayed on the Page's Update Info page.*

To hide a post from showing:

1. Hover your pointer over the post.

2. Click **Edit** (the pencil icon) | **Hide From Page**. The post will be hidden from view on the Timeline. You'll see a message on your Page where the item was posted. You can click **Undo** at this time to repost it.

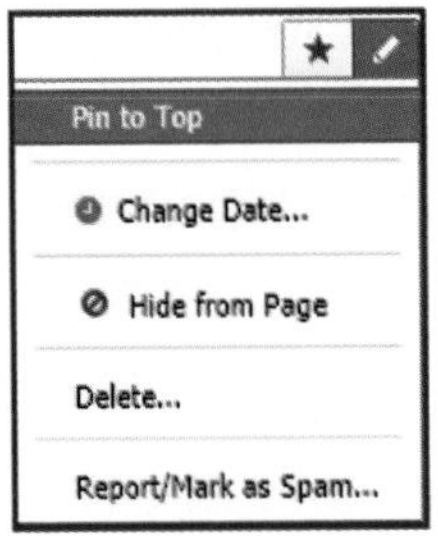

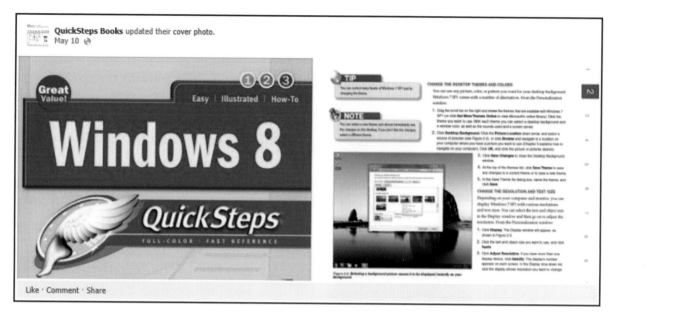

Figure 9-14: A post can be "starred," which expands it, giving it more display space.

Tip To unhide a post after you've hidden it, on the Admin Panel, click **Edit Page | Use Activity Log**, scroll to the hidden item, and click the **Hidden from Page** icon on the right.

Delete a Post

When you delete a post, it is deleted from your Timeline. There is no way to get it back. Some posts cannot be deleted.

To delete a post:

1. Hover your pointer over the post.
2. Click **Edit** (the pencil icon) | **Delete**.
3. Confirm that you want the post deleted. Click **Delete Post** again.

Schedule Your Post Time

You can create your posts and publish them later by scheduling when they are to be published. To publish your post for a specific date and time:

1. In the Write Something text box, type your post as usual.
2. Before posting it, click the **Schedule** icon.
3. Click the **Add Year** down arrow and select a year; the month will appear. Select the **Add Month** and the day will appear. Continue until you have the exact time and date you want the post published.

4. Click **Schedule**.

Block Keywords or Profanity

You can block certain keywords from being posted on your Page. When people type in the blocked words, the content is marked as spam.

1. On the Admin Panel, click **Edit Page | Manage Permissions**. The Manage Permissions pane is displayed.

2. You have these options:

- In the **Moderation Blocklist** text box type the keywords you wish to block. Separate them with commas.

- Click the **Profanity Blocklist** down arrow, and select the degree of profanity you wish to block: **None** (the default) for no blocking, **Medium** to select commonly used profanity, and **Strong** to block the strongest, most offensive words.

3. Click **Save Changes**.

Keep Track of Your Traffic

Facebook tracks some interesting statistics about the traffic crossing your Page. It tracks the size of your audience (who "Likes" you or comments on a post), whether they pass it on to other Pages, and displays reactions to posts by percentages, numbers, and graphically. An example is displayed in Figure 9-15.

1. On your Page beneath the cover photo, click the **gear icon | View Insights**. You'll see an Overview view. You have these options:

- Click **Overview** to see an overview of how widely your posts have been circulated. This is the default view.

- Click **Likes** to see who has "Liked" your page by gender and age, by country, and how many are new "Likes."

- Click **Reach** to see the demographics of the span of your reach by gender, age, and country. You can see the frequency and dates of your reach and the visits to your Page by date. You can see the number of unique visitors.

- Click **Talking About This** to see the demographics of those who have talked about your page by sharing or commenting on posts by age, gender, and country. You can see how they have talked about your posts: by the number of Likes, stories from your posts, mentions and photo tags, or posts by others.

- Click **Export Data** to download the statistics to an Excel (.xls) or comma-separated text format (.csv) file so that you can work with the numbers.

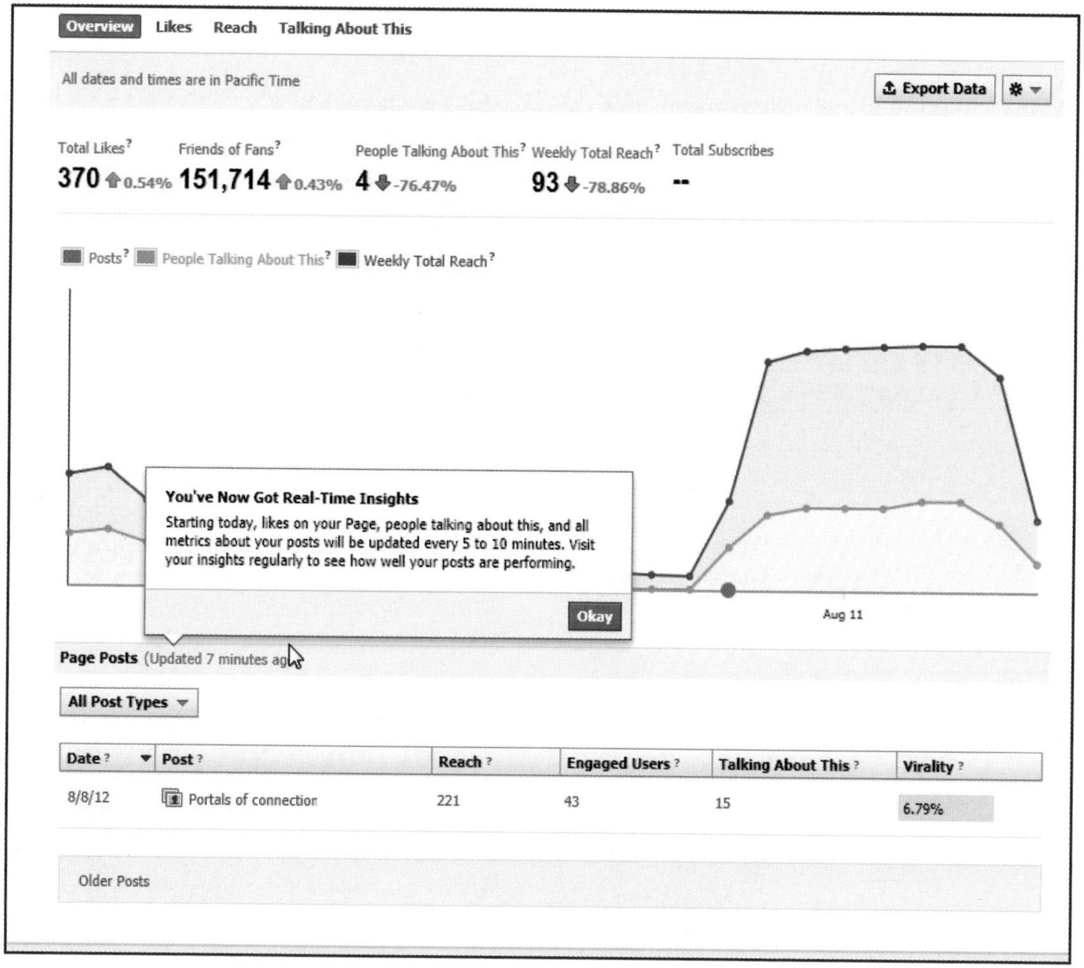

Figure 9-15: A sampling of the statistics you can see about your Page

- Click the **gear icon** to get additional information on how to understand the Insights pages.

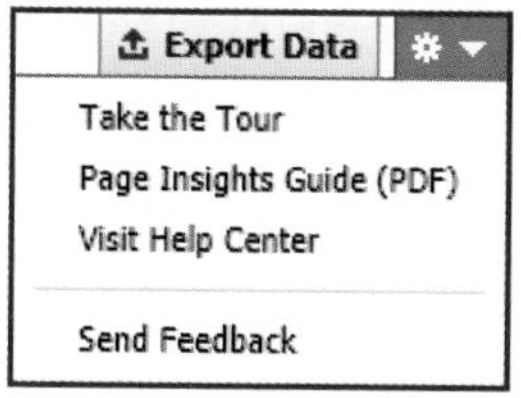

⬆ Export Data	☀ ▾
Take the Tour	
Page Insights Guide (PDF)	
Visit Help Center	
Send Feedback	

▶▶ Register a Username

As the Admin of a Page, you can request a ***username***, similar to the username for your personal Facebook page. A username is simply a shortened name for your Page that makes it easier to use as a URL to the Page. For example, in the URL http://www.facebook.com/*username* you can use a name that is the same as your business or product, making it instantly recognizable and easy to remember and reference.

The only rules are that before you can obtain a username, you must have at least 25 followers or fans. The name itself must be yours to obtain—that is, you must have the right to use the name. It must be alphanumeric with no special characters (except it can contain a period). The name cannot be generic, such as "flower" or "music." (That would allow unfair advantages to someone who could claim the URL http://facebook.com/flowers, for example.) The username must be specific to your Page.

Facebook claims that each Page can have one username specifically for it. Each Page must fit the eligibility criteria.

To get a username for your Page:

1. On your Page, click **Edit Page | Update Info** on the Admin Panel menu bar.

2. Click **Create A Username For This Page**.

3. Click in the **Enter Desired Username** text box, and type the name you want.

4. Click **Check Availability**. If necessary, repeat until you find a name you like.

5. Click **Confirm** to finalize the process.

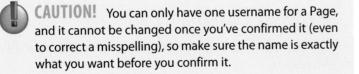 **CAUTION!** You can only have one username for a Page, and it cannot be changed once you've confirmed it (even to correct a misspelling), so make sure the name is exactly what you want before you confirm it.

 **QuickQuotes**

Nancy Watches Facebook Help Her Son

My adult son recently made a decision to go professional with his singing talent. He's had a personal Facebook page, but not being a computer enthusiast or a "small talk" communicator, he clearly needed a way to market himself more effectively. Facebook has been amazing!

Although a friend created a fan page for him, he doesn't have professional photos or videos yet, but with the help of his Mac, *Garage Band,* and a little creativity, he has learned to post videos of his performances. He has also set up an event calendar on the fan page. His connection with the music community is growing quickly. People seem to appear out of the woodwork, helping to professionalize his fan page, as well as set up a blog and a website. He successfully has booked show after show in just a few short weeks.

Finding a Facebook fan page without being a member of Facebook has been instrumental, I'm sure, in getting some private party bookings. This could not have happened as quickly without Facebook, no matter how excellent his music may be. While he is still learning, the pace has been incredible, and his fans, friends, and his mom are all hopeful.

Nancy C., 67, New Mexico

MARKET YOUR PAGE

Pages, as you'll recall, are public. They are designed to tell the world about some person or entity. You want others to see your Page. There are some ways you can make your Page more visible to others. One is simply to post updates. See "Post Status

Updates" earlier in the chapter. You can also post a Like box on your site (see "Promote the Page with Plugins"), create an ad, or get a Badge.

⏩ Promote Your Page with an Ad

Promoting ads on Facebook is not free. But you set the price you're willing to pay for an ad. Your price is entered into an auction type of process, where ads compete for valuable Facebook space in the right column. The higher your bid, the more likely your ad will be displayed. The less you are willing to pay, the less likely an ad will show results. However, the total price you pay will most likely be less than your budgeted amount, since Facebook charges you for what the ad actually costs, not what you're willing to pay for any individual display of an ad. Prices change as the auction sifts through the display possibilities and competing bids for the space.

An ad for your page is easy to create. The two primary items to think about are the 135 characters of text and the image that you use in the ad. To make the ad work for you, you should identify who you want the ad to attract and form your words accordingly. The image, the most dominant part of your ad, should be attractive and appropriate to the organization.

1. In the Admin Panel, click **Build Audience | Create An Ad**. The Advertise On Facebook page is displayed, as shown in Figure 9-16. On the right is an ad preview. As you change your ad, it is reflected in the preview.

2. You have these options:

   - **Choose a Facebook Destination** This is where the viewer will end up when they click your ad. It should be your Facebook Page or the URL for an external website.

   - **What Are You Promoting** Choose what you are promoting; for example, in Figure 9-16 the choice is between promoting a Page or a post on the Page.

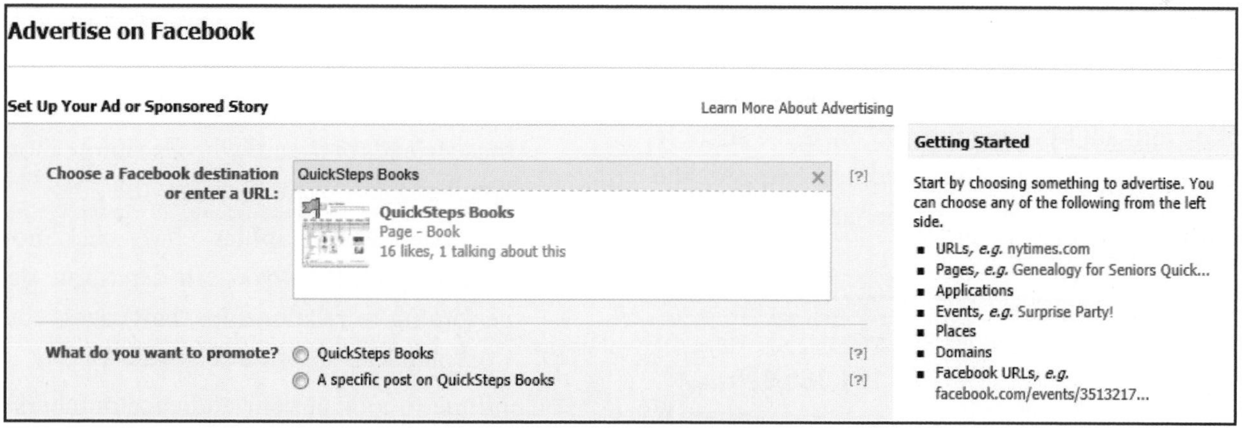

Figure 9-16: The first step in creating an ad is to design it with Facebook's help.

- **People Will See**   Choose between Facebook Ads, which is a typical ad for your business, cause, or person (and is probably what you want), and sponsored stories about your friends liking your Page or posting. When you click this a new panel pops up.

- **Headline**   The title of the ad defaults to the title of the Page. You cannot change it if you are advertising a Page.

- **Text**   The body's standard text is contained in the text box. If you want to change it, click in the text box and replace the default text with your own text. It can be no more than 135 characters in length.

- **Image**   Find an image for the ad for the Page, click **Browse**, and find the photo or graphic you want. It must be no greater than 100 (wide) × 72 (tall) pixels. If it is of a different size, it will be resized. Animated and Flash images are not supported.

- **Landing View**   Click the down arrow and choose where a reader will land when they click your ad.

3. When the preview contains the content you want, scroll down. You'll see the audience selection portion of the advertising form.

4. In the Choose Your Audience section, you can narrow the focus of your ad. By doing this you make the ad more effective—more specific to a targeted audience. All the targeting options are optional—perhaps advisable, but not required. You have these options:

> **Note**   As you narrow the audience for an ad, you'll see the numbers for your estimated audience decrease on the right.
>
> **Audience**
> **161,385,920** people
> ■ who live in the United States

- **Location**   Identifies where people live. If you have a pizza parlor in Denver, for example, you'll use a different location than if you sell cell phones internationally.

- **Demographics**   Determines the specific age and gender of people who will see your ads. An ad for this book, for instance, would allow any gender over the age of, say 55, to be specifically targeted. I would not require an exact age match, so would leave the check box unchecked.

- **Precise Interests and Broad Categories**   In the Precise Interests section, identify, using keywords, what interests your viewers will have. Think of all the keywords you can that might narrow the reach of the ad to be more directly targeted to those you want to see it. In the Broad Categories section, scroll down and select the broad categories that match the interests of your targeted population.

- **Connections**   Allows you to specify the connection to the Page of those who will see it. Do you want people who already know of it and like it to be targeted for repeat business or new events? Or do you want people who don't know about you to see your ad? The Friends Of Connections setting restricts the audience to only those friends of friends who also know about your Page. You'll probably want to ignore this.

- **Advanced Demographics**   If you click **Show Advanced Targeting Options** you can determine demographics pertaining to relationships, languages, education, and workplaces, as shown in Figure 9-17.

5. Continue to look at your audience numbers in the right column.

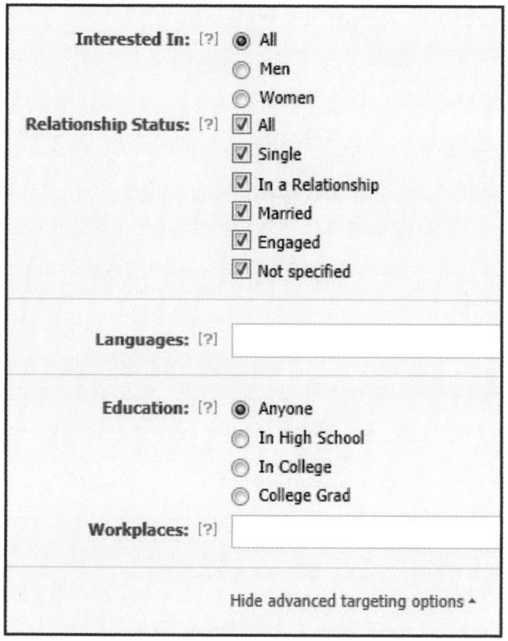

Figure 9-17: *You can use Advanced Demographics to narrow your audience even more.*

6. Scroll down for the objective part of the ad. This allows you to choose between billed for people who see the ad or story, or who actually click on the ad or sponsored story. If you choose **Click On My Ad Or Sponsored Story**, you'll see a suggested bid to the right.

Audience

33,705,080 people
- who live in the United States
- age 55 and older

Suggested Bid

$1.09–$2.37 USD

7. As you scroll down further, you'll see the campaign, pricing, and schedule part of the ad. You have these choices:

- **Account Currency**   Sets the currency you want to use.
- **Account Country**   Sets your country.
- **Account Time Zone**   Sets your time zone.
- **New Campaign Name**   Names the current ad campaign. This helps you identify which ad produces which results. It makes tracking your ad or sponsored stories easier.
- **Campaign Budget**   Sets a budget for the ads. You can set the budget to be for the lifetime of the campaign or per day.
- **Campaign Schedule**   Have the ad run continuously by retaining the check mark in the check box. If you clear the check mark, or if you choose a lifetime budget (in the Budget menu), the schedule will show the beginning and ending date and time for the campaign to run.

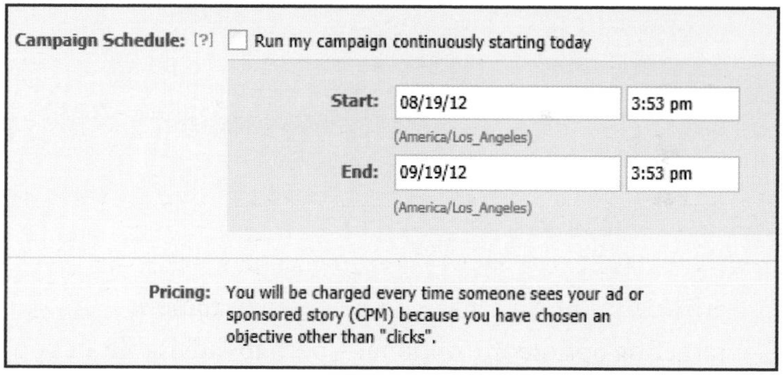

- **Pricing** The default is "simple pricing," wherein Facebook manages your budget and tries to maximize the display of ads during the campaign. You will not be charged more than your budget. You'll not want to set your bid at the minimum or your ad will not be shown very often. The higher your bid, the more your ad is displayed. Remember that you're competing with others for space in someone's left column.

8. When you're ready, click **Review Ad**. You'll be shown a preview of the ad and the specifications you've set. An example is shown in Figure 9-18.

9. When you are ready, click **Place Order**.

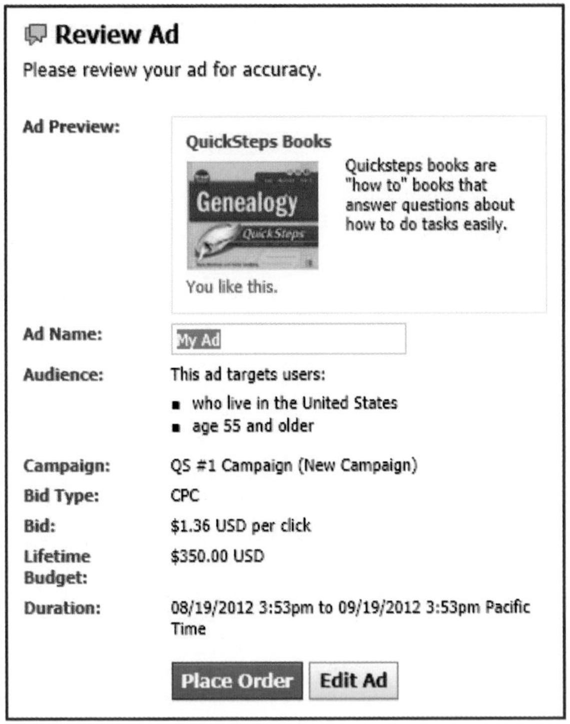

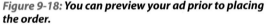

Review Ad

Please review your ad for accuracy.

Ad Preview:

QuickSteps Books

Genealogy
QuickSteps

Quicksteps books are "how to" books that answer questions about how to do tasks easily.

You like this.

Ad Name:	My Ad
Audience:	This ad targets users: ■ who live in the United States ■ age 55 and older
Campaign:	QS #1 Campaign (New Campaign)
Bid Type:	CPC
Bid:	$1.36 USD per click
Lifetime Budget:	$350.00 USD
Duration:	08/19/2012 3:53pm to 09/19/2012 3:53pm Pacific Time

Place Order   **Edit Ad**

Figure 9-18: **You can preview your ad prior to placing the order.**

Chapter 10

Assuring Your Security and Getting Help

The degree to which you are comfortable on your computer and the degree to which you are comfortable using Facebook are determined by how secure you feel with such use. This, in turn, is dependent on the security of your computer, what you do to keep safe on the Internet, and the settings you choose in Facebook. We'll discuss each of these in this chapter, as well as look at how to best use the support features of Facebook. Both of these subjects, security and help, were discussed briefly in Chapter 1 and several other chapters to get you started. Here we will expand on that information and more fully cover it.

SECURE YOUR COMPUTER

When you first read the words "Secure Your Computer," you may think about how to protect it from being stolen. That *is* a consideration—a computer is like any other valuable item and needs to be protected. Here, though, we are talking about what takes place on your computer and who does it.

In this book we look briefly at the common measures you can use to protect yourself. To go further and learn more about security in Windows 7, see *Windows 7 for Seniors QuickSteps,* by Marty Matthews and published by McGraw-Hill/Professional (also *Windows 8 QuickSteps* will soon be out by the same author and publisher).

Examine Your Computer Security

Windows 7 has an excellent resource to check many of your computer's security precautions that is part of the Action Center, as you can see in Figure 10-1. To open the Action Center and review the security settings:

1. Click the **Action Center** icon in the notification area at the bottom-right corner of your screen, and then click **Open Action Center**.

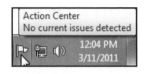

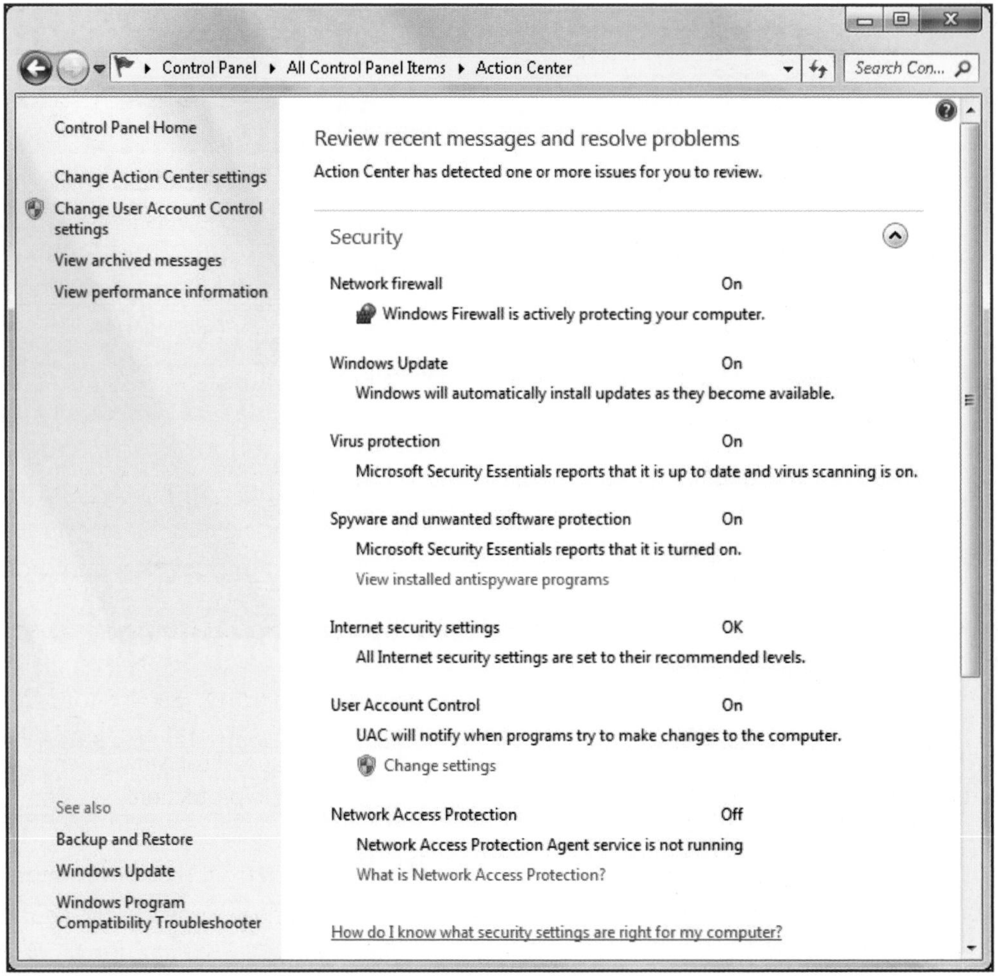

Action Center
No current issues detected
12:04 PM
3/11/2011

Control Panel ▸ All Control Panel Items ▸ Action Center
Search Con...
Control Panel Home
Change Action Center settings
Change User Account Control settings
View archived messages
View performance information
See also
Backup and Restore
Windows Update
Windows Program Compatibility Troubleshooter
Review recent messages and resolve problems
Action Center has detected one or more issues for you to review.
Security
Network firewall
On
Windows Firewall is actively protecting your computer.
Windows Update
On
Windows will automatically install updates as they become available.
Virus protection
On
Microsoft Security Essentials reports that it is up to date and virus scanning is on.
Spyware and unwanted software protection
On
Microsoft Security Essentials reports that it is turned on.
View installed antispyware programs
Internet security settings
OK
All Internet security settings are set to their recommended levels.
User Account Control
On
UAC will notify when programs try to make changes to the computer.
Change settings
Network Access Protection
Off
Network Access Protection Agent service is not running
What is Network Access Protection?
How do I know what security settings are right for my computer?

Figure 10-1: You can check and change your security settings through the Action Center in the notification area, shown with the Security section open.

2. Click the **Security** down arrow in the upper-right corner of the window, and then scroll down and review the various settings that are in place (in the next section, we'll look at making changes to some of these settings). Figure 10-1 shows, for the most part, the recommended Windows 7 settings, which are the defaults. Here is a quick review of the settings:

- The **Network Firewall** is a programmable barrier between your computer and the Internet or other computers on a local area network (LAN) with you. Its purpose is to allow the things you want to come into your computer while blocking things that you don't want. The default settings in Windows 7 have the Windows Firewall turned on, and do a pretty good job of blocking bad stuff and letting good stuff through for most people. We recommend that you leave it this way.

- **Windows Update** automatically downloads and installs any updates Microsoft has for Windows, such as security patches when a vulnerability is found. By default this is turned on so both downloads and updates are automatic. This is the recommended setting.

- **Virus** and **spyware protection** are programs that are always running in the background looking for harmful programs or events that can damage your computer or the information that is stored on it. Windows 7 (or any version of Windows) does not come with virus protection and you must download it, either for free or at a cost. You need to do that—you'll see how in the next section.

- **Internet security settings** allow you to select how you want Internet Explorer (IE) to react to various security situations. IE comes with defaults installed for these settings that are good for many people. In the next section you'll see how to change these if you wish.

- **User Account Control** (UAC) watches what is happening on your computer and if it sees a program trying to make a change on the computer, it stops all activity, tells you about the situation, and asks you if you want to allow the prospective change to take place. For example, if you are trying to install a program, UAC will ask you if you want to do that. You can turn off UAC, but that is strongly not recommended.

- **Network Access Protection** looks at computers on a LAN and determines if they have enough protection in operation to not threaten the network and other computers connected to it. If the computer does not have enough protection, it is prevented from using the network. This normally is only used in larger installations and is probably not something you need to be concerned with.

3. To learn more about these items, click the links in the Action Center. When you are ready, click **Close** (the X in the upper-right corner of the window) to close the Action Center.

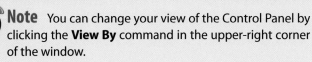 **Note** With the firewall, virus protection, and spyware protection you can install more than one program to handle the protection. Running two or more programs to handle a particular threat, however, is not recommended because it can slow down your computer without any real gain in protection.

Note You can change your view of the Control Panel by clicking the **View By** command in the upper-right corner of the window.

▷▷ Use Password Protection

Depending on how your computer was set up, you may or may not have to enter a password when you start. If you do not have to worry about someone else using your computer— for example, a desktop computer kept in your home—you probably don't need password protection. On the other hand, if you are concerned about kids, grandkids, or others using your computer when you don't want them to, then you need to password-protect it.

Passwords are the primary keys used to allow some people to use a computer and to keep others away. While there are recent alternatives to passwords, such as fingerprint readers on some computers, most computer protection depends on passwords.

Create a Password

You can create a password that will then be required to use your computer.

1. Click **Start** and click **Control Panel**. In Category view, click **User Accounts And Family Safety**, and then in any view click **User Accounts**. (If your Control Panel is in Large or Small Icon view, look in the upper-right corner—you will be able to click User Accounts directly without the intervening screen.) The User Accounts window opens.

2. If it is not your account that you want to add a password to, click **Manage Another Account** and click the account you want to change. In your account or in the other account (this cannot be the Guest account because that cannot have a password), click **Create A Password**. The Create Password window will open, as shown in Figure 10-2.

Make changes to your user account

Create a password for your account
Change your picture
Change your account name
Change your account type

3. Type the new password, click in the second text box, type the new password again to confirm it, click in the third text box, type a nonobvious hint to help you remember the password, and click **Create Password**.

4. Close the Make Changes To Your User Account window.

Figure 10-2: Passwords not only control entry onto the computer, but also such items as encrypted files, certificates, and other passwords. If you change or delete a password, you will lose all items that are based on the password.

Change a Password

It is a good idea to change your password periodically in case it has been compromised.

1. Click **Start** and click **Control Panel**. In Category view, click **User Accounts And Family Safety**, and then in any view click **User Accounts** (you can click this directly in either Large or Small Icon view of the Control Panel). The User Accounts window opens.

2. If it is not your account that you want to change, click **Manage Another Account**. If needed, type a password, click **Yes**, and click the account you want to change. In your account or in the other account that opens, click **Change Your Password**.

3. In your account, type the current password, and click in the second text box. In either your or another's account, type a new password, click in the next text box, and type the new password again to confirm it. Click in the final text box, type a nonobvious hint to help you remember the password, and click **Change Password**.

4. Close the Make Changes To Your User Account window.

Remove a Password

If you move a computer to a location that doesn't need a password—for example, if it is not accessible to anyone else, or if you want to remove a password for some other reason—you can do so.

1. Click **Start** and click **Control Panel**. In Category view, click **User Accounts And Family Safety**, and then in any view click **User Accounts** (you can click this directly in either Large or Small Icon view of the Control Panel). The User Accounts window opens.

2. If it is not your account in which you want to remove the password, click **Manage Another Account**. If needed, type a password, click **Yes**, and click the account you want. In your account or in the other account that opens, click **Remove The Password**.

3. If it is your account, type the current password, and, in any case, click **Remove Password**.

4. Close the Make Changes To Your User Account window.

> **Tip** For a password to be **strong**, it must be eight or more characters long; use both upper- and lowercase letters; and use a mixture of letters, numbers, and symbols, which include ! # $ % ^ & and *. It also should *not* be a recognizable word, name, or date. Instead of a password such as "mymoney," consider using something like this: "my$Money23."

▶▶ Lock a Computer

By default, when your screen saver comes on and you return to use your system, you must go through the logon screen. If you have added a password to your account, you have to enter it to get back into the system, which is a means of preventing unauthorized access when you are away from your running computer. If you don't want to wait for your screen saver to come on, you can click **Start**, click the **Shut Down** right arrow, and click **Lock**; or you can press ⊞ (the Windows flag key)+**L** to immediately bring up the logon screen, from which your screen saver will open.

> **Note** "Locking your computer" means that the view of your screen is obscured by either your screen saver or the logon screen, and if you have implemented password protection, a password must be entered to use the computer.

Depending on your environment, having to go through the logon screen every time you come out of the screen saver may or may not be beneficial. To turn off or turn back on the screen saver protection:

1. Right-click the desktop and click **Personalize**. Click **Screen Saver** in the lower-right corner of the window.

2. Select or deselect **On Resume, Display Logon Screen**, depending on whether you want to display the logon screen when someone tries to use your computer (see Figure 10-3).

3. Click **OK** to close the Screen Saver Settings dialog box, and close the Personalization window.

Figure 10-3: To lock your computer, you must password-protect it, put it into "lock" mode when you leave it unattended (this happens automatically when the screen saver comes on), and display the logon screen when you return.

STAY SECURE ON THE INTERNET

Your connection through your computer to the Internet is your doorway to the cyberworld. It allows you to communicate with others through email and social networking; it allows you to shop for virtually anything without leaving your home; and it provides an enormous resource for gathering information and news. It also is a doorway that can let in things that can harm you, your computer, and your data. It is like the front door to your house—you need it to see and interact with other people, but it also has locks on it to keep out the people you don't want to let in. Similarly, there are a number of barriers you can place in the way of people who want to do damage via the Internet.

Understand Internet Threats

As the Internet has gained popularity, so have the threats it harbors. Viruses, worms, spyware, and adware have become part of our vocabulary. Look at each of these threats to understand what each can do and how to guard your computer and data, as described in Table 10-1.

> **Tip** *Malware* is a catch-all term for viruses, worms, spyware, adware, and any other harmful Internet critter.

> **Note** You don't necessarily have to buy several separate programs to handle the various forms of malware; some programs can do more than one thing.

Table 10-1: Security Issues Associated with the Internet and How to Control Them		
Problem	**Definition**	**Solution**
Virus	A program that attaches itself to other files on your computer. There are many forms of viruses, each performing different, usually malevolent, functions on your computer.	Install an antivirus program with a subscription for automatic updates, and make sure it is continually running.
Worm	A type of virus that replicates itself repeatedly through a computer network or security breach in your computer. Because it keeps copying itself, a worm can fill up a hard drive and cause your network to malfunction.	
Trojan horse	A computer program that claims to do one thing, such as play a game, but has hidden parts that can erase files or even your entire hard drive.	
Adware	The banners and pop-up ads that come with programs you download from the Internet. Often, these programs are free, and to support them, the program owner sells space for ads to display on your computer every time you use the program.	Install an anti-adware program.
Spyware	A computer program that downloads with another program from the Internet. Spyware can monitor what you do, keep track of your keystrokes, discern credit card and other personally identifying numbers, and pass that information back to its author.	Install an antispyware program.

⟫ Use an Antivirus or Security Program

To counter the various Internet threats, you need to install an antivirus or security program. A number of such programs are available, both free and at a cost. You can buy these in computer stores and on the Internet. There is a lot of variability in the pricing, and the opinion of which is the best also varies widely. Table 10-2 shows a few of these programs with which I have had direct experience. The best thing for you to do is go on the Internet and do a search of "antivirus software reviews." Look for the toptenreviews.com site—it gives you a quick comparison, but look at several sites and read the reviews, because there is considerable difference of opinion. When you have decided on the program you want, determine the version to get. Most companies have a basic antivirus program, an Internet security program, and an overall security program. My opinion is that the Internet security programs are a good middle ground. Finally, do some price hunting, making sure you are looking at the version you want. At the time this was written, Amazon.com, for example, was offering substantial discounts (as compared to purchasing on the company's website, shown in Table 10-2). There have been mail-in rebate deals that allow you to get the program for the price of shipping after the rebate.

Note AVG's free edition provides only basic antivirus protection. Microsoft's Security Essentials is more robust, but still less than the Internet Security offerings, although we believe that it provides what the majority of users need and we are using it on several of our computers.

CAUTION! There are two simple rules for Internet security: (1) Don't give out your Social Security number, your mother's maiden name, or your passwords to anybody you have the slightest doubt about; and (2) if a proposition is too good to be true, it probably isn't true. A third rule is harder because you may need it to purchase items on the Internet, but be cautious when giving your bank account or credit card numbers to any organization you are not sure about. In the latter case, a credit card is better than a debit card or bank account number because you have more recourse.

Table 10-2: Antivirus and Security Programs

Name	Website	List Price (as of 8/2012)
AVG Antivirus Free Edition	free.avg.com	Free
AVG Internet Security 2012	avg.com	$54.99 for one PC, one year
BitDefender Internet Security 2012	bitdefender.com	$69.95 for three PCs, one year
Kaspersky Internet Security 2012	kaspersky.com	$64.95 for three PCs, one year
Microsoft Security Essentials	microsoft.com/security_essentials	Free
Norton Internet Security 2011	Symantec.com	$49.99 for three PCs, one year

⏵⏵ Control Internet Security

Internet Explorer allows you to control three aspects of Internet security. You can categorize sites by the degree to which you trust them, determine how you want to handle cookies placed on your computer by websites, and set and use ratings to control the content of websites that can be viewed. These controls are found in the Internet Options dialog box.

Click the **Internet Explorer** icon on the taskbar, click the **Tools** icon on the right of the tab row, and click **Internet Options**.

Categorize Websites

Internet Explorer allows you to categorize websites into zones: Internet (sites that are not classified in one of the other ways), Local Intranet, Trusted Sites, and Restricted Sites (as shown in Figure 10-4).

From the Internet Options dialog box:

1. Click the **Security** tab. Click the **Internet** zone. Note its definition.

2. Drag the slider up or down to select the level of security you want for this zone.

3. Click each of the other zones, where you can identify either groups or individual sites you want in that zone. Click **OK** when you are finished.

Handle Cookies

Cookies are small pieces of data that websites store on your computer so that they can remind themselves of who you are. These can save you from having to constantly enter your name

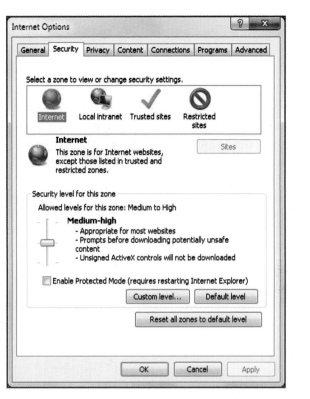

Figure 10-4: Internet Explorer allows you to categorize websites into zones and determine what can be done within those zones.

and ID. Cookies can also be dangerous, however, letting people into your computer where they can potentially do damage.

Internet Explorer lets you determine the types and sources of cookies you will allow and what those cookies can do on your computer (see Figure 10-5).

From the Internet Options dialog box:

1. Click the **Privacy** tab. Select a privacy setting by dragging the slider up or down.

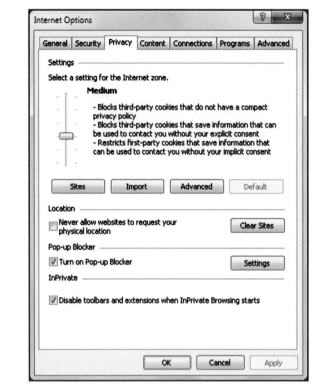

Figure 10-5: Determine how you will handle cookies that websites want to leave on your computer.

2. Click **Advanced** to open the Advanced Privacy Settings dialog box. If you wish, click **Override Automatic Cookie Handling**, and select the settings you want to use.

> **Note** A first-party cookie is one generated by the website you are visiting. A third-party cookie is one generated by an entity other than the website you are visiting. An example of a third-party cookie is one created by an advertiser on the page you are viewing.

3. Click **OK** to return to the Internet Options dialog box.

4. In the middle of the Privacy tab, you can turn off the pop-up blocker, which is on by default (it is recommended that you leave it on). If you have a site that you frequently use that needs pop-ups, click **Settings**, enter the site address (URL), click **Add**, and click **Close**.

5. At the bottom of the Privacy tab, you can determine how to handle InPrivate filtering and browsing. See the Note on InPrivate later in this chapter.

Control Content

You can control the content that Internet Explorer displays. From the Internet Options dialog box:

1. Click the **Content** tab. Click **Enable** to open the Content Advisor dialog box. Individually select each of the categories, and drag the slider to the level you want to allow. Detailed descriptions of each area are shown in the lower half of the dialog box.

2. Click **OK** to close the Content Advisor dialog box.

3. When you are done, click OK to close the Internet Options dialog box.

> **Note** Protected Mode—which you can turn on or off for each zone at the bottom of the Security tab (the notice for which you'll see at the bottom of Internet Explorer)—is what produces the messages that tell you a program is trying to run in Internet Explorer or that software is trying install itself on your computer. In most cases, you can click in a bar at the bottom of the Internet Explorer window if you want to run the program or install the software. You can also double-click the notice at the bottom of Internet Explorer to open the Security tab and turn off Protected Mode (clear the **Enable Protected Mode** check box).

Note Internet Explorer 8 and 9 have added a new way to browse and view sites, called **InPrivate**, that keeps a browsing session private. It is opened by clicking **Safety** on the tab row of IE 8 or clicking **Tools** and then **Safety** in IE 9 and then in either case clicking **InPrivate Browsing**. This opens a separate browser window with this in the address bar: `InPrivate  about:InPrivate  ⌕ ⌄ C ×`. While you are in this window, your browsing history, temporary Internet files, and cookies are not stored on your computer, preventing anyone looking at your computer from seeing where you have browsed. In addition, with InPrivate filtering, also opened from the Safety menu in the tab row, you can control how information about you is passed on to Internet content providers.

STAY SECURE IN FACEBOOK

To get the most out of Facebook, you must share information about yourself. To do that, you must feel comfortable that your information won't be misused. Facebook gives you a number of ways to do that. Among these are choosing the information and photos to put on your site, choosing who your friends are, determining what you will let your friends and others see, and taking other protective measures.

▶▶ Choose Information to Enter

The very first step to staying secure on Facebook is to carefully consider the information you enter into Facebook. Some, like your name and birth date are required, but most is your choice and you can choose whether to display your birth date. There are two considerations in determining the information to put up:

- What is your purpose or objective in putting up the information?

- If it gets in the wrong hands, what could someone do with it?

CAUTION! Don't put information on Facebook you don't want to be at least somewhat public. Mistakes are made— by you, by Facebook, or by others—that might affect access to your information. So if there is something that you really don't want the majority of people to see, don't put it on Facebook. Even if you restrict the information to your friends, you could unthinkingly accept a friend request (a good reason to think carefully about this) that discloses information to that "friend" that you wouldn't otherwise want disclosed.

Consider Your Facebook Objectives

Look at the reasons you are using Facebook and how that relates to the information you put up. For example, if you would like to contact your high school or college classmates, it is probably logical to put up the schools you attended and years you graduated. A similar situation exists with friends you have worked with, been in clubs with, or lived near, indicating that you might want to, respectively, enter where you have worked, clubs you have belonged to, and/or places where you have lived. The important point is to consider how the information you put up will be beneficial to what you want to do with Facebook.

Review What Can Be Done with Information

Be pragmatic for a moment and consider what can be done with the data you put on Facebook. For example, what is someone going to do with the fact that you graduated from a university in 1972? It does date you, but that is generally not a problem for seniors. In the same vein, listing the organizations for which you have worked, clubs to which you have belonged, and places you have previously lived (your current location should be more protected) cannot be easily used against you unless there is some negative connotation connected with them. For all the items you put on Facebook, ask yourself, what can someone intent on being malicious do with those items, and be realistic about it.

> **Note** I am not totally at ease about revealing graduation dates—that makes birth dates more accessible, and that is a real no-no. Graduating from college is different from high schools, since people don't necessarily graduate at the expected time. But I would be very cautious about taking any action that can lead you to reveal your birth date.

▶▶ Choose Your Friends

Probably the most important decision you make on Facebook is choosing who to make your friends, because you can separate what you display to your friends and what you display to everyone else. This is really asking yourself on every friend request, either from them or from you to them, whether you want to display the information you put on Facebook to that person. For the most part, you probably want to be fairly discerning about who you make your friends. See Chapter 3 for more discussion of this subject.

> **Tip** If you decide to befriend lots of people, then you might consider a discipline of assigning each to a list at the time you befriend them, allowing you to control who sees what. So if you want to be friends with someone but don't want them to see everything, simply put them in a list that is restricted on what they can see. See Chapter 3 for more info about lists.

Although when you first befriend someone is when you can best decide how to treat them (regardless of who initiates the friend request), Facebook always allows you to unfriend the person or assign them to an appropriate list.

1. On your Timeline page, click **Friends**. A list of all of your friends will be displayed.

2. Scroll down until you see the person you want to unfriend or assign to a list. Hover your mouse over the name of the person to open their pop-up information.

3. Hover over **Friends**, click **Unfriend | Remove From Friends | Okay** to confirm the removal.

4. You can also assign the individual to one of the displayed lists or click **Friends | Show All Lists** and add the person to one of the additional lists by clicking the list. The Restricted list might be a good alternative to unfriending.

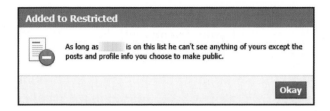

> **Note** Refer to Chapter 3 to see how to use lists to organize your friends.

Select Personal Information to Display

In addition to your choosing what to enter in the first place, Facebook provides many controls to determine what information is displayed and to whom. When you originally set up your Facebook account, you were required to state whether you are male or female and to enter your birth date. This might bother you, but you can choose whether to display this information. It is important that you judiciously use both choices, where you have them, of the information you put on Facebook, as well as displaying only what you are comfortable with.

You can see a wealth of details about how the information you put on Facebook is shared and how you can control it (see Figure 10-6).

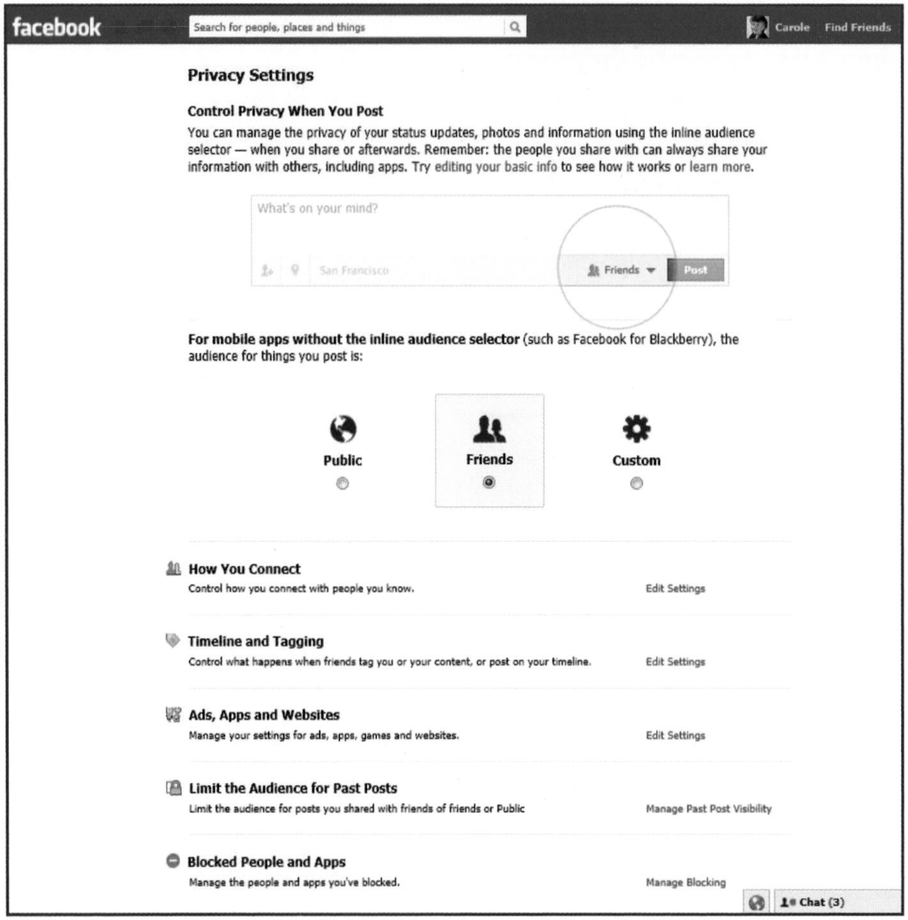

Figure 10-6: Facebook provides a lot of information about your privacy and a number of settings to control it.

Note Some information is treated as if you set your audience selector for it to be public—that is, available to anyone on Facebook. This information is your name, profile pictures, cover photos, gender, networks, username, and user ID. Your birth date is used (not displayed) to filter you for ads and sponsored stories. See "Manage Use of Your Name in Ads" for how to restrict this.

1. Click the down arrow to the right of **Home**, and then click **Privacy Settings** to open the page shown in Figure 10-6.

2. At the bottom right of the first paragraph, click **Learn More** to open a discussion of how sharing works, as shown in Figure 10-7. Click the links at the bottom of each of the numbered paragraphs for further information. After reading each of these, click the browser's **Back** button to return to How Sharing Works Now.

3. When you are done reading about sharing, click **Profile** at the top of the page to see how to control what is in your profile and who can see it.

4. When you are ready, click the browser's **Back** button twice to return to the Privacy Settings page.

Facebook's privacy settings control how the data you put on Facebook is displayed and to whom. These settings are divided into the following:

- **Control Privacy**   Sets a default for mobile devices, etc., that don't have audience selector icons. (Normal audiences are selected at the time of posting, defaulting to the previous audience selected—for example, if I selected Friends last time, that is the current default.)

- **How You Connect**   Controls the information used to find you.

- **Timeline And Tagging**   Controls who can see information and what happens when you get tagged or someone posts on your Timeline.

- **Ads, Apps, And Websites**   Establishes the settings for using applications, games, and websites.

- **Limit The Audience For Past Posts**   Limits the visibility of posts you shared in the past.

- **Block People And Apps**   Allows you to block people, App invitations from a specific person, event invitations from a specific person, and applications.

Control Privacy

Facebook provides three avenues to control the privacy of your information, as shown in the top half of Figure 10-6: controlling your basic information; controlling individual posts, photos, locations, and events; and setting a default that stands behind all that you do.

1. On your Timeline, you can control your basic information by clicking **About** on the left under your profile picture and clicking **Edit** opposite Basic Info, or from the Privacy Settings page, by clicking **Editing Your Basic Info**. In either case, the page shown in Figure 10-8 opens.

2. In the Basic Info box you can control both what information is entered and displayed, but also for each type of information, who it is displayed to. For example, for your birthday, if you click the down arrow opposite **Show My Full Birthday On My Timeline** you can choose *what* to show, while clicking the **Audience Selector** down arrow on the right of the Birthday area you can control who sees

Figure 10-7: It is worthwhile to take the time to read about how to control the information you share on Facebook and possibly view the videos at the end of the page.

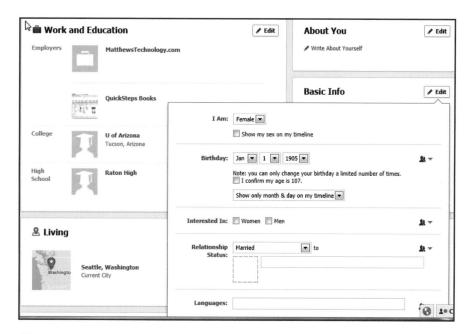

Figure 10-8: Your privacy on Facebook is controlled by establishing with whom you share your information.

it. (If you choose not to show your birthday at all, you will not see the icon for choosing who sees it.)

Birthday: Jun ⌄ 28 ⌄ 1952 ⌄

Show my full birthday on my timeline
Show only month & day on my timeline
Don't show my birthday on my timeline

3. For each category of information an Audience Selector icon is displayed allowing you to select your audience. Facebook starts out with five groups of people that you can show your information to:

🌐 Public
✓ 👥 Friends
👥 Friends except Acquaintances
🔒 Only Me
⚙ Custom

☆ Close Friends
🏠 Family
See all lists...

- **Public**   Your information is shared with *anyone* on the Internet.

- **Friends Except Acquaintances**   Information is shared only with friends not in the Acquaintances list. This is a way to restrict access for people you really don't know that well.

- **Friends**   Your information is limited to your friends, plus if you tag someone your information is displayed to that person and their friends.

- **Only Me**   You are the only person who can see this information unless you tag someone, and then they will be able to see the information.

- **Custom**   You can limit your information to one or more specific individuals or lists and/or hide it from one or more specific individuals or lists.

- **List Names**   There are two default lists, Close Friends and Family, but you can view all your lists.

4. If you haven't already, go through your basic and other information, enter what you want in each category, and then select the audience that can see it.

5. When you are done with the Basic Info box, click **Save Changes**.

6. When you have completed making all the desired custom settings, click **Back** in your browser to return to your Timeline page.

Note Remember you can control the privacy of each post you make by clicking the **Audience Selector** down arrow on that post and choosing the group you want to see it.

Change How You Connect

Facebook has a group of settings, accessed from the Privacy Settings page, that aid or block people from finding you. The default, and Facebook's recommendation, is that you allow everyone to see or do these items. You may want to consider, though, how they relate to your objectives and sense of security.

1. Click the down arrow to the right of **Home** and click **Privacy Settings**.

2. On your Privacy Settings page, opposite How You Connect, click **Edit Settings**. The How You Connect dialog box opens.

3. Review each of the items, and consider whether you want to limit the access to the people indicated.

4. Click the **Audience Selector** down arrow for the settings on the right, and choose the one that is correct for you.

5. When you have made all the changes you want, click **Done** to return to the Privacy Settings page.

Control Timeline Posting and Tagging

Facebook provides several settings that allow you to control who can post and see the posts on your Timeline, how you want tagging of you handled, and whether you want to review both of these before they appear on your Timeline.

1. Click the down arrow to the right of **Home** and click **Privacy Settings**.

2. On your Privacy Settings page, opposite Timeline And Tagging, click **Edit Settings**. The Timeline And Tagging dialog box opens.

3. Review each of the items, and consider how you want to handle each of them.

4. Click the down or right arrow for the settings on the right, and choose the one that is correct for you, returning to the Timeline And Tagging dialog box when you leave it.

5. When you have made all the changes you want, click **Done** to return to the Privacy Settings page.

Set How Ads, Apps, and Websites Access Your Data

By default, once you begin using applications (Apps) such as MyCalendar and We're Related, games like FarmVille and CityVille, and websites such as Bing and Pandora, they can access your name, profile picture, friends list, and information you choose to share with everyone. The Apps, Games, And Websites privacy page, though, gives you some degree of control over what is shared, as you can see in Figure 10-9. For the sake of brevity, both Facebook and this book use the word "App" to describe applications, games, and websites.

1. Click the down arrow to the right of **Home** and click **Privacy Settings**.

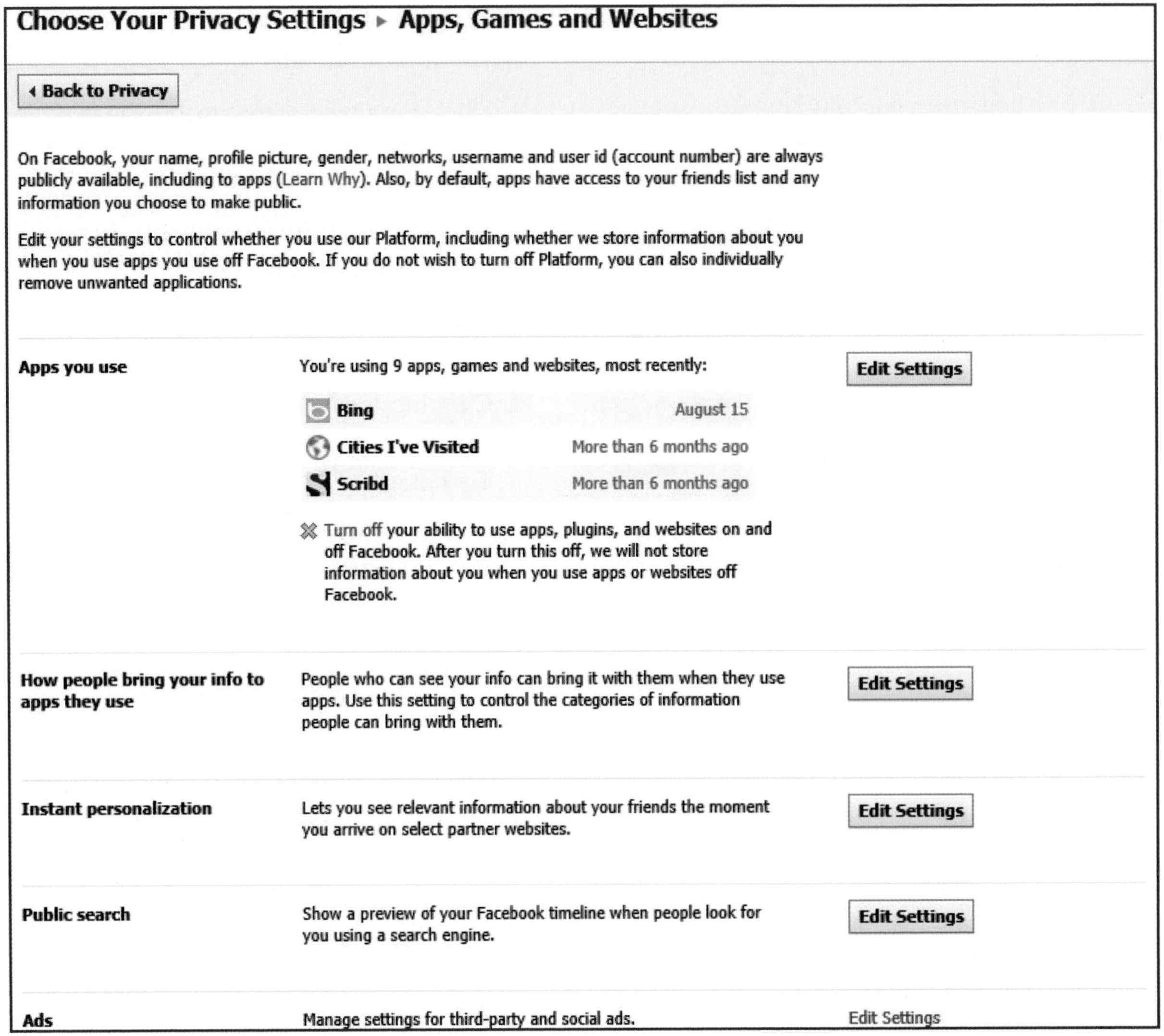

Choose Your Privacy Settings ▸ **Apps, Games and Websites**

◀ **Back to Privacy**

On Facebook, your name, profile picture, gender, networks, username and user id (account number) are always publicly available, including to apps (Learn Why). Also, by default, apps have access to your friends list and any information you choose to make public.

Edit your settings to control whether you use our Platform, including whether we store information about you when you use apps you use off Facebook. If you do not wish to turn off Platform, you can also individually remove unwanted applications.

Apps you use	You're using 9 apps, games and websites, most recently:	**Edit Settings**
	◉ **Bing** — August 15	
	🌐 **Cities I've Visited** — More than 6 months ago	
	Ⓢ **Scribd** — More than 6 months ago	
	✖ Turn off your ability to use apps, plugins, and websites on and off Facebook. After you turn this off, we will not store information about you when you use apps or websites off Facebook.	
How people bring your info to apps they use	People who can see your info can bring it with them when they use apps. Use this setting to control the categories of information people can bring with them.	**Edit Settings**
Instant personalization	Lets you see relevant information about your friends the moment you arrive on select partner websites.	**Edit Settings**
Public search	Show a preview of your Facebook timeline when people look for you using a search engine.	**Edit Settings**
Ads	Manage settings for third-party and social ads.	Edit Settings

Figure 10-9: Facebook provides good control of the Apps you are using and what information they get from your site.

2. On your Privacy Settings page, opposite Ads, Apps, And Websites, click **Edit Settings**. The Apps, Games, And Websites page opens.

3. Click **Edit Settings** opposite Apps You Use. This opens a list of Apps you use. It gives you the option of limiting some of the information that the App uses, but not all of it, or removing the App.

4. Click **Edit** opposite the App whose settings you want to change. You'll see that some information is required, while you can exercise limited control over other information, as you can see in Figure 10-10. If supplying the required information is unacceptable to you, choose **Remove App**. When you are done with an App, click **Close**.

5. It is a good idea to check all the Apps you are using to fully understand what you are sharing. When you are ready, click your browser's **Back** button.

6. Click **Edit Settings** opposite How People Bring Your Info To Apps They Use. A dialog box opens listing all the settings that are available to Apps when your friends use them. This is a good time to evaluate what settings you will use with your friends. We suggest limited access to your personal information. Click the check boxes to turn

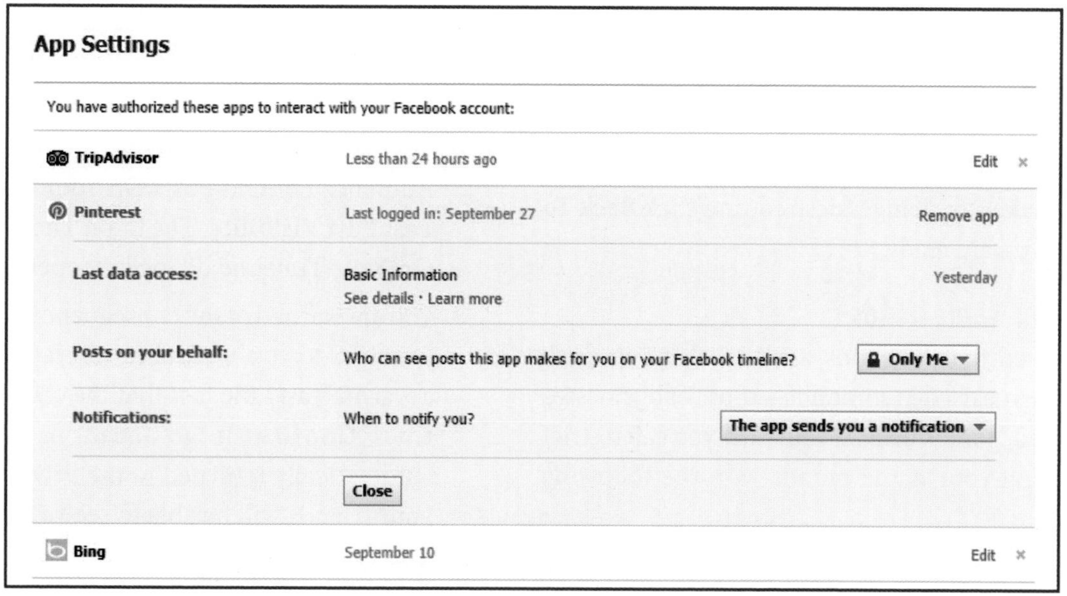

App Settings

You have authorized these apps to interact with your Facebook account:

TripAdvisor	Less than 24 hours ago		Edit ✕
Pinterest	Last logged in: September 27		Remove app
Last data access:	Basic Information See details · Learn more		Yesterday
Posts on your behalf:	Who can see posts this app makes for you on your Facebook timeline?	🔒 Only Me ▼	
Notifications:	When to notify you?	The app sends you a notification ▼	
	Close		
Bing	September 10		Edit ✕

Figure 10-10: Other than removing the App, you have very limited control over what it does with your information.

them on or off (a check in the check box indicates you are sharing that information), and click **Save Changes** when you are ready.

> **How people bring your info to apps they use**
>
> People on Facebook who can see your info can bring it with them when they use apps. This makes their experience better and more social. Use the settings below to control the categories of information that people can bring with them when they use apps, games and websites.
>
> ☐ Bio   ☐ My videos
> ☐ Birthday   ☐ My links
> ☐ Family and relationships   ☐ My notes
> ☐ Interested in   ☐ Hometown
> ☐ Religious and political views   ☐ Current city
> ☐ My website   ☐ Education and work
> ☐ If I'm online   ☐ Activities, interests, things I like
> ☐ My status updates   ☐ My app activity
> ☐ My photos
>
> If you don't want apps and websites to access other categories of information (like your friend list, gender or info you've made public), you can turn off all Platform apps. But remember, you will not be able to use any games or apps yourself.
>
> [Save Changes] [Cancel]

7. Open the remaining settings on the App privacy page to review them, make any changes desired, and click **Back To Privacy** when you are ready.

Manage Use of Your Name in Ads

You may be surprised that Facebook assumes that you don't mind having your name used in some ads—those of businesses or Pages you've "liked," for instance. If you want, you can restrict Facebook from using your name on ads with the following settings:

1. Click the down arrow to the right of **Home** and click **Privacy Settings**.

2. On your Privacy Settings page, opposite Ads, Apps And Websites, click **Edit Settings**. The Choose Your Privacy Settings page opens.

3. To the right of Ads, click **Edit Settings** again.

4. Under Ads Shown By Third Parties, click **Edit Third Party Ad Settings**. Click the down arrow and choose **No One**. Then click **Save Changes**.

5. Under Ads And Friends, click **Edit Social Ads Setting**. At the bottom, click the down arrow and select **No One**. Click **Save Changes**.

6. Click the Facebook logo to return to your Home page.

Limit the Audience for Past Posts

The best way to limit the audience for old posts is on an individual post basis by simply changing the audience. Facebook, though, does give you the option of setting the audience for all of your past posts to friends only.

1. Click the down arrow to the right of **Home** and click **Privacy Settings**.

2. On your Privacy Settings page, opposite Limit The Audience For Old Posts On Your Timeline, click **Manage Past Post Visibility**. The Limit The Audience For Old Posts On Your Timeline dialog box opens.

3. You are warned of the consequences (really not that bad). If you want to go ahead, click **Limit Old Posts**. You again get a warning and the fact that the change cannot be undone. Click **Confirm** to go ahead, or click **Cancel**. You are automatically returned to the Privacy Settings page. Only your friends will be able to see your older posts.

Block People and Apps

Facebook allows you to identify individuals and Apps from whom you specifically do not want friend, App, and event invitations. You can also block Apps from contacting you and using your information, as you can see in Figure 10-11.

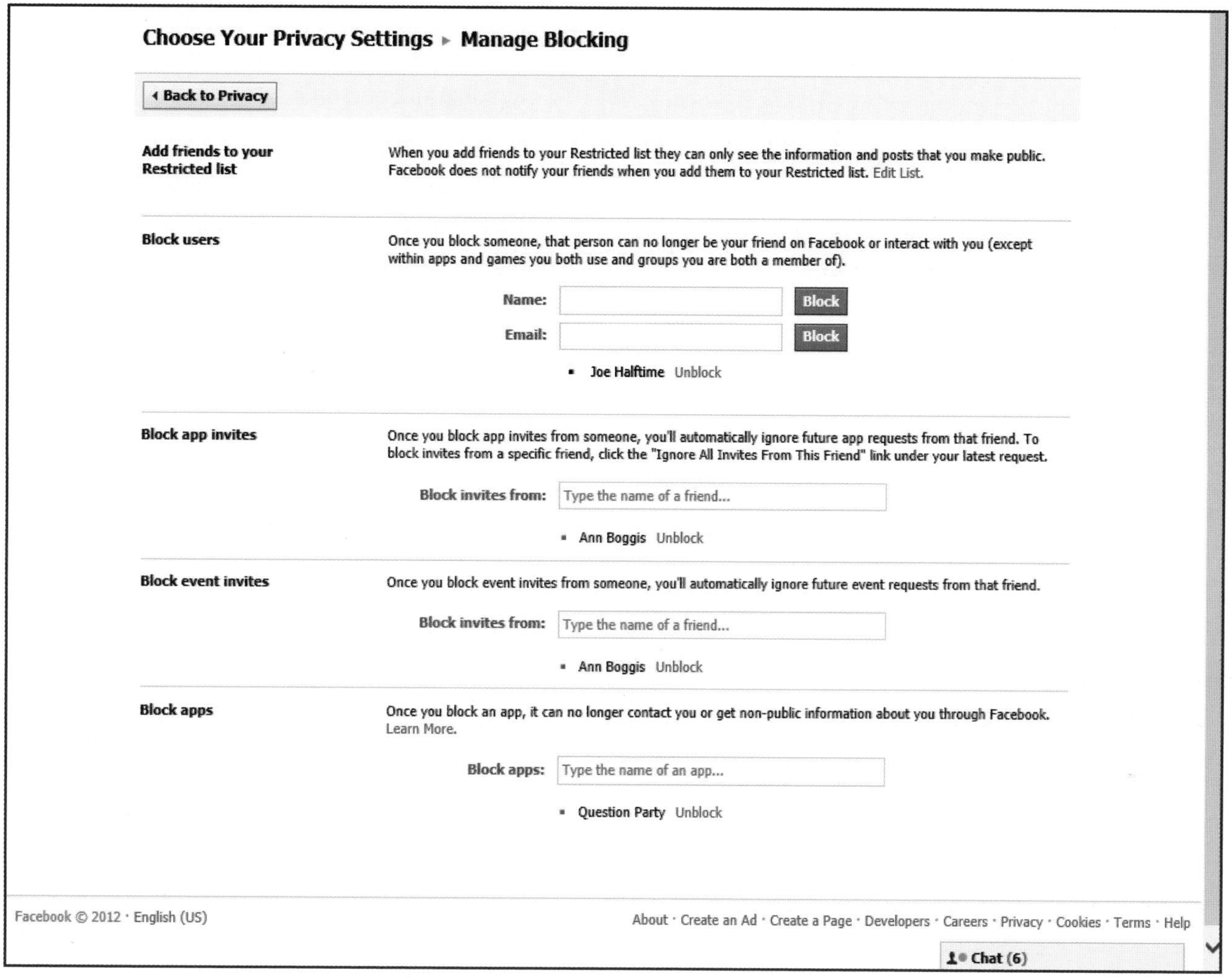

Choose Your Privacy Settings ▸ Manage Blocking

◂ Back to Privacy

Add friends to your Restricted list

When you add friends to your Restricted list they can only see the information and posts that you make public. Facebook does not notify your friends when you add them to your Restricted list. Edit List.

Block users

Once you block someone, that person can no longer be your friend on Facebook or interact with you (except within apps and games you both use and groups you are both a member of).

Name: [   ] Block

Email: [   ] Block

▪ Joe Halftime Unblock

Block app invites

Once you block app invites from someone, you'll automatically ignore future app requests from that friend. To block invites from a specific friend, click the "Ignore All Invites From This Friend" link under your latest request.

Block invites from: [Type the name of a friend...]

▪ Ann Boggis Unblock

Block event invites

Once you block event invites from someone, you'll automatically ignore future event requests from that friend.

Block invites from: [Type the name of a friend...]

▪ Ann Boggis Unblock

Block apps

Once you block an app, it can no longer contact you or get non-public information about you through Facebook. Learn More.

Block apps: [Type the name of an app...]

▪ Question Party Unblock

Facebook © 2012 · English (US)

About · Create an Ad · Create a Page · Developers · Careers · Privacy · Cookies · Terms · Help

👤● Chat (6)

Figure 10-11: People and Apps that you do not want to interact with can be specifically blocked.

1. Click the down arrow to the right of **Home** and click **Privacy Settings**.

2. At the bottom of the Privacy Settings page, opposite Blocked People And Apps, click **Manage Blocking**. The Manage Blocking page opens.

3. First you are reminded that in place of blocking a friend, you can put her or him on the Restricted list. To do that click **Edit List | On This List | Friends**, select the friend to be added, and click **Finish**.

4. Click in the **Name** or **Email** text box in the Block Users area, type a name or email address, and click **Block**. You may see these actions:

   - If you have entered a name, the Block dialog box will open to give you a list of candidates matching the name you've entered. If you do, in fact, want to block one of the candidates, click **Block**. The name is listed below the text box. Click **Unblock | Confirm** to remove the block against the person.

   - If you have entered an email address, the address will be entered below the text box. Click **Remove | Confirm** to remove the email address from being blocked.

5. Click in the text boxes opposite **Block App Invites, Block Event Invite**, or **Block Apps**; type a name; and press **ENTER**. The name will go in a list below the text boxes, where you can click it to unblock it.

6. When you have completed entering the people and apps you want to block, click **Back To Privacy** to return to the Privacy Settings page, and then click your Home or Timeline page to continue with Facebook.

Index

time played, 124
time to go, 124
uploading from computer, 118–119
uploading from video sites, 120–122
viewing, 124–125
volume control, 124
views, filtering in left column, 28
virus and spyware protection, 209, 213

W

Wall
downloading photos to, 110
explained, 21
uploading photos to, 105

Wall activity, seeing, 30–31
web mail, using to set up account, 7–10
webcam
recording videos with, 123–124
taking profile picture with, 39–40
websites
categorizing, 215
setting access to data, 225–228
Windows Live Mail, using, 186
Windows Update, 209
worm, defined, 213

Y

yourname, using Facebook as, 195

Z

Zynga games
Café World, 168–170
CityVille, 162–165
Texas HoldEm Poker, 165–168